Creative Writing in America

Creative Writing in America

Theory and Pedagogy

Edited by

Joseph M. Moxley
University of South Florida

National Council of Teachers of English
1111 Kenyon Road, Urbana, Illinois 61801

Staff Editor: Robert A. Heister

Cover Design: Doug Burnett

Interior Design: Tom Kovacs for TGK Design

NCTE Stock Number 09268–3020

Library of Congress Cataloging-in-Publication Data

Creative writing in America : theory and pedagogy / edited by Joseph M. Moxley.
    p.   cm.
    Includes bibliographies.
    ISBN 0–8141–0926–8
    1. English language—Composition and exercises—Study and teaching—United States. 2. English language—Rhetoric—Study and teaching—United States. 3. Creative writing (Secondary education) 4. Creative writing (Higher education) I. Moxley, Joseph Michael. II. National Council of Teachers of English.
PE1405.U6C7   1989
808'.042'07073—dc20   89-34713
                                             CIP

Contents

Acknowledgments

I thank all of the writers who have kindly and freely shared their time and expertise to write chapters for this book. I wish to express my special appreciation to Eve Shelnutt for being a vital source of inspiration and support. Also, I thank David Jauss for his insightful and helpful commentaries. In addition, I thank Tom Ross, our chair, and my colleagues in the Department of English at the University of South Florida.

I could not have envisioned this book without guidance and encouragement from Charlie Moxley, David Kranes, Art Efron, Don Murray, Ed Hirshberg, and Rita Pollard. Finally, for her constant support, I thank my bride, Pat Hemmens Moxley.

Preface

This book is for high school and college teachers who are interested in how creative writing can be taught effectively. Composition researchers and teachers, students and aspiring writers can also benefit by learning the composing strategies of the successful writers included in this book. In twenty-three original chapters, prominent novelists, poets, editors, and playwrights discuss practical classroom methods that can help aspiring writers understand the need for critical, avid reading; a variety of prewriting, revising, and editing strategies; the creative process; the fundamental aspects of craft.

I have asked these authors and editors to share their advice and expertise on how teachers can best "nurture" writing improvement, because practical questions about teaching creative writing have been virtually ignored. At present, no debate rages in professional journals as to whether creative writing programs are providing students with the necessary writing skills, knowledge of the composing process, or background in literature needed to write well. Although professional writers frequently have criticized the workshop method, few have recommended viable alternatives. Yet there is evidence that our discipline is preparing to undergo a paradigm shift, a period of self-reflexiveness in which we question our theories and practices. The recent, unprecedented dialogue about the value of literary theory to creative writers in the 1987 and 1988 issues of the *AWP Newsletter* (*Associated Writing Programs Newsletter*) indicates an emerging interest in pedagogy and theory. Gerald Stern, a professor at the Iowa Writers' Workshop, has reported grassroots interest throughout the country in developing alternatives within the broad confines of the workshop method:

> Everywhere I go the workshop instructors are designing strategies to revivify workshops, to make them more exciting or more directed for the students, to make them more bearable for the instructors. There is a doubt about the procedure, almost a kind of crisis. One teaches literature, one provides subject matter, one form. (1987, 6)

There are indeed questions not only about practice, but also about audience and purpose. Each year thousands of students throughout

America enroll in B.A., M.A., M.F.A. and Ph.D. programs in creative writing. The growing popularity of these programs now threatens the elitist assumption that only those students who clearly possess the ability and desire to succeed as professional writers should enroll in creative writing workshops. Certainly, some students take our courses because they are possessed by a need to write, a need to express their thoughts, feelings, and experiences. Motivated by a love for language, an active imagination, or a powerful feeling of dissonance, some of our students are prepared to shape their lives around their writing goals. However, many students at both the high school and undergraduate levels enroll in creative writing courses not because they wish to pursue a career as professional writers, but because they wish to develop their writing ability, to learn more about who they are and what they can do, to test the limits of their imagination.

Presumably academic training in fiction, poetry, playwriting, and screenwriting enables students to meet and discuss aesthetics, the creative process, and ambitions. These courses also allow students to share their writing with a small group of people in a supportive, challenging environment. Many prominent writers—such as Robert Bly, Philip Levine, Mark Strand, David St. John, Donald Justice, W. D. Snodgrass, Richard Hugo, W. P. Kinsella, Raymond Carver, Carolyn Chute, and Jayne Anne Phillips—are graduates of American creative writing programs, particularly of the world-renowned Iowa Writers' Workshop.

Although workshop courses in poetry and fiction date back to the 1890s and were part of the curricula at various universities, such as Harvard and Oregon, the first workshop program per se was the one founded at Iowa in 1936. Since then, creative writing departments have prospered throughout the country. Presently, the *AWP Catalogue of Writing Programs* lists 279 college and university undergraduate writing programs, and 29 M.F.A. programs with an emphasis in creative writing. Greg Kuzma predicts that "within five years there will be a creative writing program available for anyone in America within safe driving distance of his home" (1986, 349). And, as Dave Smith explains, we have good reason to celebrate these developments:

> More practically, we do not expect to make *all* students into Miltons. The biology major does not often become a Darwin. But we help students to realize that language is a living, vital reality; *it is what we possess to experience and shape reality.* . . . *Creative writing is one of the few formal opportunities in education for self-*

discovery and self-creation. It leads a student less to right answers than to right questions. It creates more intelligent, informed, and responsible readers by immersing them in the actual process of imaginative exploration and accomplishment. Creative writing engenders, or ought to engender, an appetite for excellence in the dramatic images of man. In an age dominated not only by the shallow and delusionary images perpetrated by television, and movies and pulp books, but also by the anarchists and polemicists of fringe culture, good instruction demonstrates the historical successes and failures of ideas, actions, beliefs, dissent, taste, tolerance, beauty, and knowledge. (1981, 3; emphasis added)

Despite the rapid growth and popularity of courses and programs in creative writing, pedagogical techniques have not evolved all that much. In fact, perhaps because they studied at Iowa or were trained by graduates of the Iowa Writers Workshop, most creative writing teachers at the undergraduate and graduate levels follow the same studio method established at Oregon and Iowa over ninety years ago. According to the September/October 1987 edition of the *AWP Newsletter*—based on the results of a 1978 survey—the workshop method still holds the imprimatur of the AWP as the preferred means of instruction (12). The heart of most creative programs, the standard workshop goes something like this. The writer-teacher asks two or three students to distribute copies of their manuscripts a week before the works are to be criticized in class so their peers can write comments on them and be prepared for discussion. Then, with varying degrees of authority, the writer-teacher guides the group's discussion by asking questions relevant to the manuscript's strengths and weaknesses. Instruction regarding the writing craft—such as choosing a point of view, setting the scene, writing dialogue, and developing a satisfying plot—typically emerges from these discussions. The copies of the manuscripts—now marked with the peers' comments—are returned to the authors at the end of the discussion.

The workshop method is a convenient and sometimes effective way to teach creative writing. Based on how artists are trained in other disciplines, such as painting and music, the workshop enables aspiring writers to rub elbows with accomplished professionals. An extremely flexible technique, this approach provides the community, audience, and criticism that some inexperienced writers need. Indeed, when the workshop is comprised of critical readers—the kind of readers many writers hope to reach when they publish—and when these readers feel free to provide immediate, critical feedback, students can learn to escape their own perspectives and better understand the need for, and possibilities of, revision. Mirroring the organic flow of the creative process, teachers can improvise as they go along, directing the group's discussion along pertinent aesthetic lines. When guided by sensitive, experienced teacher-writers, this method can be highly effective.

However, despite these advantages, the workshop method has a few limitations. For example, by focusing primarily on revising and editing, the workshop fails to address prewriting strategies. Given that many professional writers such as Donald Murray report that they spend as much as eighty-five percent of their time searching for ideas and rehearsing possible alternatives, our omission of prewriting strategies is particularly troublesome. In short, the implied assumption of the workshop methodology is that students already know how to gather, shape, and revise material. Without defining aesthetic criteria for evaluating manuscripts, most teachers direct the group's analysis by asking, "Does the text work?" As Eve Shelnutt mentions in the opening chapter, by proceeding in this manner, the workshop presumes that students already know how to write, that they are capable of determining whether a piece "works," that they are familiar with traditional and contemporary literature, that all they need to master the craft is a little practice before a critical, peer-audience. Perhaps this product-oriented methodology is appropriate when the workshop consists of handpicked graduate students—students who have truly mastered a variety of prewriting, revising, and editing strategies, as well as the fundamental techniques of craft.[1] However, we need to reconsider whether most graduates, undergraduates, or high school students possess the necessary critical faculties or knowledge of craft and literature to approach learning in this manner.

Our discussions of the fundamental techniques of creative writing—or even, for that matter, the basics of grammar—should not be left solely to the haphazard winds of group discussion. After all, amid the competition in the workshop for "the star!" position, even the boldest students are sometimes reluctant to mention aspects of the craft that they do not understand. Even one student—if forceful, articulate, and extremely negative—can shatter the ambience of openness that is essential to critical inquiry. And the meeker students are inclined to shy away from submitting experimental work, work that goes against the grain of what other students in the class are producing. Still other students may fear sharing autobiographical pieces that are close to their hearts and painful to discuss, though the development of such subjects could lead to powerful literature. Indeed, it seems possible that some students, in tune with the academic tradition of writing for the teacher, may present manuscripts in workshops that please the teacher or group more than the writer.

By organizing instruction around editorial discussions of students' completed works, this method can fail to introduce students to a variety of original plots, themes, treatments. In part, then, the workshop can close in on itself, restricting students by encouraging them to write for each other rather than for themselves or in response to literary traditions or for commercial audiences. As Donald Hall satirizes in his description of the *MacPoem,* the result can be a little like fast food: the workshop story, poem or drama can satisfy the immediate desires of the audience, but it can also be flawed by the bland sameness of the assembly line and lack the substance to have lasting nourishment. Finally, the workshop method limits the amount of writing students compose because of the time-consuming nature of large group discussions.

Because of these problems, some prominent novelists, editors, and poets have criticized writing teachers for not being rigorous enough. For example, Ted Solotaroff, Senior Editor at Harper and Row, believes writing programs are propagating *a culture of narcissism:*

> The tacit deal that is cut with the students whose enrollment pays for the program and its faculty is that since we can't give most of you a career, we won't ask much of you. We will mostly let you *critique* each others' work and sit in a few seminars where you'll have to do some reading but that will still leave you with plenty of time to concentrate on your handful of stories or poems, to teach perhaps an introductory writing course, and to hang out with the other writers. (1987, 9)

William Gass has also criticized the workshop method for not being sufficiently demanding:

> The students . . . write like one another. . . . Only the exceptional instructors push their students much. No one is required to do exercises on the practice fields of fiction. No one is asked to write against the little grain they've got. Relations grow personal before they grow professional. And the community perceives each poet as a poet, each writer as a writer, making them members in this social sense, although they may not have written a worthy word. Here many hide from academic requirements and from intellectual challenge. There are always shining exceptions, of course, but on the whole the students show little interest in literature. They are interested in writing instead . . . in expressing a self as shallow as a saucer. (1987, 34–35)

Solotaroff and Gass are not alone in their criticisms. For example, Greg Kuzma believes that the creative writing teacher "no longer teaches the few who really care and are dedicated to the art, the few and the best; he teaches the average and the many. The writer no longer works in the fierce light of the scrutiny of the ages—and the scrutiny of the scholars—the quality of one's writing is no longer a concern" (1986, 344). According to Kuzma, encouraged by "the ecstasy of being associated with a growth industry," writing teachers and administrators have wrongfully lowered their standards:

> The result of what may seem like a series of small compromises, a little yielding here and there to expedience, readjusting our ideals to comply with the budget, looking the other way, whistling while our backs are turned, being friendlier than we would be normally, accepting that which is contentedly mediocre in place of the work of high ambition which we had formerly expected and indeed demanded, lowering our academic standards to make room for the swarms of new students our budget requires, is finally, in sum, a large betrayal. (345)

As teachers in a discipline, we need to address these sharp criticisms; we clearly must assess our practices, goals, assumptions. In particular, can a program that relies on critiquing student work as the primary means of writing instruction provide students with an understanding of the composing process or the solid background in technique and literature that they'll need to write well and be critical thinkers? How can we prepare students to write well?

The following twenty-three chapters suggest procedures and advice that teachers can use to establish the groundwork that aspiring writers need. While intending to shorten the apprenticeship of student writers, each essay explores different classroom exercises that should provide students with a variety of composing strategies. Taken as a whole, these authors and editors make the following recommendations: (1) student writers must be readers—a background in literature and criticism enables student writers to identify and produce creative work; (2) academic training in writing must be rigorous and diverse; (3) student writers must have an understanding of the composing process and a knowledge of a variety of composing strategies; and (4) student writers must master the fundamentals of craft.

The need for writers to be active readers is stressed more than any other recommendation. In fact, John D. MacDonald, Stephen Minot, David St. John, and Dewitt Henry suggest in their chapters that students cannot create works of art, much less popular fiction or poetry, if they are not avid readers and aware of literary trends and genres. Creative writing programs that rely on reviewing student manuscripts in workshops as the principal means of instruction may fail to introduce students to the more original possibilities of theme and form. If students ever hope to publish or produce truly creative work, they must know enough about the marketplace to distinguish M.F.A. literature from New York literature. We can help students understand contemporary styles, themes and alternatives by exposing them to some important literary magazines.

Second, the academic training of student writers must be rigorous and diverse. Writers need to be capable, knowledgeable, critical thinkers. As David Jauss, Robert Abel, Eve Shelnutt, Dewitt Henry, and Valerie Miner point out, students need to be competent in a variety of genres, well read, knowledgeable, and capable of making a living with their words, images, ideas, knowledge.

A third critical component of a writer's education should be a background in the composing process. To work as professionals, students need more than to hear their poems and stories criticized five or six times. To overcome writer's block, to develop innovative work, and to learn a variety of ways to revise their work, students need to learn the ways professional writers draw on experience, "inner speech," the unconscious, the "right brain," images, literature and research to generate stories, poems, or plays. To find strategies that work best for them, we need to introduce students to a variety of prewriting techniques, in addition to developing our methods of showing students how to revise and edit their manuscripts.

Fourth, student writers must learn the fundamentals of craft, such as developing believable characters, realistic scenes, dialogue, and original plots. Researching material, analyzing the content of a literary journal, writing query letters or submitting manuscripts for publication should be a part of each student writer's training. As Valerie Miner mentions, the myth of the isolated writer in the garret must be replaced with an understanding of the role of the writer in the publishing world.

Naturally, theorizing that things ought to be done is much easier than explaining how these things can be accomplished. However, these twenty-three chapters do more than theorize: they explain practical procedures that teachers can profitably employ to teach students the fundamentals of craft, the art of critical reading, and the strategies to generate, structure, refine, and publish writing.

The five chapters in the first section address some important assumptions, goals, and problems. In the first chapter, Eve Shelnutt describes the weak intellectual climate, the in-bred curriculum, and second-rate status of most creative writing students as evidence that we need to take a more rigorous interdisciplinary approach. Shelnutt argues that creative writing teachers must work together with literature and composition professors, and she proposes several innovative ways literature professors and creative writing teachers can jointly explore the creative process. Next, I examine ways in which we can use the research and recommendations of composition theorists and practices of professional writers to engage students in their creative process and to show them the generative power of their active, forming, critical minds.

George Garrett traces contemporary practices to the sixteenth century and the precepts of the standard classical education. Garrett analyzes the people and institutions who shaped the beginning and growth of creative writing programs, and he explores the impact of instruction in creative writing on American literature, discusses problems with current publishing procedures, questions the implications of desktop publishing, calls for alternatives to the traditional workshop method, and clarifies the need for new techniques to teach literature.

While citing the advice of Keats, Flaubert, García Márquez, Welty and other authors, David Jauss presents over forty aesthetic principles that underlie writing instruction (as well as contemporary literature).

The fourteen chapters in the second section are primarily concerned with ways of generating material. Ron Carlson presents a series of assignments that teachers can use at the beginning of the semester to establish a rigorous tone; to avoid general, vague discussions; to help students identify their aesthetic predispositions. The late John D. MacDonald argues that writers must be "compulsive and omnivorous readers," that we must introduce students to the rigors of the writing profession and the need to entertain an audience. In chapter 7, Stephen Minot picks up where John D. MacDonald leaves off. Agreeing that beginning writers must first be "omnivorous readers," Minot differentiates "active reading" from "passive." He describes what most professional writers look for when they read fiction, how they find new work, and how they recall what they have read over the years. Creative writing teachers, Minot argues, demonstrate through their own enthusiasm how writers remain active students of literature all their lives.

While giving great emphasis to the importance of regular writing, the next four chapters explore distinct sources of inspiration: writing in different genres; addressing different audiences; freewriting to take advantage of the generative nature of language; plotting and outlining; and identifying emotional subjects and situations. While Elizabeth Winthrop stresses the importance of daily writing, she often finds it inspiring to alternate among children's books, young adult novels, and adult novels. When writing, Winthrop remains receptive to new story ideas, and she suggests that exploring themes in children's books often helps her address similar subjects in adult fiction. Donald Murray contends that student writers must overcome the misconception that theme precedes story and the notion that writing involves transcribing what is already known. Murray encourages writers to experience the generative nature of language by writing quickly: "acceleration of prose causes those accidental connections between what is known and what is suddenly remembered." While suggesting writers must balance the need for planning with the joy of discovery, Murray encourages student writers to start with two characters speaking with each other: "not meaning, idea, theme, or thesis; not literary style or voice; not background or setting; but character against character. All else comes from that. . . ." In contrast, Marion Zimmer Bradley advises student writers to plan their stories before leaping into composing. Bradley believes students can plot an entire novel in a writing workshop by summarizing their story in one sentence, by defining what the main character wants, and by determining the final outcome, point, and climax of the story. For Sheila Schwartz the impulse for her novels and stories stems from emotion; she suggests that realistic characters develop naturally when writers explore a situation that exorcises old wounds or redresses old grievances, or brings "clarity to unresolved events of the past."

The following three chapters explore innovative methods of transforming personal experiences into fiction. Wayne Ude presents a set of point-of-view exercises that help students learn the way point of view shapes a story, that teach students to distance themselves from characters and situations drawn from personal experience, and that illustrate the importance of revising. Next, Eve Shelnutt explores an innovative alternative to the traditional writing workshop, an alternative that takes the focus of instruction away from the product and redirects it toward the process. In particular, Shelnutt describes certain memory exercises; prose models and anecdotal accounts by the authors of these models that address the sources of their material; student essays; and student essays on the sources of their stories that can help students transform personal experiences into fiction. Robert

Abel's engaging discussion of his apprenticeship reminds us of some of the benefits of formal academic training in writing, and he discusses some of the personal experiences that compelled him to write.

William Holinger reviews some important conventions of dialogue in fiction and suggests techniques for prewriting and revising dialogue. David Kranes offers guidelines for teaching playwriting. David St. John argues that creative writing teachers must introduce students to "a wide range of literary periods, not simply that of contemporary poetry." St. John suggests that aspiring poets must be familiar with Yeats, Eliot, Williams, and Stevens so that they don't write on trite, conventional subjects or "write the sing-song metrics of greeting cards, bad rock songs" and so forth. Finally, Mimi Schwartz examines the effect of teachers' commentaries on student writing, and she explores how expository writing teachers can profitably employ many of the practices that creative writing teachers use in order to encourage experimentation and awareness of how form follows function.

The three essays in section three explore the final stages in the composing process—revision, editing, and publishing. Alan Ziegler analyzes the types of literary feedback, the dynamics of criticism, and some ways to teach revision and editing. Valerie Miner explains the procedures and results of her "Writers in Society" course in which students are placed in publishing houses, writers' organizations, magazines, literary agencies, and radio programs. Miner's course is designed to consider aesthetic, economic, and technical issues in writing and publishing fiction in order to break through the myth of the isolated artist and to deal with the writer as a member of society. Because they provide a breadth of models of the best contemporary fiction, DeWitt Henry suggests that literary magazines should be required reading in writing workshops. Henry classifies the top thirty-seven literary magazines into six categories; explains how he assigns magazines and uses them in the classroom; reviews the many benefits students receive by doing internships with magazines like *Ploughshares;* and provides guidelines for submitting manuscripts.

Chapter 22 consists of some important aphorisms about generating and revising material, about steps in mastering the craft, and about strategies that teachers can use to help students become independent, objective critics of their work. In the final chapter, based on the advice of the authors in this book and on that of other writers and scholars, I summarize some important theoretical assumptions and recommendations for writing teachers and writing program directors about teaching creative writing, and I suggest some areas for future research and inquiry.

Last, in the appendix, Marion Perry reviews the requirements of twenty-eight M.F.A. programs in creative writing. In particular, Perry reports the number of hours required, the number of years in residence, and the number of hours needed in literature, interdisciplinary, language, thesis, and workshop courses.

While our primary aim is to provide teachers with innovative classroom techniques that will shorten the apprenticeship of student writers, we also hope that this book will stimulate a dialogue among creative writing, literature, and composition teachers about how we can improve writing instruction. In order to develop an effective curriculum, one which can enable creative writing students to produce significant works, or secure positions as editors and thinkers, we must assess our hidden assumptions, experiment with new approaches, and study the strategies and experiences of successful professional writers.

Before closing, I would like to mention that *Creative Writing in America: Theory and Pedagogy* is not meant to be a cookbook for producing literary luminaries. No one will ever be able to prescribe the precise steps method. Inspiration, talent, originality—these are elusive qualities, qualities that teachers cannot dispense. Yet, to prepare our students to plumb the depths and mysteries of their own creative processes and talents, we must establish a supportive environment for experimentation and discovery; we must ensure that we have provided students with knowledge of the composing process, the fundamental techniques of creative writing, literature and critical reading.

Joseph M. Moxley
University of South Florida

Notes

[1]It is, in fact, interesting to note that in a single course at Iowa, several now well-known writers were enrolled, including W. D. Snodgrass, Philip Levine, Donald Justice, Robert Dana, Donald Peterson, Henri Coulet and Jane Cooper (see Solotaroff 1987, 9).

Works Cited

"AWP Guidelines for Creative Writing Programs and Teachers of Creative Writing." *AWP Newsletter*, September/October 1987: 12.

Gass, William H. "A Failing Grade for the Present Tense." *New York Times Book Review*, October 11, 1987: 1, 32, 34–35, 38.

Hall, Donald. "Poetry and Ambition." *AWP Newsletter*, February/March 1987: 1–2, 4–5, 10–13.

Kuzma, Greg. "Comment: The Catastrophe of Creative Writing." *Poetry* 148 (September 1986): 342–54.

Murray, Donald. "Teach Writing as a Process Not Product." In *Learning by Teaching*, 14–39. Upper Montclair, N.J.: Boynton/Cook Publishers, Inc., 1982.

Smith, David. "Notes on Responsibility and the Teaching of Creative Writing." *AWP Newsletter*, May 1981: 1–3, 7.

Solotaroff, Ted. "The Literary Campus and the Person-of-Letters." *The American Poetry Review* 16 (July/August 1987): 7–10.

Stern, Gerald. "Life is Not a River—Some Thoughts on Teaching Poetry." *AWP Newsletter*, November/December 1987: 6–9.

I Assumptions, Problems, Prospects

There are countless writer-teachers around the country who burn energies seeing others to maturity. They work out of a reverence for the possibilities of the imagination, and they resist all temptations to become propagandists. They listen more than they talk and, in that sense, are less teachers than students. They work in that hazy time between wish and fulfillment, employing a knowledge of techniques, the tradition, recent movements in contemporary fiction, and so forth, to bring the student to a better realization of his or her own work.

—Philip F. O'Connor, *Itinerary One*

1 Notes from a Cell: Creative Writing Programs in Isolation

Eve Shelnutt
Ohio University

In a recent issue of *Salmagundi* devoted to the topic of intellectuals, William Pfaff, a political writer for *The New Yorker*, argued that "the intellectual life and teaching have always been connected, but never more so than in the United States today." Yet, as a teacher in a university Master of Fine Arts creative writing program, I barely recognize his description of academe.

The intellectual life professionally is something I sense from behind an invisible wall. Muted celebrations of the mind seep in occasionally from the literature and composition programs. But for teachers of creative writing and M.F.A. students in writing, the intellectual life has, I believe, never been so disconnected from our niche in the university. Of this writers' community, William Gass claims, "Here many hide from academic requirements and from intellectual challenge" (1987, 34).

Critics of the more than 280 graduate and undergraduate writing programs in colleges and universities across the country would no doubt answer that they never expected "real" writers to emerge from the cocoon of academe, much less intellectuals from among those writers. Perhaps a similar sentiment among European academicians accounts for writing programs being largely an American phenomenon. Other critics would state that they never conceive of writers of fiction and poetry as intellectuals in the first place. The myth that Mark Twain never read much still has coinage, and we enjoy the image of the garreted writer wrestling more with his anguish than his intellect, although even anguish is an outmoded substitute for a writer's work since Tama Janowitz, Jay McInerney, and others of what is being called "The Brat Pack" are promoting glitter instead. In this climate, Lionel Trilling's statement in *The Liberal Imagination* that "intellectual power and emotional power go together" reads as a non sequitur. Any critic of M.F.A. programs *has* a right to be skeptical, no matter what he or she expected.

The unsettling fact is that in America the majority of new, "serious" imaginative writing is being produced by writers trained in M.F.A. programs staffed by teachers who themselves are products of M.F.A. programs.

The intellectual climate in these programs ceases to be of provincial concern when publishers, the reading public, and alumni of M.F.A. programs are congruent. Of university M.F.A. programs, Gass writes, "It has been in their interest to feed their students into the commercial world of publishing . . ." (1987, 32). Moreover, when so many aspiring writers and publishing teachers are gathered under the umbrella organization of the Associated Writing Programs (AWP), which concerns itself, among other things, with developing connections with publishers, it becomes difficult to discern how much the publishing industry is influenced by writing spawned in M.F.A. programs. Jayne Anne Phillips, Ray Carver, and Bret Ellis are products of university writing programs, and their imitators, who also publish, are many.

Conversely, it is equally hard to discern how much M.F.A. students and their teachers are influenced by current publishing practices. Bret Ellis's young-writer-makes-good story may be the contemporary prototype. His writing instructor, Joe McGinnis, of *Fatal Vision* fame, helped Ellis cut a 400-page novel, the potential for which McGinnis had discovered in Ellis's nonfiction writing, down to a saleable two hundred pages, which editor Robert Asahina then accepted. Says Asahina, "Bret came along at a time when there was great interest in what young people were up to. It was young people he was writing about, and he was young himself" (Sheppard 1987, 77). Asahina was following a current trend when he added, ". . . he was young himself," since it is the practice now to promote the writer as heavily as the product. When Carolyn Chute's *The Beans of Egypt, Maine* appeared, Chute's own story of poverty received as much attention as her novel: *she* was obviously saleable.

The success in sales of Ellis's *Less Than Zero* not only proved that McGinnis and Asahina knew the marketplace, it spawned a second novel by Ellis, *The Rules of Attraction*. Of both, reviewer Terrence Rafferty wrote, "The only reason his two raw, fumbling novels have been published is, of course, that they contain large, even toxic, doses of the elements that stimulate sales: lots of sex, lots of drugs, brand names on every page, and a cynical tone that's perfect for readers who want to lap up the decadent behavior and then feel righteously shocked at its emptiness" (1987, 142).

Presumably writing instructor McGinnis counts Bret Ellis as a success, and other Bennington students are sure to follow with their versions of what Rafferty calls "yuppie lit." Of writing students, Gass writes, "Because few of the young people I met had the romantic aspirations my generation had, I decided they lacked ambition. I was wrong. They have plenty of ambition, but it is of a thoroughly worldly and commonsense kind: they want to make it" (1987, 38). The outmoded aspirations to which Gass alludes were to produce writing that wouldn't make a professor of, say, Joyce or Faulkner or even Barth shudder.

If New York publishers can be counted on to help certain young writers "make it" despite the merits of their work, aren't university and small presses still protective of quality writing? Certainly university and small presses are where many writers *have* to turn but that fact does not of itself assure quality.

Unlike scholars of literature who write *for* university presses, mindful of the traditional standards for the publication of scholarly work, creative writers usually send their work to university presses only after it has been rejected by Harper and Row, Morrow, Viking, and so on. In the genres of short fiction and poetry, a publisher, commercial or university, will be more likely to consider a manuscript when its author has a proven track record in magazines. Book publication, then, often reflects instead of *corrects* literary standards.

It is necessary to look at the literary journal to assess the literary climate; it is in this market that all but a few writers begin, and it is from here that they will branch out into book publication. Prior to the establishment of the National Endowment for the Arts, the number of literary journals in America was modest and, like *The Partisan Review*, were begun by intellectuals as forums for the exchange of ideas, which included ideas lurking in fictional and poetic forms. When government money became available, the number of literary journals multiplied, especially since the states were also entering the arts business. And the infusion of federal and state money for the arts coincided with the development of M.F.A. programs. Hordes of new writers who had been encouraged by the availability of new programs in which to study writing suddenly needed journals in which to publish.

Too, writing teachers working toward tenure, writing students seeking both professional experience and credentials, and English departments seeking to validate the seriousness of new writing programs discovered that beginning and working on literary journals served them well.

With writing students aiming to "make it" by publishing first in literary journals before an assault on New York publishers, with new journals serving mainly mundane purposes such as program validation, what happened in many journals was a splitting off of creative writing from intellectual discourse. A majority of literary journals publish only fiction and poetry. Many that publish nonfiction prose limit it to book reviews, personal essays, and interviews with writers. Scholarly discourse *about* writing was now the province of what was called the "academic" or "scholarly" journal, in only a few of which could be found fiction and poetry. Moreover, so great is the deluge of imaginative writing, editors of the separate "literary" journals of fiction and poetry found that it was often expedient to use students to sort through the ubiquitous manila envelopes and present to them only "the best," despite the fact that students making initial decisions about quality often had minimal knowledge about literary traditions and were students *because* they were still working to learn the craft of writing.

What a number of new literary journals began most glaringly to reflect was what Jacques Barzun has called "a surfeit of art," which many of the journals, as a matter of policy, did not want to investigate—the "positive" book review was sought, on the basis that a negative review was not constructive either to the writer or the reading public. And the polarity—"positive" versus "negative"—made it clear that the very investigative nature of scholarly discourse had not only been abandoned but forgotten. It is from this situation in academe that small publishers receive book submissions.

As "suppliers," M.F.A. programs need to be studied. Yet M.F.A. programs' faculty and students appear to be in no position to raise the relevant questions. Why, and what can be done, requires some background.

Let me borrow from Leozek Kolakowski, Senior Research Fellow at All Souls College at Oxford, the definition of an intellectual as a person whose vocation it is "to make the proper use of words" (1986, 233). That definition seems encompassing and provocative enough to contain creative writers, and if a skeptical reader cannot imagine speaking of such writers as Ray Carver, Ann Beattie, Carolyn Chute, and Bobbie Ann Mason as intellectuals, the same reader may be willing to admit V. S. Naipaul, Nadine Gordimer, J. M. Coetzee, and Ruth Prawer Jhabvala to its ranks, noting, meanwhile, that none are American nor products of M.F.A. programs.

As a teacher of creative writing, I am interested in students who aspire to the quality of work produced by Naipaul, Gordimer, Coetzee, and Jhabvala, even if I believe that most students will not become writers. Enough will, as a cursory reading of the contributors' notes of any literary journal will demonstrate. In fact, many writers begin to publish while still enrolled in M.F.A. programs, a fact I will return to later.

But whether few or many M.F.A. students will go on to become professional writers, I am concerned about a growing climate of anti-intellectualism among writing students who will, at the least, be readers and job-seekers, parents, and voters.

Prior to the epidemic of new M.F.A. programs that raged during the 1970s, creative writers in the university were men of letters—consider The Fugitive School—whose relationship to imaginative writing was profoundly linked with the study of literature as an indicator of a society's well-being. It is obvious that critical writing and imaginative writing were seen by Ranson, Tate, and Warren as symbiotic, and the university still houses a number of such writers who do not, alas, often teach in M.F.A. programs—William Gass and Saul Bellow are two.

That teachers in M.F.A. programs need no longer aspire to be men and women of letters is a phenomenon coinciding, roughly, with the growth of M.F.A. programs. This trend in academe away from intellectual concerns is, I believe, now being taken as a given not only by critics of writing programs, but also by English departments that shelter such programs by giving support to established writers in the form of teaching positions and by awarding teaching assistantships to M.F.A. students for the staffing of, predominately, freshman composition courses. Writers outside the university term the academic writers' positions "havens," without, I daresay, realizing that the "haven" is also from intellectual discourse.

Since experience has shown me that an almost aggressive anti-intellectualism exists in a number of M.F.A. programs, I am interested in exploring the predicaments of M.F.A. students in relation to the university community of thinkers because I think that M.F.A. students are being ill-served. They, in turn, by serving the needs of publishers and a television-age readership, are changing the face of contemporary American writing.

I have never been interested in the question that has plagued M.F.A. programs since their inception, namely, *can* creative writing be taught? The question puts teachers of writing immediately on the defensive and seems of little practical value—M.F.A. programs will doubtless continue to exist. Indeed, a number of English departments owe their fiscal security to writing programs. And since student demand for space in these programs grows yearly, the relevant questions seem to me to be, *what* are we teaching students who come to us wanting to learn how to write fiction, poetry, and nonfiction? And how does what we teach or fail to teach affect contemporary literature?

The University of Iowa, which developed the first writing program more than fifty years ago, instituted what was to become the blueprint for hundreds of writing programs, namely the "workshop" method, whereby students discuss their own writing around elbow-worn tables, "as if," said one of my students, "we already knew *how* to write." So mythologized has that roundtable become that Boston University, in an advertisement for its M.F.A. program, declares of its workshops, "All of these are held in the same small room, which allows, through its dusty window, a glimpse of the Charles River."

The workshop constitutes the core of a student writer's curriculum. As guidelines published by the AWP state, "The 1978 AWP survey indicated that most teachers of writing felt they were most effective in the workshop format . . ." (1987, 12). It is not always the case in M.F.A. programs that students take fewer literature than writing courses (see the appendix in this book)—the required number of hours devoted to literature courses varies widely from program to program. Nor is it true that a program's stated number of credited workshop hours is always indicative of the true emphasis of the workshop format. Some courses not indicated strictly as writing workshops are, in fact, workshops, in that the focus is on discussion of student writing. And many writing students audit additional workshops in order to experience the ambience or to obtain additional "feedback" on their writing.

What makes the M.F.A. students' situations signally different from those of M.A. or Ph.D. students—students who usually make up two-thirds of the enrollment in literature courses taken by M.F.A. students—is that M.F.A. students, as a result of spending time in writing workshops, lack the background necessary for placing newly encountered texts in a historical context. Some literature professors are vocal about M.F.A. students' lack of preparation for the material they will encounter in graduate literature courses and speak of M.F.A. students "dragging down" the quality of literature courses.

In recent years, as the teaching of composition became a task for the specialist, writing students employed as teaching assistants began to divide their non-workshop time between literature studies *and* courses in the theory of teaching composition, courses often required by the terms of their employment. These seminars in composition theory arose not only in response to the interests of M.A. and Ph.D. students of composition, who sought to master what had become a theory-laden field of study, but also in response to English departments, which needed some assurance that student teachers understood how to teach composition in its new configuration, especially as freshman and advanced composition once again became, in many universities, a required subject, staffed primarily by teaching assistants.

M.F.A. students are a beleaguered lot, pulled between course requirements in creative writing, including the completion of a book-length manuscript, and requirements in literature and composition theory, as well as the demands of the twenty to forty freshmen they teach each term.

If, after thirteen years of teaching creative writing at the university level, I have come to believe that M.F.A. students are largely separated from the broader intellectual life of the university, and if I see this separation as augmenting publishers' economic moves away from quality literature, I have also concluded that the separation and its consequences are not the fault of writing students but a result of the structure of English departments that contain literature, composition, and writing programs. In short, writing students are hapless victims. Their writing teachers are victims too, I think, but perhaps willing victims, a point I will return to.

Here let me be specific about what I perceive to be the writing student's intellectual isolation. Recently one of my best fiction writers told me that, after four years in the undergraduate writing program and two years in the M.F.A. program, while taking the required courses in literature, writing, and composition theory, she had no confidence in her ability to write an essay for a general, non-scholarly but literate audience and *no* ability to write a critical article for a scholarly journal. And she was baffled and angry because, through her own writing, she had acquired an interest in writing *about* writing but lacked the skills and background in critical theory.

In the fall of 1987 I taught a course designed to help M.F.A. students learn how to write essay reviews and critical essays about literature. I discovered that none of the students wrote confidently or even passably about literature. They struggled with discursive prose as well as, in some instances, with grammar and punctuation. They confronted the meagerness of their backgrounds in literature by which they might assess a novel or story collection and place in any perspective a trend in contemporary writing. Yet they were affectingly diligent and earnest as they revised and began to try to fill the gaps in their educations. What was required of me was great diplomacy: M.F.A. students do not like to expose their ignorance and are a long way from demanding they be better taught.

The course, "Readings in Contemporary Fiction," is designed to give writing faculty great leeway in how it will be taught; some may focus on *oral* reports about contemporary fiction. As a group, M.F.A. faculty themselves are a long way from believing that the writing students they teach would benefit from knowing how to use the traditions of scholarly discourse. Too, writing instructors usually teach elective courses and veer away from designing courses that M.F.A. students may deem difficult or peripheral to their completion of the required creative thesis.

To say that M.F.A. students' backgrounds in theories of criticism are weak is not to say that all M.F.A. students envision themselves as competing with traditional scholars of literature, although some may and have—Joyce Carol Oates and Cynthia Ozick are fiction writers who move with ease between creative writing and scholarly discourse. But M.F.A. students who seek to write essay reviews and general essays about literature for a general but literate audience are at a disadvantage if they approach the assessment of literature as if criticism had just been invented. And students who may never, upon graduation, write *about* writing are nonetheless at a disadvantage as *creative* writers if they lack sufficient training by which to evaluate the implications of new formal devices in writing that begin as fads. Young writers' reliance on the present tense in fiction and on narrators' colloquial voices are examples, I believe, of devices that have been adopted apart from an examination of how they affect other fictional techniques. Yet, if students in M.F.A. programs are not presented with the means by which to ask searching questions about imaginative forms, how will universities continue to make a distinction between the kind of education provided in a university setting and that provided by commercial schools of writing?

Specialization in English departments has severely fragmented English studies. It was this concept of specialization, in fact, that made the study of creative writing as a university-taught discipline conceivable in the first place. This specialization, which may or may not have benefited English departments as a whole, has made it especially difficult for the M.F.A. students it created to study the history of critical theory to discover how they may use various theories to think and write about imaginative writing. *How* texts are talked about in the literature courses M.F.A. students take alongside Ph.D. students is often determined by an individual professor's specialized interest and by the *school* of criticism that the professor studied in graduate school. As an M.F.A. student takes courses from a variety of literature professors, that student may become simply confused without a historical context within which to place the discourse of a specialty. Indeed, an M.F.A. student may find that perceiving a way into *any* scholarly discourse is difficult.

Intimidated, baffled, rebuffed, M.F.A. students turn inward to their own writing as if it *must* exist in a vacuum.

If M.F.A. students experience isolation in literature courses, they also carry it into writing workshops, or perhaps it is more accurate to say that, in writing workshops, intellectual isolation is programmatically reinforced. Material in workshops is primarily student writing or writing by young contemporaries such as Carver, Beattie, Chute, Tobias Wolff, Phillips, and others. Of his encounter with M.F.A. students' penchant for the newest writing, William Gass writes, ". . . they hand me a list of a hundred authors each named Ann (or Anne). My enthusiasm wanes—for Musil, for Proust, for Literature" (1987, 34).

What M.F.A. students are doing is reading their "competition," with encouragement of M.F.A. faculty. While it may be difficult to discern why instructors encourage such myopia, it is clear to see that M.F.A. students feel they *must* keep up with current trends on contemporary literature even if keeping up means there is no time left for Musil or Proust. They know they can hardly compete for jobs teaching composition with M.A. and Ph.D. students whose specialty composition is, and their degrees, unless they continue in the M.A. and Ph.D. programs, preclude their seeking jobs in literature. All M.F.A. students can imagine is publishing fiction, poetry, or nonfiction while working at marginal jobs to support an ambition they steadfastly maintain despite fierce competition. "What are the *stars* doing," they ask, not, "what do *I* want to write?"

Locked out of the traditions of literary discourse, out of hope for teaching positions, out of a deep appreciation for literature itself, M.F.A. students *are* second-class citizens in English departments. If they can be seen huddled in tight circles reminiscent of Conestoga wagons under attack, their stances are not gratuitous.

Again and again M.F.A. students are taught that they must study and work in the intellectual ghettos of English departments. Finally they come to agree, largely, that it is their proper place—they were never meant, heaven forbid, to become creative writers *and* thinkers too. This lesson has come in the subtlest forms, since effective teaching is often subtle. I have mentioned already the lessons of the current marketplace; the lessons of departments offering a specialized discourse while providing the M.F.A. student insufficient introduction to it; the M.F.A. programs' focus on contemporary writing; and the lessons of the job market.

Another significant lesson comes from M.F.A. programs' *allegiance* to the separation of writing students from literature and composition programs, especially writing programs which doggedly subscribe to AWP guidelines for such programs. These published guidelines (last printed in the September/October 1987 issue of *The AWP Newsletter*) make principle of circumstance.

Clearly, in a number of statements, they indicate a desire of writing programs to *remain* outside the influence of English departments' literature and composition programs. To quote from the guidelines on the tenure process, "AWP believes that writing program faculty, who as creative writers are best qualified to make assessments of a candidate's work, should be given the responsibility of making professional decisions about their peers, and that their evaluations of the candidate, and their recommendations, should be given the utmost weight in the review process." Under "Additional Recommendations" is this: "AWP believes that writers should have the major voice in decisions concerning the hiring and retention of creative writing faculty, admission of students to the writing program, the awarding of degrees in writing, the writing program's budget, and the allocation of physical resources. AWP believes that writers in the academy are best qualified to make such judgments in regard to creative writing programs" (1987, 12).

To assess what is being stated in these guidelines, it is important to note first that many writing programs include journalism as a field of study which is then, according to language of the guidelines, termed "creative writing," presumably because recent journalism has incorporated techniques from fiction. Second, it is interesting to note that in the phrase, "writers in the academy are best qualified to make judgments in regard to creative writing programs," the qualifier "creative" has been dropped in the first instance because it is *assumed* that the reader of the guidelines will know that "writer" *means* "creative writers." Yet writers abound in literature and composition programs, and it could be argued that some post-structualist critics (consider Ihab Hassan's *Paracriticisms*) have adopted techniques from fiction at least as often as journalists. Moreover, journalism courses as well as creative writing courses have encouraged writing in the forms of journals and personal memoirs, thereby blurring the distinctions between the writing performed by many composition students and "creative" writers.

What seems obvious in the somewhat confusing terms of the AWP guidelines, adopted by "a majority of the graduate degree programs in creative writing in the United States," is that M.F.A. programs are sending two clear messages to English departments: *"We will define writing"* and *"Stay off our turf."*

The seemingly endemical antagonism between writing, literature, and composition faculty is a result of many complex factors having coalesced over time, including hiring practices in many M.F.A. programs. Hiring practices illuminate other practices and raise questions about the future course of M.F.A. programs, indicating, I think, the necessity for reform and even the direction reform should take.

It has long been customary in universities with creative writing programs to allow the current writing faculty to choose the new members of the writing faculty, while literature and composition faculty "rubber stamp" their decision. After all, faculty deciding on a candidate's prospective value to a department must read the work of the candidate, stay informed about a writing program's continued development, and assess how a candidate will fit into that program. Many literature faculty feel that they do not have the time required for such a judgment or that they have not read enough contemporary writing to make a judgment about the candidate's writing. Further, before AWP transformed it into a guideline, a mystique that was more elusive developed around writing programs, often floated by writers themselves; its message was, mysteries exist in the teaching of imaginative writing that only writing faculty can fathom in order to make hiring decisions.

Even when members of literature and composition faculties want to participate in the hiring of writing faculty, it is often the case that candidates for positions in literature and/or composition are considered the same year. What frequently happens is that, in a sotto voce agreement, lines of influence are drawn: "Don't tamper with my candidate, I won't tamper with yours." Such practices, however covertly practiced, solidify the isolation of writing faculty.

A more alarming offshoot of this particular form of isolationism is the possibility that writing faculty may tend to hire newcomers who do not jeopardize the egos of the writing faculty who are already in place. In a "publish or perish" university, untenured writers may feel that their positions are especially fragile, depending as they do on the whimsical nature of the imagination finding form and the form finding a receptive publisher.

Quantity of publications can be an especially thorny issue since any younger writer seeking to enter academe has had to publish voluminously even to get a foot in the door. It may be that these young Turks threaten the reputations of the older writing faculty, who began their teaching careers during less pressured times. New writers of both quantity and obvious quality can be seen as exerting unusual pressure on older writers, particularly at a time when some universities are helping solve financial strain by offering early retirement, a "nudge" most older writers do not want.

Current practices in hiring writing faculty also tend to insure that the "old boy" system of hiring former classmates or friends of friends or cohorts from a dozen AWP conventions will narrow the range of perspectives offered by a writing program. Such a tendency—entirely human but not necessarily of advantage to the university—may be followed especially when a writing program is embattled within a department: its members will seek candidates who will make them feel comfortable and who they think can be counted on to help present a "united front." And more and more writing programs are hiring writers whose books have made it big in New York. I will mention later some of the consequences of this practice; here I will suggest only that these writers are often hired without due consideration being given to their teaching experience or to their suitability to teaching or even to the quality of their work— these writers will "draw."

Since it seems detrimental to the growth of a sound writing program for a literature faculty, especially, to abstain from active and formal participation in the hiring of writing faculty, I think we must look at writing programs historically in order to understand how at least one creative writing teacher in an M.F.A. program might come to elicit concern on the parts of literature and composition faculty.

Most writing programs developed slowly, usually as a result of the interest of one or two faculty members, some student demand, and the idea that writing courses could draw revenue into English departments. Usually several faculty members who have doctoral degrees and who write fiction and/or poetry begin teaching an occasional course in creative writing. Students flock to the courses, additional faculty are hired, and in time a full-fledged program comes into existence.

Since World War II, interest in contemporary literature as an area of study within the university has increased sharply. This rise in interest was met with chagrin at some universities; only since the 1960s has Columbia, for instance, permitted dissertations on James Joyce. Slow recognition of contemporary work as appropriate for graduate study has coincided with economic problems in universities and with the development of writing programs. While literature faculties were adjusting to the insertion into "traditional" studies of highly contemporary work—film studies, minority studies, children's literature, *and* new theories of criticism—they were simultaneously asked to embrace writing programs. It was, I think, too much at one time. Curricular changes not only brought to the fore the thorny issue, still unresolved, of the "canon" but also required the hiring and tenuring of faculties whose disciplines, indeed whose very language in scholarly discourse, had an unsettling effect on faculty whose notions of English studies issued more from the Renaissance ideal than from Lévi-Strauss.

What I have sensed is that overburdened literature faculty tended to be unable to concern themselves intimately with new developments in both literature *and* creative writing. It was probably assumed for the sake of expediency that debates about direction and quality in writing programs mirrored those in literature. I think the assumption was wrong.

First, writing programs developed slowly, almost invisibly, until embracing a full-fledged program meant more or less approving of that which was already in place. And the Iowa program was the model. Did not students in the Iowa program publish poems in *Harper's* and *Atlantic*, a question asked without, it seems, a real understanding of how those magazines, among others, were changing to reflect the taste of a more general and probably less educated audience.

But, more significantly, writing programs are an American phenomenon. Debate at whatever level of intensity could not be augmented by Continental thought. The loss was and is, to my mind, enormous.

There are no theorists of the teaching of creative writing equal to the theorists in literature and composition. While the *AWP Newsletter* prints interesting, if lightweight, essays about writers and occasionally about the position of writing programs within English departments, the marked absence of essays about the *teaching* that creative writers do within English departments underscores a passivity lurking behind one of the AWP's "Additional Recommendations," which follow the more formal guidelines: ". . . most teachers of writing felt they were most effective in the workshop format. . . ." This statement is followed simply by a recommendation that workshops have no more than fifteen students. But questions abound: "Effective" at doing what? Based on what assumptions about and knowledge of world literature? "Effective" as a teacher within what vision of the student writer as prospective professional? The assumption could easily be, in such a vacuum, that most teachers of creative writing find the workshop format effective because it is the only format they know. Yet there are other methods. (See chapter 6 for only one example.)

Within individual writing programs (and I have been a member of three and a guest of many), I have discovered little debate about teaching methods, including those of the workshop; about the positions of writing programs within departments, although the desire for complete autonomy is often voiced; about curricula; about the requirement of the thesis, and so on. Most often changes appear to happen in this way: students, overburdened as they are, rally together to complain about a literature or composition course requirement; the director of writing, ever mindful of keeping enrollments high, rallies the staff, and pressure begins to be exerted to keep the M.F.A. student happy *in the way that the M.F.A. student suggests.*

The trend, in fact, is away from complex discussion, even the possibility of discussion. As increased funding is poured into writing programs, more money becomes available for hiring "name" visiting writers and new faculty. The glossy brochures advertising M.F.A. programs emphasize not the programs' curricula but the luminosity of the programs' "star" writers, as if there is necessarily a direct correlation between fame and teaching ability. The latest trend, in fact, is to hire very young writers, with or without teaching experience, who have a book from a New York publisher—and often one book is enough. After all, a "star" can give a student's manuscript to an agent or editor to be heard, while a writing teacher whose national reputation is modest may simply ask the student to consider a variety of revisions. The brochures and magazine advertisements for some writing programs are now listing magazines in which the program's *students* have published. A writing program builds a record of student publication: all must be well with the writing program. Debate is *not* encouraged.

Indeed, M.F.A. faculty who are not sanguine about the M.F.A. programs in which they work must be careful about voicing reservations since, historically, writing programs are said to be embattled, isolated from the literature and composition programs, and in competition for funds that are often awarded by deans to programs within departments which appear especially healthy. The message from writing program directors explicitly and from administrators implicitly is, "Present a united front, a cheerleading section."

Yet what is distressing about this pattern of development in writing programs is that the currently defined indicators of a program's health or weakness have not been questioned. While critics go to scholarly journals and symposia for enlightenment about their colleagues' work—journals which will not often be advertised in *The New York Times Book Review* and with circulations of, at best, several thousand—English departments' personnel, tenure, and promotion committees bow to the East when evaluating the promise and accomplishments of writing faculty. And if writing faculty do not like this fact they nevertheless encourage it when they lobby for the magic a "star" writer will bring to a program as guest or staff. This practice of demonstrating particular excitement when a candidate has a New York publisher continues despite lip service to the impeccable aesthetic and intellectual standards of such "small" journals as *Prairie Schooner, The Virginia Quarterly Review, The Georgia Review, Salmagundi,* and *The Partisan Review,* to name a few of the perhaps two dozen excellent literary journals. The excuse often is that *deans* give less credence to literary journals, which may be the case. If so, it is understandable since the heady proliferation of mediocre literary journals, begun by a number of universities as substantiation of writing programs' value and visibility, helped devalue even the best journals.

Student publication as an indicator of a program's health is something I have not heard debated among writing teachers as being, possibly, a two-sided issue. Nor is it likely to be debated as long as M.F.A. programs advertise their programs by touting student publication. This advertising strategy is waged both within and outside of English departments; it has become a standard method by which writing programs tell literature and composition programs how well they are doing. Yet we know that it is not difficult for an average M.F.A. student to learn to write well, even "professionally," any particular type of story, poem, or nonfiction piece. What is much more difficult is to expand one's capabilities, to push the limits, to begin to discover how form can be molded to reflect a personal worldview. Such expansion of vision often requires that a student experiment and, invariably, produce awkward work on the way to a broader understanding and polishing of forms. Nevertheless, students are pressured to publish: publication will ensure renewal of a fellowship, help the writing program advertise itself, and possibly open the doors to New York. What most students do while preparing their theses and submitting work to publishers is to eschew experimentation in favor of refinement of what they already do well.

When *The New York Times Magazine* ran a story about the Iowa writing program on its fiftieth anniversary, the writer focused on the "stars" the program had produced as well as those it had lured to teach in the program. In response, a former student wrote to the magazine, "There is nothing wrong with encouraging success. But the purpose of the workshop is to stave off the realities of the marketplace for a few years, give students a chance to find their own voices, their concerns, allow them to be *students*." But John Legget, former director of the Iowa Writers Program, seems to confirm the assumed rightness of a student's narrowing down when he said, "What we're [the teachers] meant to do, really, is to help students refine their skills. 'You can't do children,' we say, 'but the old people in that piece came off fine.' We can stop them from doing what they don't do well and hope that next time they'll play to their strengths."

These students are in their early twenties, a time when pushing their limits may be the most valuable course to take. A writing teacher who doesn't keep his or her eye trained on the publications of students may instead envision the student writer at age thirty-five, when the writer who couldn't "do" children may have found a *need* to know techniques by which children can be rendered fictionally.

The book-length M.F.A. thesis requirement may similarly constrain students. Since many programs require the thesis to be of "professional quality," the question is, what, of that which a writing student needs to know in order to embark on a career as an imaginative writer and, in some cases, on a career as someone who also writes *about* writing, is being sacrificed for the thesis? There *are* trade-offs, yet I have not heard any discussion in writing programs or English departments or read delineations in the *AWP Newsletter* of what these trade-offs may be.

Nor have I heard discussion among teachers of writing about how to help students arrive at an understanding of broad theories of aesthetics that they may need in mid-career and that they will certainly need if they want to be responsible for their work. V. S. Naipaul's essay on Conrad is a fine example of a writer's search for an understanding of form placed against a backdrop of both tradition and a writer's need for form's plasticity as a response to experience over time. This ability to examine his writer's position is what many critics, correctly I think, believe Hemingway lacked and sorely needed. For students lacking experience and perhaps an inclination to examine a creativity they are taught is fragile, it is nevertheless possible to suggest questions they will no doubt encounter as they develop in relation both to themselves and to form. On the simplest level, what does a writer do when the roman a clef stories have all been written? More difficult but worthy are considerations of a writer's attitude to language and form as carriers *in themselves* of political and social assumptions as well as methods by which subtle social and political affects are or can be expressed in imaginative writing.

As literature faculty who read Continental works know, the traditional "face" of literature is changing rapidly, partly in response to post-structuralist criticism, which has questioned not only the definition of *text* but the uses to which texts are put. And American writers have been responding. Yet it is not clear whether their response is reflective merely of the word from "out there" that something new is afloat (which would account for the seeming naivete of much contemporary writing by the very young) or whether theirs is a considered response to a changing world and its assumptions about language and form.

But if M.F.A. students and their faculty knit themselves into tight cocoons of unexamined curricula, of defensive responses to literature and composition programs, and of provincial views of success in the field of writing, how are they to participate not only in a worldwide community of writers, but also in a global community of thinkers?

Let me illustrate my point. The so-called "blue collar" novel or story is currently a fad in American fiction, coexisting with what reviewer James Wolcott has identified as "the young and the wasted" fad exemplified by Ellis's two novels (1987, 13). The fad has spilled over into poetry, there termed "working-class poetry." In fiction, Ray Carver's stories are an example, as is Russell Bank's *Continental Drift*. A class below the working class was featured in Carolyn Chute's *The Beans of Egypt, Maine,* which alerted young writers and New York publishers to the fact that a first, slim work of fiction could vault a writer to fame. In an intellectual vacuum, students are not prone to ask hard questions raised by this fad, such as, are middle-class readers for whom the books are marketed having primarily a voyeuristic experience when reading about the lower class or, if not, what aspects of form mitigate voyeurism? Are these fictions political documents that exaggerate characters' traits to make a point? What is the effect of this exaggeration, if it exists, politically and socially? Should an imaginative writer be concerned with fiction's social and political effect? How does a reader evaluate cliches attached to characters of a class unfamiliar to the reader? And so on and so forth.

What is even more striking about the writing of Nadine Gordimer than her material is her refusal to underestimate the intelligence of either her characters or her readers, since to do so would obfuscate the true dangers of the struggles her fictions reflect. But many M.F.A. students have not read Gordimer, and the question is, can they evaluate Carver or Chute in such a vacuum?

From my perspective within an M.F.A. program, what is most exciting intellectually in English departments is happening in literature programs. It is also not surprising that there is a relationship between the economics of Ph.D. programs and new ideas. Ph.D. students, searching for material to investigate which had not been overplundered, were placed almost naturally in the position of having to seek newness. European critics' investigations into semiotics and the use of anthropological data to criticism linked graduate students and faculty in literature to the oldest and newest views of language, form, and humankind's relationship to both. That alarmists over the post-structuralists' "cold" relationship to texts have set up a hue and cry is merely a response that usually accompanies change, since, after all, it was not, as some writing faculty have supposed, a contagious disease the French offered, but simply some interesting ways to consider certain literary texts and readers' relationships to them.

A number of writing faculty, while looking to the American publishing scene for indications of how matters stood for them intellectually and economically, behaved as if *their* students, fragile vessels of creativity, were not, if they had anything to do with it, going to be exposed to the thing—whatever it was. One such response was carried in the September/October 1987 *AWP Newsletter*. "Tell them ["those fatcat professors of creative writing"] to hire someone who will teach you to write intelligent and analytical practical criticism of difficult, actual literary texts," writes Peter Stitt, editor of *The Gettysburg Review* and a former teacher in the creative writing program at The University of Houston (1987, 3).

While the message to literature programs is clear ("... the new breed of theorists want to be seen as the custodians of a body of knowledge so rarefied that ordinary mortals cannot be trusted with its secrets," Stitt writes), what may not be so clear to the M.F.A. students who read the *Newsletter* is that Stitt wants thinking about language and its forms frozen in time. In music this would be like freezing out Alban Berg or Donald Harris.

The question is, how are M.F.A. students to learn to feel confident as *thinkers* as long as M.F.A. faculty behave as intellectual provincials? Knowing of and thinking about contemporary theories of criticism does not mean an M.F.A. student must embrace the theories, which Peter Stitt believes were adopted by certain literature faculty simply as a ploy to grab power in English departments. The M.F.A. student may want to consider new ways of thinking about literature when encountering new literary works, such as V. S. Naipaul's *The Engima of Arrival* and Kundera's body of work, which demonstrate that writers, as Naipaul has written, "change the form of narrative because every civilization reveals its dynamic in a special way" (Von Barloewen 1985, 32).

If M.F.A. students felt more sure of themselves intellectually— rather than feeling protected *from* intellectualism by their M.F.A. faculty—it is possible that they would also feel more sure economically. Most current M.F.A. students are headed toward trades upon graduation—proofreading, copyediting, advertising, or public relations work. They are unable to conceive of themselves as finding work as *thinkers*. Yet, V. S. Naipaul is a perfect example of someone who could support himself as a writer because he was able and willing to write in a number of forms, discursive and creative, and to trust his ability to think. It is a European tradition.

It is possible that our current M.F.A. students will document a peculiar time in education, when creative writing was the fashion apart from cultural grounding. They are our new nouveau riche.

I do not think that it would be easy for M.F.A. programs to broaden the base of their concerns. But I also think that English departments that maintain creative writing programs must not wait for writing faculty to signal their willingness to expand their conceptions of education for creative writing students.

It is time, I think, for literature faculty especially to ask themselves if they are now able to concern themselves with what is happening in writing programs. This would require sloughing off traditional disdain, no matter how well founded, and seeking actively to invite M.F.A. students and faculty into a community of intellectuals. But how?

The means could be as varied as the minds that think creatively about the problem. To suggest only a few:

- Writing and literature faculty could team-teach courses in the history of literary criticism, including post-structuralist criticism, with the writing faculty member encouraging M.F.A. students to see relationships between the ways they, as imaginative writers, think about writing and the various theories of criticism by which literature has been studied.

- In an M.F.A. program's reading series, imaginative writers reading from their own fiction or poetry could be alternated with imaginative writers or critics reading papers *about* contemporary writing. This type of series by visiting writers could be alternated with a similar series by student writers.

- M.F.A. faculty could be encouraged to design new methods of teaching writing as alternatives to the workshop methods and to do so with a focus on contemporary *world* literature.

- Literature and writing faculty could cooperate in designing courses for M.F.A. students which would ensure those students' ability to write critical essays on both works of literature and on trends in contemporary writing.

- The requirement of the M.F.A. thesis could be questioned, and an alternative means of evaluating M.F.A. students' development as writers could be studied.

- New approaches to advertising M.F.A. programs could be studied, and new methods of substantiating a writing program's development and "health" could be devised.

- A focus on student publication could be replaced by a focus on students' taking responsibility for envisioning, planning for, and studying for professional writing careers.

- Literature faculty could help M.F.A. faculty devise reading courses for M.F.A. students which would help those students place trends in contemporary writing within a context of historical developments in form.

- M.F.A. programs with their own literary journals could determine to publish not only writing in imaginative forms but also critical articles about imaginative writing, if the journals are without such articles. New types of journals could be conceived to reflect current debates about form and technique—possibly publishing commentary on the imaginative writing that appears in the journals, with guidelines that ask the authors to write specifically about form and technique in their commentary.

- M.F.A. programs could sponsor conferences about the teaching of imaginative writing.
- Literature and composition faculty could become fully involved in the hiring of M.F.A. faculty, with an eye toward the M.F.A. students' need to be a part of the university's intellectual community.

The possibilities are, of course, numerous, and they can multiply exponentially if an atmosphere exists in which creative thinking about the teaching of imaginative writing eventually becomes benign. And this work on the part of literature faculty need not, I think, be selfless. All that is required as an impetus is the realization that writing spawns writing; that M.F.A. students will publish; and that how deeply students think will affect the future of American literature.

Since I think that much of what I have said in this chapter will be seen as heretical by writing faculty (we *are* accustomed to praising ourselves; we *are* by and large a self-satisfied group), it is possible that literature faculty who become involved in M.F.A. programs should prepare themselves to hear writing faculty scream bloody murder all the way to the baptism.

But writing programs do not need to produce *more* writers, contrary to all the trends in universities that tout "bigger" as "better." (Our M.F.A. students do not need to be held hostage in the economic crises of English departments—their economic plights are dire enough). Writing programs need to produce *better* writers for whom the latest fads in fiction and poetry are to be questioned; writers who envision themselves in a community of intellectuals—a global community of writers who are able to question American publishing practices and their effects on literature; writers who know they have a cultural heritage; and writers who can envision producing that which can become a cultural heritage instead of a dispiriting literary era.

Works Cited

Atlas, James. "V.S. vs. The Rest." *Vanity Fair* 50, no. 3 (March 1987): 64–69.

"AWP Guidelines for Creative Writing Programs and Teachers of Creative Writing." *AWP Newsletter*, September/October 1987: 12.

Gass, William H. "A Failing Grade for the Present Tense." *New York Times Book Review*, October 11, 1987: 1, 32, 34, 35, 38.

Kolakowski, Leozek. "The Polish Intellectual: Response and Discussion." *Salmagundi* 70–71 (Spring-Summer 1986): 233.

Rafferty, Terrence. "Advertisements for Themselves." *The New Yorker*, October 26, 1987: 142–46.

Sheppard, R. Z. "Yuppie Lit: Publicize or Perish." *Time*, October 19, 1987: 77–79.

Stitt, Peter. "Writers, Theorists, and the Department of English." *AWP Newsletter*, September/October 1987: 1–3.

Von Barloewen. "Naipaul's World." *World Press Review* 32, no. 4 (April 1985): 32–33.

Wolcott, James. "The Young and the Wasted." *Vanity Fair* 50, no. 9 (September 1987): 24–32.

2 Tearing Down the Walls: Engaging the Imagination

Joseph M. Moxley
University of South Florida

I believe our primary role as writing teachers should be to engage students in one of the world's most natural endeavors: the creative process. Engaging students' imaginations requires an interdisciplinary approach, one which brings together creative writing, literature, criticism, and composition. As Donald Hall argues, everyone loses when writing, reading, and interpretation are compartmentalized into mutually exclusive areas of specialization:

> The separation of the literature department from the writing department is a disaster; for poet, for scholar, and for student. The poet may prolong adolescence into retirement by dealing only with the products of infant brains. . . . The scholars of the department, institutionally separated from the contemporary, are encouraged to ignore it. In the ideal relationship, writers play gadfly to scholars, and scholars help writers connect to the body of past literature. (1987, 10–11)

The general segregation of creative writing from literature and composition corrodes the development of a literary culture. In our eagerness to pursue intellectual territory germane to our disciplines and interests, we have established mutually exclusive lexicons, subjects, journals, and methods of inquiry. Our students—who need help seeing connections among ideas, events, books, and traditions—are told they should take literature courses to read, expository and technical writing courses to write nonfiction, fiction writing workshops to write fiction, poetry workshops to write poetry, speech courses to make speeches, critical thinking courses to think, research methods courses to interview people or survey attitudes, and psychology courses to study behavior in a systematic way.

Naturally, there is much good in this specialization: each discipline clearly deserves and requires special attention. Yet, the process of writing transcends many of the distinctions among disciplines. As a fundamental mode of thought and self-expression, writing integrates, organizes, connects, and stimulates perception and learning. Just as we expect students to listen to lectures and read materials, so we should expect writing to be at the center of any college or high school education.

Our zeal for specialization and analysis has confounded our ability to perceive useful parallels between creative writing, expository writing, and literature. For example, David Smith reminds us that the term "creative," when applied solely to fiction, drama, or poetry, is largely a misnomer: ". . . all writing that has interest, value, passion, durability, and vision is necessarily creative" (1981, 2). Whether composing monthly feasibility studies, poetry, screenplays, or the great American novel, writers are engaged in a natural, organic process of forming meaning.

Our passion for specialization has encouraged us to divide and subdivide what should be considered to be an *integrative* and *generative* process of discovering and shaping meaning. All writing carries the seeds of creativity: when our images and concepts develop, combine, and connect and take shape in the form of words, writers discover and construct their meaning. Language is not "a set of molds into which we pour our incandescent thoughts" (Berthoff, "Speculative Instruments," 114). Meaning finds form in language when writers have a dialogue with their texts, when they ask questions about genre, character, purpose, tone, and audience. In hopes of providing us with a more holistic model of composing, Donald Murray ("Teach Writing as a Process," 24) challenges us with a vision he asks us to imagine multiplied "a thousand times or more for each draft of an essay or story" (see the accompanying illustration; original version copyright 1980 by National Council of Teachers of English):

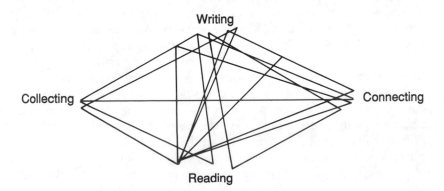

Murray believes that connecting and collecting are a natural consequence of perception: "As we collect a piece of information, we immediately try to connect it with other pieces of information" (21). And he hypothesizes that the tension between the generative nature of writing and the more critical nature of reading influences how we connect and collect ideas:

> Reading seems to involve criticism. We make comparisons; we look for immediate clarity, for instant grace. *Just as connecting can control collecting too effectively and too early, so reading can suppress writing.* The writer has to develop new forms of reading, to read loosely at first, to give the piece of writing space so that the embryonic patterns of meaning which are making shadowy appearance can have time to come clear. (23; emphasis added)

Murray's model forcefully illustrates our need to establish an interdisciplinary approach, one which recognizes the interactive and dynamic nature of reading and writing, one which accounts for each writer's personality, personal background, and sociocultural experiences. In short, writers do not live in a vacuum and we cannot afford to blind students with tunnel vision. As educators, we must be careful not to confuse the single cell for the organism.

Creative Writing and Composition

Because Eve Shelnutt has already examined ways creative writing teachers and students could benefit from an interdisciplinary approach that brings literary and critical study into its proper relation with writing (see chapter 1), I will narrow the following to exploring ways composition theory and research and the anecdotal accounts of professional writers can inform the practices of students and teachers of creative writing. While many creative writing teachers and artists have tended to enshrine and mystify the creative process, composition theorists have been charting common patterns of how writers generate and refine material by studying the planning, prewriting, revising, and editing practices of professional and student writers. These studies have greatly enhanced our understanding of how the generative nature of language guides writers; how writing promotes thinking and learning; how writers draw on unconscious images, the right hemisphere of the brain, felt sense, personal experiences, and literature to develop material.

Given creative writing teachers' relative lack of interest in pedagogy, it is ironic to note that composition theorists' interest in writing as a mode of thinking, prewriting and editing heuristics, peer criticism, and a Socratic, nondirective approach emerged from the inherent advantages of the workshop method and from studies of professional writers' composing behavior.

As a whole, composition research and the anecdotal accounts of professional writers challenge us to reconsider our theories of creativity and practices. Ultimately, our increased understanding of what writing involves suggests that creativity is the natural consequence of learning, involvement, and commitment. For this reason, I believe we need to reevaluate the assumption that only a chosen few are capable of creative writing or creative thinking.

Creative Writing, Mysticism, and Alienation

As a culture, we tend to cloak the creative process in a mantle of mysticism. Artists are considered by many to be weird, supernatural beings who are living on the edge of sanity, who must live in dark garrets in order to create meaningful work. For example, Allan Bloom contends, "A man who can generate visions of a cosmos and ideals by which to live is a *genius,* a demonic being" (1987, 181). Valerie Miner aptly describes this elitist syndrome in chapter 20: "We cultivate an antagonism toward the artist and develop a sado-masochistic relationship with him or her. Often we demand that as proof or penance for the art, the writer be addicted, psychotic, desperately unhappy or suicidal."

Though some elements of the creative process are indeed mysterious and though some creators are geniuses, emphasizing the mysterious nature of creativity erects walls around our writing classrooms. With a dismissive wave of a hand, we should not foster the myth that writers are born, that you cannot teach someone to be a talented writer. The price of our lack of pedagogical and theoretical inquiry is isolation and divestment: many students don't enroll in writing courses because they've been trained to think they're neither creative nor gifted. Still others avoid writing (and literature) courses because they perceive English and writing to be an esoteric discipline, an artistic (or even magical) activity dependent solely on divine inspiration. In Arthur Applebee's nationwide study of writing in American secondary schools, he discovered that very little creative writing is being assigned: only 8.2 percent of the 182 ninth graders' writing that he examined and only 7.2 percent of the 167 eleventh graders' writing that he examined involved writing stories or poems. Apparently, rather than being asked to explore their own experiences, American high school students are expected to summarize, report, and sometimes analyze given information. A similar and earlier study of 1,992 British students' writing samples, completed by James Britton and his colleagues, suggested that British students' academic opportunities for creative expression diminish as students grow older: 17 percent of the sixth graders' writing, 23 percent of the eighth graders' writing, 24 percent of the tenth graders' writing, and 7 percent of the twelfth graders' writing could be classified as poetic or creative. In agreement with Applebee's findings, Britton discovered that students are not given much opportunity to write fiction or persuasive or theoretical writing—writing that demands much imagination, commitment, self-involvement or extensive revision. For many, schooling involves being trained to follow the rules, to listen instead of asking questions, to sit quietly at a desk and passively listen to a teacher who spends two-thirds of the class' time lecturing (Barnes 1976). Schooling primarily teaches students to sort information in multiple-choice, true-false tests, and short-answer forms. Reality and truth are considered to be quantifiable, divisible by true-false, a-b-c-d objective tests.

We obviously need to ask why *more* creative writing isn't taught in the schools. As Aldous Huxley cautions, we must ask why our educational system discourages creative and critical thinking:

> Why is it that in most children education seems to destroy the creative urge? Why do so many boys and girls leave school with blunted perceptions and a closed mind? [sic] A majority of young people seem to develop mental arteriosclerosis forty years before they get the physical kind. (1963, 202)

Even though most of them will not go on to become the next Bellow, Tyler, Calvino, Hemingway, or whoever, all of our students can learn that they have imaginative minds. In addition, some experience writing literature enhances students' ability to read and appreciate literature or to criticize and interpret texts.

The first step toward engaging students begins with developing a curriculum that addresses their interests and provides them with opportunities for composing. And then, as John Gardner has warned, we must encourage risk-taking and independence: "In a bad workshop, the teacher takes the place of students' critical imagination" (1983, 86).

Thought and Language

When we're teaching writing, we're not involved in an esoteric activity. Writing not only stimulates thought, but is itself a significant mode of thought, a way of generating ideas. As Janet Emig has observed, writing exercises the three factors that encourage learning which Jerome Bruner defined: "(1) enactive—we learn 'by doing'; (2) iconic—we learn 'by depiction in an image'; and (3) representational or symbolic—we learn 'by restatement in words'" (1977, 124). Furthermore, because it involves the hand, the eye, and the brain, writing is a remarkably "multi-presentational mode for learning" (125). Writing provides "a unique form of feedback, as well as reinforcement . . . because information from the *process* is immediately and visibly available as that portion of the *product* already written" (125). This fact allows writers to review how their ideas developed when they become blocked, thereby promoting more analysis and synthesis. As with successful learning, writing is self-rhymed, engaged, committed.

According to Lev Vygotsky, thought and language stem from separate genetic roots. As children learn more language, language becomes abbreviated, more personalized and egocentric. Eventually language becomes so condensed that it bonds with thought at a subterranean level, creating what Vygotsky called "inner speech." Based on his observations of children, Vygotsky hypothesized that the more language, scientific concepts, axioms and metaphors we know, the more fully developed our inner speech and thinking can become:

> Thought development is determined by language, i.e., by the linguistic tools of thought and by the sociocultural experience of the child. Essentially, the development of inner speech depends on outside factors. . . . The child's intellectual growth is contingent on his mastering the social means of thought, that is, language. (1962, 51)

If Vygotsky's assumptions are correct, the more students listen to the voice in the back of their minds and the more opportunities they have to tell stories or write poems about their experiences and learning, the more fully developed their thinking and language will become.

Recursive Composing Strategies

Studies of students' and professional writers' composing processes have led away from prescriptive, linear models. Janet Emig, Sondra Perl, Maxine Hairston, Linda Flower, and John Hayes (among others) have observed that writers refer to their memory, plan, hesitate, reread, and assess the rhetorical situation throughout composing. The work of these and other composition researchers has caused us to reject the think-and-then-write paradigm as well as the linear—plan, prewrite, write, and revise—model of composing. For example, we now recognize that writers perform global revisions when rehearsing possible subjects and treatments.

With our heightened understanding of the dynamic, recursive nature of composing, we can help students try new strategies when writing. For example, John Gardner's recommendation might inspire a student writer who always attempts to compose a finished product on the first draft:

> Fiction, like sculpture or painting, begins with a rough sketch. One gets down the characters and their behavior any way one can, knowing the sentences will have to be revised, knowing the characters' actions may change. It makes no difference how clumsy the sketch is—sketches are not supposed to be polished and elegant. All that matters is that, going over and over the sketch as if one had all eternity for finishing one's story, one improves this sentence, now that, noticing what changes the new sentences urge, and in the process one gets the characters and their behavior clearer in one's head, gradually discovering deeper and deeper implications of the characters' problems and hopes. *Fiction does not spring into the world full grown, like Athena. It is the process of writing and rewriting that makes a fiction original and profound.* One cannot judge in advance whether or not the idea of the story is worthwhile because until one has finished writing the story one does not know for sure what the idea is; and one cannot judge the style of the story on the basis of a first draft, because in a first draft the style of the finished story does not yet exist. (1983, 135–36; emphasis added)

Many students clearly need to learn how to shut off the editor and let the material flow—that is, to brainstorm and freewrite.

Although some writing theorists and most textbook authors prescribe a single composing process, others such as Jack Selzer have observed that the writer's interest in, and familiarity with, the subject and audience and other constraints (such as the writer's schedule) affect composing behaviors. Selzer argues persuasively that we need to accommodate in our teaching a variety of effective composing strategies: "Instead of prescribing a single composing model and instead of making assignments appropriate only to that model, teachers need to concentrate on expanding and directing students' composing repertories" (1984, 281). Selzer wisely argues that we need to educate students about the range of composing possibilities: "[teachers] must expose students to a variety of composing styles and actions, a variety of possibilities for planning, inventing, arranging, and revising" (282). Selzer also challenges us to develop assignments that will stimulate and exercise a range of composing activities. We clearly need more extensive research into how writing in different genres promotes creative growth and vision. If Elizabeth Winthrop's experiences are representative of the affect of writing for different audiences and purposes or creativity, then we clearly should be asking students to shape their material into multiple forms, such as the avant-garde short story, the realistic play, the confessional editorial (see chapter 8).

In her studies of the recursiveness in writing, Sondra Perl has observed that when writers reread little bits of discourse they often return to "some key word or item called up by the topic" (1980, 365) and that they return "to feelings or non-verbalized perceptions that *surround* the words, or to what the words already present *evoke* in the writer" (365). While comparing this activity, which she labels "felt-sense," to Vygotsky's conception of "inner speech" or the feeling of "inspiration," Perl suggests that writers listen "to one's inner reflections . . . and bodily sensations. . . . There is less 'figuring out' an answer and more 'waiting' to see what forms. . . . Once a felt sense forms, we match words to it" (366–67).

James Moffett, Gordon Rohman, and some other composition theorists have suggested that we should teach students to meditate in order to help them discover their felt-sense. By calling for in-class writing, journal reports, in-the-field notes or research, or by prescribing particular genres or poetic forms, we can intrude on students' usual methods and encourage new behaviors (and, of course, we can make them conscious of what they do well). Also, we can ask students to log their different ways of composing in journals and encourage open-ended discussions of their "experiments." And we can help students recognize the recursive and sometimes mysterious nature of composing by having them read interviews with professional writers in books like the *Writers at Work: The* Paris Review *Interviews* or books by professional writers about learning the craft, such as John Gardner's *The Art of Fiction*. Finally, as Jack Selzer recommends, we can have students interview each other to discover more about their composing processes.

The Scientific Method

Because of the difficulties inexperienced writers have getting started, composition theorists have proposed several ways to teach students to gather and analyze information, such as Rohman's prewriting techniques; Young, Becker, and Pike's tagmemic heuristic; Burke's dramatist pentad; Flower and Hayes's problem-solving strategies; and the journalists' questions—who? what? where? why? when? how?[1]

Because it does not draw attention away from writing, George Hillocks has argued that the most effective method to teach inquiry is to familiarize students with the scientific model. According to Hillocks, investigators in the natural sciences share the same basic strategies of inquiry as critics and philosophers: observation → description → comparison/contrast → enumerative generalizations → definitions → hypothesis. Hillocks reviews over ten years of independent investigations which demonstrate that encouraging observation and comparison promotes writing improvement and student involvement, and he has found similar results in his own research:

> Further, when one group of independent judges was asked to rate pre- and post-test compositions on a scale of creativity and another group was asked to rate them on a scale of organization and support, both sets of judgments resulted in statistically significant differences in favor of the students who participated in observational activities. (1982, 670)

Garth Boomer also believes that "human beings are born scientists." Five years of observing hundreds of teachers, students, and parents in South Australia have led him to conclude that formal research is the natural outcome of the active mind:

> In small groups, they compare and contrast each other's learning, looking for patterns and dissimilarities. Unerringly, the classic scientific method emerges: problem → observation → hypothesis → testing → evaluation. The learner runs back and forth across these "phases," but each and every piece of learning can be accommodated within the model. (1987, 9)

The emphasis Hillocks and Boomer give to involving students in observing and comparing events, objects, and people is clearly analogous to Ann Berthoff's call for engaging the active, forming imagination. While quoting Coleridge's *Biographia Literaria*—"The primary imagination I hold to be the living power and the prime agent of all human perception"—Berthoff reminds us that "imagination is properly a name for the active mind, the mind of the child making forms in the sand, the artist making forms in granite . . ." ("The Teacher as Researcher," 36). Because we all share a primordial urge to create ideas, images, or stories that are original at least for us,

Berthoff argues that we can engage students' imaginations by encouraging observation and writing:

> . . . looking, seeing, turns on the mind. When we encourage students to look and look again, we are not differentiating creative and critical writing, which should be kept together, just as composing and editing should be kept apart. . . . Students of composition and creative writing who do a lot of looking will learn that perspective and context are essential to interpretation. In short, they will learn habits of mind essential to critical and creative thinking. ("The Teacher as Researcher," 37)

In agreement with Hillocks and Boomer, Berthoff contends, ". . . the mind naturally orders by comparing and differentiating. . . . We see in terms of classes and types. . . . My point is that we do not have to teach our students *how* to abstract but *that* they abstract" ("Discovering Limits," 75). Ultimately, engaging students in observational activities affirms the organic nature of composing and perception. We need to embrace the concept that providing students with lots of opportunities to write about subjects that they care about will promote writing development more than endless hours of *talk* about writing or grammar.

Creativity, the Unconscious, and the Right Brain

I also believe that we need to inform students about the role of the unconscious and the right brain in composing. The Romantic poets and some twentieth-century artists have suggested that the unconscious facilitates creativity. Believing that their dreams are windows into the deeper recesses of the mind, some contemporary artists even wake themselves at irregular intervals during a night's sleep. Anaïs Nin says, "For creativity it is necessary to work with the unconscious which accumulates pure experience, reactions, impressions, intuitions, images, memories—an unconscious freed from the negative effect of societal evaluations" (1968, 21).

In *The Courage to Create*, Rollo May has described four attributes that characterize moments when creative ideas transcend the humdrum veneer of daily life. First, while citing Picasso—"Every act of creation is first of all an act of destruction"—May contends that the unconscious "seems to take delight . . . in breaking through—and breaking up—exactly what we cling to most rigidly in our conscious thinking" (1976, 62).

Second, May suggests that creative moments are particularly vivid, indicating "a state of heightened consciousness" (63).

Third, creative insights usually occur in response to conscious attempts at solving a problem. In other words, scientists, artists, and writers don't sit around coffee shops hoping for inspiration. Effective problem solvers are committed to understanding what they perceive to be an incomplete gestalt.

Fourth, if we're not too rigid and dogmatic, creative breakthroughs often come "at a moment of transition between work and relaxation" (66). Albert Einstein once asked a friend of Rollo May, "Why is it I get my best ideas in the morning when I'm shaving?" (64). And it is interesting to note that Einstein conceived his theory about the time-space continuum when he was sick in bed. While demonstrating the need for incubation and hard work, this fourth attribute also clarifies the need to be open-minded and willing to embrace chaos. Keats, in his definition of "negative capability," also suggested that creative artists must ". . . be capable of being in uncertainties, mysteries, doubts, without any irritable reaching for fact and reason" (Abrams et al. 1974, 705).

In addition to these attributes, many scientists and artists report that spontaneous and unbidden images often facilitate creative breakthroughs. For example, Italo Calvino argues that the creative mind leaps into the void, seeking meaning that has "no reference at the linguistic level" (1975, 79). Consider, for example, the dream of Friedrich Kekulé, in 1865, which inspired him to conceive of the cyclic structure for the molecule:

> Kekulé had been puzzling over the linkage of carbon atoms in forming the benzene ring . . . Then he dozed and saw snakes form a mouth-to-tail chain. The front snake took the hind snake's tail in its mouth. He realized the carbon atoms must be linked together in such a chain to account for the various properties of benzene and awoke with a start knowing he had solved the problem. (Horowitz 1978, 140)

In addition to illustrating the attributes of creative breakthroughs that May defined, Henri Poincaré's creative process when he theorized Fuchsian Functions also shows the effect of the explorative and retrospective nature of unconscious images. Poincaré writes in his autobiography:

> For fifteen days I strove to prove that there could not be any functions like those I have since called Fuchsian Functions. . . . One evening, contrary to my custom, I drank black coffee and could not sleep. Ideas rose in crowds . . . by the next morning I had established the existence of a class of Fuchsian Functions. . . . (1935, 36)

> Most striking at first is this appearance of sudden illumination, a
> manifest sign of long unconscious prior work. The role of this
> unconscious work in mathematical invention appears to me in-
> contestable. . . . These sudden inspirations . . . never happen
> except after some days of voluntary effort which has appeared
> absolutely fruitless. (38)

By examining the work of neurosurgeons, some composition researchers (see, for example, Janet Emig or Monica Weiss) have suggested that the inspirational flash, the much talked about "Eureka"
moment, comes about when the right hemisphere of the brain enter-
tains an insight that the ordered and logical left hemisphere has not
considered. According to neurologists, the left hemisphere—the
dominant, rational sphere—controls speech, language, and per-
ceives the world in a logical, critical, sequential way, while the right
hemisphere is more intuitive, visual, emotional, and capable of perceiving holistic patterns. Viewed from this perspective, what the Romantic poets called the unconscious may actually be stimulated right
hemispheric activity.

Perhaps in time research will provide us with some visual exercises that will stimulate the right hemisphere. Perhaps oil painting
and drawing and screenwriting courses will become recommended
for student writers. Meanwhile, we certainly need to inform students to be receptive to unbidden images and exploratory, metaphorical thinking. Our classrooms and assignments must encourage
students to take breaks from writing in order to help them understand the recursive nature of composing.

The Shape of Content

In this age of utilitarianism, many creative writing programs have
courageously resisted courses in commercial fiction. And though I
agree that we must do much more than provide vocational training
and that we must provide a strong, rigorous background in the humanities, I also believe that we should introduce students to the expectations of popular genres such as horror, suspense, mystery, science fiction, fantasy, and children's literature. If we are ever going
to compete with Blockbuster Video and other VCR superstores, if
we are going to stop escalating illiteracy rates, then I think we need
to broaden the base of "academic literature." Ultimately, our goal as
teachers is not to prescribe a particular literary form. We shouldn't,
for example, teach literary fiction as if that's all there is. If students
want to write science fiction, historical novels, romance, or some

other kind of commercial fiction, we should help them to realize their goals, while educating them about the range of alternatives. Creativity takes many forms.

At the same time, our students must learn that successful writers shape form in response to content. Form never exists without content, although form can suggest content. This, of course, is one of the reasons why we cannot rely solely on prose models for teaching writing. In fact, many creative writers reject all they have read when they sit down to write. Instead of mimicking work they admire, creative writers turn their focus inward toward the depths of inner speech. Rather than relying on prose models or literary traditions, the creative mind turns from the familiar:

> We seem to be hemmed in by peer groups, hedged by tradition, struck dumb by archetypes; to be other-directed, outer-directed, over-directed. We are the organization man. It is not allowed that we may think for ourselves or be different or create something better than that which was before. . . . One only need remark that *all art is based upon nonconformity.* (Shahn 1976, 76; emphasis added)

Many creative writers look inside, assessing what they've internalized, as opposed to mimicking what they admire:

> A story may be "workshoppy" because the writer (or the teacher) has too often thought from the literature student's point of view rather than from the writer's, so that instead of working like a storyteller, beginning with what happens and why, and only gradually moving . . . to the larger issues (how this story is in some way every human story, an expression of a constant or universal theme), the student writer begins with theme, symbolism, etc., in effect working backward from his imagined New Criticism analysis of a story not yet in existence. (Gardner 1983, 88)

> Every writer at some point must go through an analytical period, but in time he must get his own characteristic solutions into his blood, so that when confronted by a problem in a novel he's writing he does not consult his literary background. He feels his way to the solution; rather than drawing back from the fictional dream to look at what he's doing, he solves the problem by plunging deeper into the dream. (Gardner 1983, 115)

In short, creative writers look into themselves to find their content and form. As J. D. Salinger points out in *Seymour—An Introduction,* writers examine their hearts by questioning what they would want to read:

> Please follow your heart, win or lose. . . . When was writing
> ever your profession? It's never been anything but your re-
> ligion. . . . If only you'd remember before ever you sit down to
> write that you've been a *reader* long before you were a writer.
> You simply fix that fact in your mind, then sit very still and ask
> yourself, as a reader, what piece of writing in all the world Bud-
> dy Glass would most want to read if he had his heart's choice.
> The next step is terrible, but so simple I can hardly believe it as I
> write it. You just sit down shamelessly and write the thing your-
> self. (160–61)

Contrary to the rhetorical paradigm, writers like Aldous Huxley
don't bother with thoughts of external audiences when they're writing: "I've never made a point of writing for any particular person or
audience; I've simply tried to do the best job I could and let it go at
that" (Huxley 1963, 200). Wallace Fowlie writes in *The Age of Surrealism*, ". . . the modern artist has had to learn that the universe
which he is going to write or paint is in himself. He has learned that
this universe which he carries about in himself is singularly personal
and unique as well as universal" (1950, 29). By following their intui-
tion after reading copiously, writers find the universal in the particular:

> By obeying the improvisations born of emotions, by abandoning
> myself to digressions and variations, I found an indigenous
> structure, a form of organic growth, like crystal formations. In
> this world of the unconscious there is an inevitability as logical,
> as coherent as any found in classical drama . . . a plot in which
> it is our originality, our individuality, which gives surprising
> endings which never resemble each other . . . form created
> organically by meaning and born of an individual character. . . .
> It is when we use will and force to impose an artificial structure
> that we become sterile. (Nin 1968, 28–29)

Revisions and Critical Reading

Along with exploring ways to generate material, we also need to develop methods to teach students to be critical readers and editors of
their own writing. One of the chief distinctions between professional and student writers is that professionals perform multiple revisions, while many students expect to write well after one or two
drafts. In our writing workshops, we clearly must encourage revision by giving students sufficient time to look and look again at their
writing and by helping students see alternative ways to develop
their material. Rather than relying on one large group, we can sepa-

rate students into groups of three, thereby allowing each student to receive and provide more responses. By showing students samples of texts by professional writers, who have written multiple drafts or who have addressed the importance of revision, we can help students understand that revision is *an opportunity* to shape and discover intentions instead of *punishment* for being "incorrect." For example, James Thurber reports that he often rewrote a short story at least fifteen times:

> *Interviewer:* Then it's rare that your work comes out right the first time?

> *Thurber:* Well, my wife took a look at the first version of something I was doing not long ago and said, "Goddamn it, Thurber, that's high-school stuff." I have to tell her to wait until the seventh draft, it'll work out all right [*sic*]. I don't know why that should be so, that the first or second draft of everything I write reads as if it was turned out by a charwoman. (1977, 88)

Ernest Hemingway also stressed rewriting:

> *Interviewer:* How much rewriting do you do?

> *Hemingway:* It depends. I rewrote the ending to *Farewell to Arms,* the last page of it, thirty-nine times before I was satisfied. (1963, 222)

In order to promote revision we need to establish an ambience of critical thinking and critical reading in the writing classroom. By providing substantive responses to their fiction and by assigning revisions, we can help students distinguish local revisions—sentence-level changes such as spelling, word choice, and syntax—from important global revisions—changes which involve large-scale deletions and additions, and changes in tone, style, and organization.

Methods of Response

Like treading across a mine field, responding to student writing can be an awfully tricky process. On the one hand, we want to provide feedback that will help the student identify significant problems; and yet, we also need to be careful that we do not provide too much feedback and appropriate the student's text. Indeed, despite our best intentions, our responses to student papers can be more pernicious than instructive if we're overly judgmental.

As Sommers and Brannon and Knoblauch have argued, we need to decipher *the writer's intentions* and propose (when pertinent) several alternatives to realizing these intentions. Our function is not to compare a student's text with some unwritten, pre-verbal "ideal text." We cannot presume to know the *only* way to improve a text:

> But basically what teachers need to teach students is *not* how to fix a particular story but how to figure out what is wrong with the story and how to think about alternative ways of fixing it. . . . I've frequently worked with writing assistants—young writers with successful first novels—whose inexperience as teachers led them to focus on finding the best solution to problems in writing placed in their care. . . . In case after case, when I myself looked at the student's work later, I felt there were a number of possible solutions to the problems—alternative solutions whose relative value must depend on the student writer's preferences—and that in suggesting only one solution, the one he himself would choose, my assistant had done an unwitting disservice to the student. *What the beginner needs to learn is how to think like a novelist.* What he does not need is a teacher who imposes his own solution, like an algebra teacher who tells you the answer without showing how he got there, because it is *process* that the young writer must learn. . . . (Gardner 1983, 87)

We need to treat all student writing as emerging texts, rather than as completed products. After all, how many of us could complete a final draft of a story in two weeks (or even twelve or fifteen weeks)? Ultimately, our goal is to teach students to adopt the critical role writers assume when they ask questions about their work. We can best encourage risk-taking and commitment by omitting grades on individual manuscripts and by assigning a "pass" or "fail" at the end of the semester. Like many other writing teachers, I would prefer never to assign grades on individual manuscripts because grading transforms our effective roles as coaches into less productive roles as judges. It would, however, be foolhardy to ignore that most students are accustomed to receiving grades and that some students write primarily for grades. Thus, I assign grades for those students who are dependent on them, even though I am familiar with over thirty years of research which has demonstrated that *evaluative* commentaries do not seem to improve student writing (Moxley, "Responding to Student Writing," in press).

Productivity

Professional writers commonly cite *regular writing* as crucial. For example, John Gardner asked students in his novel writing workshops to present an outline for a novel at the beginning of the course and then called for a chapter each week: "Of the ten students in the course, eight later published their novels" (1983, 91). In chapter 6, John D. MacDonald argues that students should write 5,000 words per week, and in chapter 8, Elizabeth Winthrop explains that she is inspired by writing in different genres on similar themes. Marion Zimmer Bradley reminds us, in chapter 10, that time spent on task doesn't correlate absolutely with the success of the fiction. Yet, we must also remember that *regular* writing isn't necessarily *voluminous* writing. We all have different rhythms and often the speed at which we develop meaning is dependent on the number of risks that we're taking. Fine writers like Hemingway, Flaubert, and Joyce, for example, were known to put in eight-to-ten hour days to produce *a page*.

A recent study that Robert Boice conducted determined that "behavioral techniques actually facilitate writing that will be subjectively judged as creative" (1985, 473). Boice divided twenty-seven college professors into a control group, a spontaneous writing group, and a contingency writing group, and he asked the subjects to record the number of pages produced and the number of original ideas that occurred while writing. Boice asked the participants in the control group "to defer all but the most urgent writing tasks for exactly 10 weeks" (475). For three weeks the participants in the spontaneous group were asked to "write when you feel like it." Thereafter the spontaneous group was encouraged to write more and "to establish regular writing times five days per week" (475). After a ten-day baseline period, the participants in the contingency group were instructed to "produce three written pages each day, one of which could be a rewrite of the previous day's output" (476) to avoid paying a $15 fine to a despised organization, such as the Ku Klux Klan. As expected, when examining the participants' log entries of writing performed, Boice found the contingency group was eight times more productive once the contingency condition was established. Most surprising, however, was that the subjects in the contingency group reported discovering *more creative ideas than the control or spontaneous groups* (see table 1).

Boice also observed that the academicians typically paused when a new idea occurred and reflected on how the new idea could guide the next day's writing. These results reinforce Hemingway and others like him who advise writers to stop only when they know what will come next:

> You write until you come to a place where you still have your juice and know what will happen next and you stop and try to

live through until the next day when you hit it again. (Hemingway 1963, 221)

Facilitating a Paradigm Shift

Along with their colleagues in the literature and creative writing departments, however, composition theorists tend to resist an interdisciplinary approach. Tired of fighting the disdain of literature professors and of being treated like second-rate intellects, and in response to the demands of a growing body of significant research, some composition scholars believe that composition can only overcome its "second-rate" status by severing ties with the literature program. In her keynote speech to the 1985 Conference of College Composition and Communication, Maxine Hairston argued, "we are fighting losing battles. . . . The time has come to break those bonds, not necessarily physically . . . but emotionally and intellectually" (1985, 273). Hairston added, "We have a sense of purpose and a camaraderie that energizes the profession. But I also see us stunted in our growth because we are not able to free ourselves from needing the approval of literature people" (274).

Although the walls in English departments that separate creative writers, literature professors, literary critics, and composition scholars are not easily scaled, we must tear down the arbitrary boundaries and firmly establish professional writing programs that are informed by the dynamics of the creative process. After all, without theory for teaching writing, we have no compass to direct or evaluate our activities, no way to understand why some exercises succeed while others fail. Our theory for the art of teaching writing should assume that creativity is the natural consequence of diligence, commitment, and involvement. In order to meet the myriad needs of writing students, we need to inform each other, rather than retreat from each others's disciplines.

Surely, we don't want to be like the maid who doesn't do windows, a plumber who doesn't crawl under houses, a house painter who doesn't do ceilings. We are, after all, a family dedicated to language, creativity, self-expression, and critical thinking. Together, we carry the treasures of the humanities, the keys to the mind. We must remember that narrow-mindedness promotes narrow-mindedness, and, in the worst instances, narrow-mindedness discourages that spirit of eagerness, of creative play, that is essential to creativity, learning, and development. Greater interdisciplinary commu-

Table 1

Creativity Output: Mean Number of Ideas Listed Per
Scheduled/Potential Working Day

Group	Before Scheduled Writing Phase	Scheduled Writing Phase
Control	0.1	0.1
Spontaneous	0.2	0.6
Contingency	0.4	1.2

(Source: Boice 1985, 477.)

nication among our related disciplines will invigorate our practices,
our students, our culture.

Notes

[1]For a complete review of these and additional prewriting strategies see
Erika Lindemann, *A Rhetoric for Writing Teachers*, Second Edition (New York
and Oxford: Oxford University Press, 1987).

Works Cited

Applebee, Arthur N. *Writing in the Secondary School*. Urbana: NCTE, 1981.

Barnes, David. *From Communication to Curriculum*. London: Penguin, 1976.

Berthoff, Ann E. "Discovering Limits." In *The Making of Meaning*, 73–79.
Upper Montclair, N.J.: Boynton/Cook Publishers, Inc., 1981.

———. "Speculative Instruments: Language in the Core Curriculum." In
The Making of Meaning, 113–26.

———. "The Teacher as Researcher." In *The Making of Meaning*, 30–40.

Bloom, Allan. *The Closing of the American Mind*. New York: Simon and
Schuster, 1987.

Boice, Robert. "The Neglected Third Factor in Writing: Productivity." *College
Composition and Communication* 36 (December 1985): 472–80.

Boomer, Garth. "Addressing the Problem of Elsewhereness." *Reclaiming the
Classroom: Teacher Research as an Agency for Change*, edited by Dixie Go-
swami and Peter Stillman, 4–13. Upper Montclair, N.J.: Boynton/Cook
Publishers, Inc., 1987.

Britton, James, et al. *The Development of Writing Abilities* (11–18). London:
Macmillan, 1975.

Calvino, Italo. "Myth in the Narrative." Translated by Erica Freiberg. In *Surfiction,* edited by Raymond Federman, 75–81. Chicago: The Swallow Press, 1975.

Emig, Janet. "Writing as a Mode of Learning." *College Composition and Communication* 28 (May 1977): 122–28.

Fowlie, Wallace. *The Age of Surrealism.* Denver and Chicago: The Swallow Press and New York: William Morrow and Company, Inc., 1950.

Gardner, John. *The Art of Fiction.* New York: Alfred A. Knopf, 1984.

———. *On Becoming a Novelist.* New York: Harper and Row, 1983.

Hairston, Maxine. "Breaking Our Bonds and Reaffirming Our Connections." *College Composition and Communication* 36 (October 1985): 272–82.

Hall, Donald. "Poetry and Ambition." *AWP Newsletter,* February/March 1987: 1–2, 4–5, 10–13.

Hemingway, Ernest. "Interview with George Plimpton." *Writers at Work: The* Paris Review *Interviews,* Second Series, edited by George Plimpton, 215–40. Middlesex, England and New York: Penguin Books, 1963.

Hillocks, George. "Inquiry and the Composing Process: Theory and Research." *College English* 44 (November 1982): 659–73.

Horowitz, Mardi J. *Image Formation and Cognition.* New York: Appleton-Century-Crofts, 1978.

Huxley, Aldous. "Interview with George Wickes and Ray Frazer." *Writers at Work: The* Paris Review *Interviews,* Second Series, edited by George Plimpton, 193–214. Middlesex, England and New York: Penguin Books, 1963.

Keats, John. "Letter to George and Thomas Keats." In *The Norton Anthology of English Literature,* vol. 2, edited by M. H. Abrams, et al., 704–6. New York: W. W. Norton & Co., Inc., 1974.

Knoblauch, C. H., and Lil Brannon. "Teacher Commentary on Student Writing: The State of the Art." *Freshman English News* 10 (Fall 1981): 1–4.

May, Rollo. *The Courage to Create.* New York: Bantam Books, 1976.

Moffett, James. "Liberating Inner Speech." *College Composition and Communication* 36 (October 1985): 304–8.

Moxley, Joseph M. "Responding to Student Writing: Goals, Methods, Alternatives." *Freshman English News,* in press.

Murray, Donald. "The Interior View." In *Learning by Teaching.* Upper Montclair, N.J.: Boynton/Cook Publishers, Inc., 1982, 7–31.

———. "Teach Writing as a Process Not Product." In *Learning by Teaching.* 14–39.

Nin, Anaïs. In *The Novel of the Future.* New York: The Macmillian Company, 1968.

Perl, Sondra. "Understanding Composing." *College Composition and Communication* 31 (December 1980): 363–69.

Poincaré, Henri. "Mathematical Creation." Translated by George Halsted. In *The Creative Process,* edited by Brewster Ghiselin, 33–42. New York: The New American Library of World Literature, Inc., 1955.

Salinger, J. D. *Raise High the Roof Beams, Carpenters* and *Seymour—An Introduction.* Boston: Bantam Books, 1968.

Selzer, Jack. "Exploring Options in Composing." *College Composition and Communication* 35 (October 1984): 276–84.

Shahn, Ben. *The Shape of Content.* Cambridge, Massachusetts and London: Harvard University Press, 1976.

Smith, David. "Notes on Responsibility and the Teaching of Creative Writing." *AWP Newsletter,* May 1981: 1–3, 7.

Sommers, Nancy. "Responding to Student Writing." *College Composition and Communication* 33 (May 1982): 148–56.

Thurber, James. "Interview with George Plimpton and Max Steele." In *Writers at Work: The* Paris Review *Interviews,* First Series, edited by Malcolm Cowley, 83–98. Middlesex, England and New York: Penguin Books, 1977.

Vygotsky, Lev S. *Thought and Language.* Edited and translated by Eugenia Hanfmann and Gertrude Vakar. Cambridge, England: MIT Press, 1962.

Weis, Monica R. "Current Brain Research and the Composing Process." In *The Writers Mind: Writing as a Mode of Thinking,* edited by Janice Hays, Phyllis Roth, Jon Ramsey, Robert Foulke, 25–34. Urbana: NCTE, 1983.

3 The Future of Creative Writing Programs

George Garrett
University of Virginia

Prophecy is not my strong suit. In the absence of any demonstrable prophetic gifts, and with the full knowledge that, whatever the future may be, it is, by definition, not exactly a continuation or even an extension of the present as we know it, but something else, something which can only be *imagined* and may be well beyond the boundaries of any imagination floating around in present time. My best bet is to try to know where I really am and where I have really come from before I pretend to imagine and predict where we may find ourselves sooner or later. I remember one time in the army, years and years ago, watching a colonel open up a map and spread it out on the hood of a jeep to study it. He studied it long and hard, then briskly folded it up, turned and issued crisp orders for his infantry battalion. And off they (we) went, full pack and everything, humping to follow his commands. Only trouble was he had read the map upside down. So off we went, many miles in the wrong direction, before somebody figured out what had happened.

Moral? Nothing really profound or heavy. Just this. You can get yourself pretty thoroughly lost, in time and space, if you don't know where you are or where you have just come from. How is this relevant to creative writing and writing programs? First of all, there is a certain amount of misinformation masquerading as assumed history, as the story of creative writing in America. Some of it is just accidental, an inevitable reaction to the experience of what a writer friend of mine calls "The Book of Lobster and Forgetting." Other distortions of the past derive from the simple and familiar error of working backward from our present state of things, comfortably imagining that somebody planned or intended things to be the way they are now—the commonplace *progressive fallacy*.

I don't want to waste a lot of time and space on this (or the reader's patience), but there are a few things that really ought to be set straight. First, we need to recognize that there is a very old and long tradition of what we are doing. A good many years ago—I forget when, but it was the first time the Associated Writing Programs ever held its annual meeting in Denver—novelist and poet John Williams, who was then our new president, gave the opening talk. He read from a sixteenth-century teachers' handbook. What he read to us was a curriculum built around what we now call "creative writing," what they called "composition" (among other things). In the days of the standard classical education, education in and about the classics, the composition of original Latin poetry and prose was one of the key elements. This practice continued for as long as the classics were the heart and guts of education. Thoreau, for instance, came out of exactly this kind of system, as did so many of the American nineteenth-century writers, and a few elders of the twentieth-century tradition. Robert Frost, for example, was largely self-educated, but he taught himself from the classics. In any case, when we talk about the beginning and growth of creative writing in our time, within the context of institutions of one kind and another, we are really talking about a *renewal, a revival,* the return, in somewhat different form and circumstances, of an old-fashioned, centuries-old form of teaching and learning rhetoric. The aims were different, but the ways and means are surprisingly alike.

It is interesting, I think, that the somewhat disguised creative writing courses, which were offered in American colleges and universities for years before there were any official courses *named* "creative writing," were usually associated with "great books" courses, that is, de facto courses in the classics. Some or all of the students would be allowed to write poems and stories instead of papers. This was the kind of course available at Princeton in the late 1940s and early 1950s, under the direction of R. P. Blackmur and with instructors who included Randall Jarrell, Delmore Schwartz, John Berryman, and Saul Bellow. Also there were composition courses, of various kinds, that permitted or, indeed, required the students to write poems or stories. There were not really "workshops," in our sense of the word or practice of the craft, but they were usually small classes and very close to the same thing. Anyway (and as briefly as possible), long before Iowa, or anybody else, people in institutions were actively studying the craft of writing fiction and the craft of writing poetry and getting credit for their efforts. These people, pioneers in our field, deserve all kinds of credit but have received very little. Most of them are all but unknown by now. Yet they thought and encouraged a whole generation of American writers, people who are now the elders of our own scene, long before it was either easy or fashionable to do so. I mention and honor a few names here, out of memory, a few names to represent so many others: William Blackburn of Duke; George Williams of Rice; Jesse Rehder and Paul Green of Chapel Hill; R. P. Blackmur of Princeton and Allen Tate of various places, including Princeton; Meta Eppler Gilpatrick of Furman; Andrew Lytle of Florida and Sewanee (and, briefly, Iowa); John Coleman and A. K. Davis from the University of Virginia.

Now then. You have to put that fact in a somewhat larger context. The fact is that nobody *studied* modern or contemporary literature in American colleges and universities until after World War II. Following the lead of the Ivy League schools, American institutions usually ended the *formal* study of literature with the year 1900. A nice cut-off date. People read the moderns, of course, but they were not taught or studied until the late 1940s; in part because of the G.I. Bill and the millions of young Americans, back from the wars, who wanted to read the literature of their own age, and who demanded it. There were strikes and protests (really, *seriously*) in prominent schools, so that these students could read T. S. Eliot and W. B. Yeats or Faulkner and Fitzgerald and get academic credit for doing so. You just had to be there. I was there. The Old Guard resisted briefly, then surrendered with a warning. The old-timers, scholar-teachers, who, in fact, often read and enjoyed and wrote about the moderns, were concerned about the academic canon. What would be the canon of modern and contemporary literature? How would we arrive at a sense of what truly mattered and what didn't matter much, without a century or so of time to let things settle into place? We laughed at that. I thought that was the silliest thing I'd ever heard. I didn't understand what they were saying, not then and not until I, myself, had been teaching literature and writing for some years. They weren't talking about absolutes. They were thinking about the choices people would have to make as to what to teach (in fifteen-week semesters or twelve-week quarters) and what not to teach, what to leave in and what to leave out. They thought that it would lead to a whole lot of trouble if you tried to take the living-breathing contemporary literature, the art even as it was happening, *in process*, and then, by some kind of abstraction, went on to rank it and codify and classify and label it, as if your abstraction were in some way final, as if both the literature and its makers were stone dead. The Old Guard could see that this method would very likely lead to major distortions and omissions, *errors*, and to other kinds of

trials and tribulations. Almost immediately, for all of us, it was clear
that the Old Guard had been dead right about one thing. Both as
students and teachers, we in the first wave of courses in modern literature discovered that, quite aside from quality, some authors and
works were much easier or more fun to teach than others of equal
quality and importance. And by the early 1950s the last of the World
War II veterans were gone from the campuses. (The Korean veterans came and went, but were fewer in number and had much less
impact.) It was all *kids* again. There were things that the mature veterans had known, from hard experience, that the kids didn't and
couldn't know. Content quickly became less important than form.
We taught more about literary aesthetics than essential substance—
because we had to. We also tried to teach things relevant to them
and their limited experiences. Pretty soon here came *The Catcher in
the Rye* and *Lord of the Flies*. We discovered that whatever we *called*
the canon *was* the canon. We ate up the forbidden fruit, enjoyed it
thoroughly, and our eyes were opened to the possibilities of organizing and manipulating the present to be and to mean whatever we
said it was. We shared a lot more with the hucksters and tricksters
of Madison Avenue than we would ever admit, even to ourselves.
The Old Guard had, after all, almost arbitrarily invented convenient
catch-all concepts like "the Renaissance" and "the Romantic Movement," "Metaphysical" and "Cavalier Poets." We could do the same
thing here and now without waiting for posterity. The exemplary
proof of this was/is the so-called "Beat Movement." It was a completely self-invented, self-labeling literary movement. The truth is
that it was a myth first invented, then assiduously cultivated, by a
bunch of *students*. Mostly good students, really. Not street people.
Certainly not working people. They were mildly disgruntled academics who declared war on Academia and Academics, using an academic method, the identification and classification of literary
groups as "schools" and "movements," to do so. To that extent it
was cheerfully fraudulent, a shuck, and a con—which is probably
why the Press, also peopled by young folks right out of the same
Gradgrind mill, picked it up and ran with it. The Beat Movement
was in large part a big publicity stunt, the first of many among the
literati, and one of the most successful. It did have the positive effect
of creating (just as television did) a whole new crew of "Stars"—
Ginsberg, Corso, Holmes, Kerouac, and others, the whole gang—
overnight. All they did was announce that they were "Stars" and
they became so. And all this created a lively opposition to the Establishment. Oh, those guys put the fear of God into the comfortable

Literary Establishment! You want to read "Panic in the Streets?" Go and dig up some of the rear-guard essays of Donald Hall, back in the days before he decided that detente was the better form of valor. It was fun and games while it lasted. Most of the people, on both sides, with certain solemn exceptions, were only kidding around, anyway.

There were aftereffects, of course. One was/is that ever after that people realized that they could do the same thing—create an image and call it a reality. It all goes back at least to Joseph Paul Goebbels, whose fairly simple idea—one which proved painfully, murderously true—that if you say anything with enough authority and enough times, over and over again, it *becomes* the truth . . . until the next one comes along. A lot of our most ambitious (and better known) critics and poets and fiction writers have glommed onto this notion and, sometimes, made it pay off. Another, and more important thing the Beats proved—as if they had listened very carefully to the Old Guard—was that the canon is always up for grabs. Maybe it always was. At least the various and sundry minorities and special interest groups that soon came along (like hairy barbarian patrols on search-and-destroy missions from the Old Guard's point of view) in the 1960s saw that any canon, and especially the canon of modern and contemporary literature, is at best an arbitrary formulation, most likely deeply political and social in its basic assumptions, its hidden agenda of implications. And so the fight over the canon is still on and will continue. Meantime the canon is really whatever we say it is, more or less.

My favorite exemplary story of all this involves my friend Richard Dillard, a first-rate poet and novelist and one of the greatest teachers of our age, especially of creative writing. He will have to forgive me for telling it. (I hope he will.) Anyway, back twenty years and more, I was poetry editor of the University of North Carolina Press. One of the books we published—and we did some really good ones, by good people, I'm proud to say—was Dillard's collection *News of the Nile* (or, as one newspaper misprinted the title, *Nudes of Denial*). The title poem, the *real* title, was (among other things) a wonderful, knowledgeable, imaginative and imaginary exploration of Egyptian culture, ancient and modern. Well, one day, not too long after publication, the Press got an order for 600 copies of Dillard's book. They couldn't believe it—thought it was a mistake of maybe one or two zeros. A book of poetry then would sell a maximum of maybe 600 copies in its lifetime. The order was real, and it came from the University of Massachusetts in Amherst. But nobody could figure out

why they needed so many copies. Then it dawned on us that it must
be connected with some course or other. We went to the University
of Massachusetts catalogue and found that there was a great big lecture course in contemporary poetry being taught there by someone
with a very Egyptian-looking, Egyptian-sounding name. And here
was the title of the course: "Contemporary American Poetry:
Roethke, Lowell, and Dillard." We all laughed at that and so did
Richard—the idea of 600 kids at the University of Massachusetts
studying Richard's work closely and maybe mentioning it, even
quoting it, for years after to puzzled people who studied from a different canon. Get it? The final irony is that (in my opinion) Dillard
probably belongs right there.

There remains one point I can only touch on briefly. Once we
started having courses in modern and contemporary literature, *com-
merce* was deeply involved. For the most part we weren't dealing
with public domain stuff. There was *money* in it, for everybody, if
you could just get plugged into the system. The paperback revolu-
tion, beginning in the early 1950s, helped this along enormously.
There were winners and losers, among publishers, writers, anthology and textbook editors, and the like. There were big bucks for the
lucky few, the absence thereof for the losers. Where there are bucks
to be had and kept, there corruption, in many shapes and forms,
pitches its tent.

Anyway. Simultaneously with the new respectability of modern
and contemporary literature, here came, beginning in the big middle
and late 1950s, working writers, poets, and novelists, onto the faculties. Prior to World War II there had been on campus a few, a *very*
few, distinguished and mostly decorative part-time people, most notably Robert Frost, and some rare and occasional brief visitors. But
any kind of association with academic life was not a serious option
for serious writers. Faulkner and Fitzgerald, for example, wrote for
the movies for a living, and as employees, not as artists-in-resi-
dence, because that was what you could do if you had the ability to
do it. There simply were not many places for writers in academe.
Faulkner was an old man and already had the Nobel Prize when the
University of Virginia discovered he was already living in town,
anyway, and found an inexpensive place for him on the staff.

As late as 1956, when I began teaching full-time at Wesleyan University, writers were still rare on the campuses—but it was beginning. Within a decade it was to be in full bloom and boom. Everybody had a poet or two, and maybe a fiction writer also, on the
staff. There wasn't a cow college, be it ever so humble, that did not

have its courses in creative writing, usually taught by writers. R. V. Cassill had created the Associated Writing Programs. And all over the country writers were on the road giving public readings of their poems and their fiction. Even that was new. True, Frost, a cultural icon, had been reading out loud and in public for years, and, yes, Vachel Lindsay and Carl Sandburg and a very few others (Edna St. Vincent Millay for one). Frost made good money out of it, but nobody else did. Then in the early 1950s, and thanks in large part to the energy and special charisma of two very different poets, Dylan Thomas and John Ciardi, public readings began to catch on quickly.

Before the end of the 1960s, for better and for worse, the colleges, in two ways, were the main support for what was then called "serious" writing, and is now known as "literary" writing, in America: by hiring writers to be on their faculties and by encouraging the ceaseless interchange of visiting writers and readers from one campus to another. The combination of modest academic salaries plus the incremental additions that were potentially available through grants, fellowships, prizes, awards, and, above all, public readings added up to a kind of precarious security for many writers, and in some cases, the cases of the Stars, led to big bucks. Poets in America never had it so good (as long as they were thought to be good). You didn't have to be James Merrill (or, differently, Wallace Stevens) to afford the luxury of a poet's career. You could, from then on and under the wings of academic patronage, come from an ordinary, even a disadvantaged background. Indeed, for some of the poets who came along in the 1960s and after, poetry proved to be a matter of social and economic upward mobility rather than poverty or, at the least, personal sacrifice. New voices of all kinds could be heard from all sides. Whitman's dream of a democratic poetry began to come true, though there was, alas, no corresponding growth of an audience for it.

Someone may have noticed that I have not, yet, said anything much about Iowa. Let me make up for that here and now. We, all of us, owe an enormous debt to Paul Engle and to the program he created at Iowa, beginning in 1937, but not really kicking in until the post-War, G.I. Bill years, and still humming along today, though much modified by time and other personalities. It is to be remembered that there were other programs, of various kinds, even earlier than Iowa's; and various writers went to other places to study writing. An obvious example is Arthur Miller, who went to Michigan in the Depression to study writing, among other things, and to avail himself of the extravagant Hopwood Awards (which were already in place); so did John Ciardi. Iowa was not the only available choice, then, not by any means, even in the late 1930s. Under Engle's leadership Iowa grew large, influential, fat and sassy even, and served as an example for much of the rest of the country, boomed and expanded with the others in the 1960s and 1970s. It did not necessarily *improve* during all those years. After 1965, Engle, the creator, was out of the Iowa Writers Workshop and busy directing his newer creation—the International Writing Program. Under the custodial leadership of George Starbuck, the workshop did not prosper much; and, after being turned down by a number of good candidates, fell to the publisher and sometime novelist John Leggett, who, essentially and conservatively, held the line while reputation caught up with Engle's earlier accomplishment. It takes about ten years in the academic world for a reputation to catch up with the facts. Plenty of good publicity and the literary success of some good students didn't hurt, either. But the truth is (in my best judgment) Iowa was mostly marking time during Leggett's tenure, as it would have during *anybody else's* tenure because it had grown too large and unwieldy even before Leggett had gotten there. Actually, in my opinion, the years 1960-1966 were the peak and prime time for Iowa, precisely coinciding with the time there of R. V. Cassill. What will happen now, under the new directorship of Frank Conroy, remains to be seen.

One of the most significant and overlooked creative writing programs was developed in Arkansas by William Harrison and James Whitehead, both out of Vanderbilt and Iowa (Whitehead's M.F.A. is from the celebrated class of 1965). Acting like Martin Luther after he had first been to Rome, they recreated in Fayetteville a reformed version of what Iowa used to be at the outset. However, it was smaller, more selective, and much more rigorous than the original. Arkansas now ranks among the very best programs in the country and has produced some very fine writers per capita more than Iowa during the same years. Of course, if you want to allow for *per capita* evaluation—and why not?—a program doesn't *have* to be on grand scale. You would have to single out for special honor Hollins College in Virginia, with their own quiet program, begun by Louis D. Rubin, Jr., in the middle 1960s and now directed by R. H. W. Dillard. They are amazing—pound for pound the most productive writing program in America. This program, which Dillard calls "a little, teeny-tiny program" and, sometimes, "The Little Program That Could," has in its short time produced gifted, published writers such as Sylvia Wilkinson, Lee Smith, Lee Zacharius, David Huddle, John Carr, Ben Greer, Garrett Epps, Don Belton, Amanda Cockrell,

George Butler, Thomas McGonigle, Tom Whalen, and poets Henry Taylor, Lisa Ress, Jeanne Larsen, Rosanne Coggeshall, Margaret Gibson, Stephen Pett, Michael Pettit. Fall of 1987 was a fairly typical year with new books published by Hollins alums like Madison Smartt Bell (now teaching at Iowa), Jill McCorkle, Tama Janowitz, Annie Dillard, and poet Wyn Cooper. Already in press for 1988 publication are first novels by Bret Laidlaw and Cathryn Hankla. The point is that Iowa was important and still is fine and dandy. But all kinds of other places are coming along very nicely, thank you. Sooner or later reputation will catch up with the new facts. It was Robert Frost who wrote in one of his earliest poems, "Mowing": "The fact is the sweetest dream that labor knows." We need not be slaves of fact, but we can't know or tell the truth unless we are faithful to the facts.

Another thing that came to pass in the middle of the 1960s was the creation of Associated Writing Programs by R. V. Cassill. Cassill, who had been closely involved with the teaching of writing since right after World War II and continued to be so until his recent retirement at Brown, is as much a visionary as a pioneer. Everybody in the field of creative writing is in his debt whether they know it or not. In less than a generation his AWP has gone from a baker's dozen of programs to something like, give or take, 300—lots more if you choose to include all the schools, which regularly offer some courses in creative writing, and individual memberships. Cassill had the idea and began things out of his own house in Providence. There was a charter board of directors (of which I am especially proud to say I was a member). And in the very first year we had the first volume of *Intro*, edited by Cassill and published by Bantam. We had very little money, and, at first, we received no grants or support from anybody. And—it's almost funny now—a number of prominent schools didn't see the point to it and did not choose to join. Iowa wasn't interested at all, at first. *Who were all these other upstart schools, anyway?* But gradually they came around. So did the others. And then, early in the 1970s, after both Cassill and I had served our seasons as president, when we finally got some support from the National Endowment for the Arts, lots and lots of people, previously skeptical or indifferent, came on board—nothing like the inducement of a little money to arouse the interest and enthusiasm of the *literati*.

Anyway, I can assure you that nobody, not even the highly prescient Cassill, could have imagined that, in twenty years, things could have or would have turned out the way they have done.

Where we are now, the shifting present, there is both good news and bad. The good news, for writers, and for students, too, is that there are more writing courses and programs taught by writers than ever before. The good news is the popularity of these courses, especially on the undergraduate level; for at a time when reading and writing are a serious problem and a great cultural illiteracy prevails, creative writing is one antidote to toxic ignorance, all the more effective because it is somewhat disguised and different from humdrum composition courses. Students are still learning rhetoric and the habits of close reading and careful writing in creative writing courses. If nothing else, these courses serve a damage-control purpose, but they do a lot more than that. Nobody has any real, valid numbers, but it is safe to say that most of the new poets and fiction writers in America now come out of creative writing courses and programs. Among these new writers—poets, story writers, novelists—the level of technical competence (the one thing that can be directly taught) has never been higher. There has been a great flourishing of talent, and the literary magazines and small presses and university presses (albeit, often, with and depending on grants and various kinds of outside support) have responded and are publishing poetry and fiction as never before. Even the big commercial publishers have not been able to ignore all this. They need new writers, too, and now they know where to find them.

Some of the bad news? Ah, yes. Well, there are many things, new and quirky problems, to deal with. A few examples will have to do. Working backwards, then. . . .

Item. Having learned, fairly recently, to value the collection of short stories and the "literary" novel (almost a genre nowadays) as a source for new writers, the commercial houses have changed the rules slightly without really changing their game. Collections of stories and serious first novels do not sell very many copies, even under ideal circumstances and trailing clouds of rave reviews behind them. In truth, small presses and university presses can and usually do sell more copies (although much more slowly) than commercial houses because the books stay in print much longer, and because, in the whole system of publishing and distributing, the smaller publishers have less overhead to deal with. It is much easier to break even. The commercial houses are, however, in a position to manipulate the market somewhat. They can't sell any more *books* than the small presses, but they are in a position to get better and more prompt review coverage. And, with the acquiescence of the writing community, which still believes that it is better to be published by

Knopf or Farrar, Straus and Giroux than, for instance, Wesleyan University Press or Stuart Wright, the commercial houses are able to create "Stars" without regard to sales. Examples? Ann Beattie has, so far, never had a single best-selling book, but she is clearly a star and in fact is paid advances as if she were, indeed, a best-selling author. It makes sense. Chances are that the people the commercial houses have invested in *will*, like Malamud and Walker Percy, for instance, pay off handsomely in the long run. Meantime the "literary" authors have a fairly high "visibility," representing prestige and a form of advertising for the commercial publisher. "Visibility," that is, recognition and status, is important to the writers, too, not merely for ego satisfaction, but in other kinds and forms of cold cash. The more "visible" contemporary poets and fiction writers can command (as long as they remain "visible") top prices on the lecture and recording circuits. The colleges and universities are often willing to pay really large sums of money for prominent writers to come and give readings. Similarly, it is more a matter of public reputation than such finally immeasurable qualities as excellence whether or not a writer within the university system is promoted and rewarded. Book reviews are these days a normal part of the academic writer's dossier. Moreover the affiliation of writers with the educational institutions has given rise to a new wrinkle, a variation on the publish-or-perish syndrome. Writers must, of course, just like their more scholarly colleagues, publish as much and as widely as possible to keep their jobs, to gain tenure, to earn merit raises, and so forth. Even with all the little magazines and small presses, there just aren't enough places for all the writers, so it is important that some places be valued more highly than others and never mind the quality of the particular piece of work. Thus, in dollars-and-cents terms, it is better to have a poem or a story in *The New Yorker* than in *The Sewanee Review*. And better there, in the *Sewanee* than, say, *The Crescent Review* or *The Chattahoochie Review*. Of course, this hierarchy flies in the face of the facts. Judging by the various anthologies of "best" American poems and stories, one would have to say, no question, that the little magazines are very often homes for work of the highest quality. Meantime, though, except for the editors of those anthologies, everybody is pretending otherwise. To pretend to something other than the truth is not a good thing for anybody's character, especially the character of a writer. It is *convenient*—to institutions, to businesses, to writers who have managed to succeed in the system's turns—but it is false.

Nobody could really fault the new *competence* of our young writers. Or, to put it another way, it is hard to make a good case for *in-
competence*. And yet . . . at least some of that acknowledged competence is a matter of learned habits and reflexes—a *beaux arts*
mentality and finish, acceptable and finally bland. Plenty of competent work by competent artists, and already a situation which some
see as almost out of control. University of Iowa Press editor (and
poet) Paul Zimmer reports that for his contest (*not* a first-book contest), offering publication to two books of poems, he received over
500 book-length manuscripts, many of them highly "competent."
Two years ago I, myself, judged for Missouri's "Breakthrough" contest. I had six slots to fill, in poetry and fiction, and I received more
than 750 manuscripts. My rough guess was that *at least* ten percent
of them were eminently publishable and of the highest quality. It's
already an old story, though, in truth, the situation is very new.

A longer view is, perhaps, more depressing. If you stop to consider it, the majority of these manuscripts have a very good statis-
tical chance of *never* finding a publisher, of never being published.
For the writer looking for the encouragement of grants and awards
or for an academic job, that is dismal news. There is another change
to consider. There is a groundswell of criticism of writing courses
and programs. "Too many," the critics say, "not selective enough—
a kind of cloning process." Pray notice that most of these critics are,
themselves, successful teachers of creative writing who have no intention of giving up their niches or endowed chairs. They just want
to thin the ranks a little and separate the sheep from the goats. Too
many snouts (to use another metaphor) at the trough. The problem
is that their complaints have been listened to and taken seriously by
serious critics. Here, for instance, is William Tazewell in his regular
book column (January 3, 1987), which is published in a number of
major southern newspapers: "The apparent paradox is that American universities are graduating more writers and fewer readers at
the same time. But teaching 'writing' is not the same thing as teaching tax law. The best fiction is not a specialty, but speaks to the general human condition. . . ."

Meanwhile, the (already) old AWP has changed to reject all these
things. In the beginning, our emphasis was always on the students—on *Intro*, which gave them a chance to be published (and introduced some wonderful new writers—go have a look sometime)—
and on trying to help them get jobs. Now *Intro* has gone by the
way. And if you take a good look at the AWP "Job Lists," you see at
once that they are mostly addressed to writers already in the sys-

tem. There are jobs, indeed a growing number of them, for new graduates of the writing programs; but everybody knows, too, how the college towns are filling up with waitresses and busboys out of our M.F.A. programs. And now there is a whole new class of writing student, one who wanders from one program to another, hoping for something or other to change for the better, meanwhile hanging on for as long as fellowship money is available. And even for the luckiest there is the much-discussed problem: that the new generation of writers goes directly from school into teaching, thus never really leaving school. No matter how technically proficient they may prove to be as writers, what will become of the sum and substance of their work?

Well then. The truth of the present is that American writers and writing have never had it so good. And no matter how unjust and unfair the system may be, the results, the work that is being produced, are exciting. Lots of good work is being created, lots of it being published, even if only the tip of the iceberg.

But there are, as indicated, some serious negative things about the present scene, things which, even if mostly invisible or ignored, can cause some real trouble in the foreseeable future. The greatest of these may be summed up under the general category of *waste*. We live in a wasteful society. We are part and parcel of it. If we are training young writers to write well, competently, without also teaching them how to recognize and value excellence for its own sake, substantial as well as technical excellence, we are wasting their time and ours. It is a waste if we have helped to encourage young writers who can never find a place to publish their work. It is a waste to train young writers in M.F.A. programs who will never be able to find a job in their specialty. All this waste accumulates to almost toxic levels.

A lot of this must have been in R. V. Cassill's mind when, a few years ago when their national meeting was held in Boston, the AWP asked their founder and first president, for the first and only time, to address the organization. Cassill stunned them by making a strong case for the deinstitutionalization of creative writing. The writing programs were a good idea whose time had come and gone. He argued that the results of the association of writers and artists with the Academy were now more negative than positive, for everyone concerned. He urged that the AWP disband. Some people thought it was some kind of a joke. In fact it was/is a persuasive case, supremely rational if the future is in fact an extension of the present. The fact that it won't happen, that the AWP will not disband until it finally collapses (if and when) does not answer to his argument. Of course, the few who profit most, personally, from the present environment will be (and were) the last to see the reasonableness of Cassill's arguments.

I have a notion that the future is going to be very different from the present scene, and it is at least possible to invent a scenario in which the future is an improvement over the present or, at least, solves some of the intractable problems of the present even as new and, so far, unimagined problems arise. All the signs and portents are that technology is going to change, radically, the American system of publishing. The computer, in its full implications for writers and publishers, and readers too, the whole concept of "desk-top" publishing will change almost everything. And most of the changes that I can imagine are for the better. The concepts of being "in print" and "out of print" will be outmoded when retrieval is a simple process. Not merely modern and contemporary, but all literature will be, as it once was and is meant to be, *simultaneous.* Fielding and Faulkner will rub elbows with Richard Ford. Contemporary poets, each and every one of them, say Stanley Plumly, for example, will properly have to hold their own against brother (and sister) poets like Virgil and Dante, Homer and Chaucer. My point is that, in the new technologized age, newness will not be enough. And repute will mean more than the *Norton Anthology.*

The ways and means of teaching will have to change to suit the new technology and the times. One thing we can fairly well be sure of, the students of the future will still have to be taught to read and write and then be encouraged to seek and find examples of literary excellence, past and present. It seems almost certain that an increasing number of our students will come out of distinctly different ethnic and cultural backgrounds and a good many will come from other language traditions. The (reading and) writing teacher of the foreseeable future will have to be aware of other traditions and be able to accommodate to them. Yet at the same time the teacher will be one of the preservers of our own American language and its traditions. Among other things, this means we are going to have to teach more literature and demand more cultural literacy of our M.F.A. students.

I can already see that, even if things do not change and just go on being more of the same, in the near future we are going to have to come to terms with the truth that the writing *workshop* is not the only or, indeed, always the best workable model for teachers of creative writing. We are going to have to consider other kinds and forms of classwork in addition to the workshop. The workshop seems to me (at this moment) almost ideal for beginning classes and for our equivalent of the musicians' master classes. But it can be too much of a good thing, and it can create an odd dependency, a *need* for the show and tell, the give and take of a workshop, which may not be the best training for the essentially lonely enterprise of making up poems and stories. As the Existentialists were always telling us (and this applies even in this world of hot tubs), "Nobody else can take a bath for you."

And, no question, unless we want an entire generation of writers, maybe more, whose ignorance of the richness and variety of our own traditions will be simply overwhelming, we are going to have to demand that our students read a lot more widely and deeply than they do now. The basic Helen Vendler or Daniel Halpern elite-rank-and-file of contemporary poetry, for example, is not enough, not by a long shot. The beginning writer—*whether or not he/she likes it or wants it,* and most don't, because freedom of choice, and the conse quences thereof, is what they fear most—needs as many models, therefore choices, as possible. When those models exist in splendid variety (and often in contradiction of and confrontation with each other), it is a shame and another profligate waste not to be aware of this, and worse to deny the truth.

We, the teachers, have got to develop some new ways of teaching literature—*for writers.* Most often, and often appropriately, literature is taught for readers and critics. Well, we ought to *be* readers and critics, but we need to find ways to make literature more meaningful and practical to the writer. In addition to everything else, what can the beginning *writer* learn from *Tom Jones*? What can a contemporary poet learn from "The Miller's Tale"?

To endure, maybe even prevail, in the future, we are going to have to learn how to question everything, most of all our most cherished assumptions. We are certainly going to be required to give the truth, with all its loose ends and ragged edges, more chance to be known than we have allowed in the present. If we have to topple a few cultural icons and even break a few hearts (remembering always that the hardest hearts are the ones most easily broken), so be it. The future is always built upon the bones of the present. The question, which all the real prophets asked, is, "Can these bones live?"

4 Articles of Faith

David Jauss
University of Arkansas at Little Rock

Teaching fiction writing is in at least one way like writing fiction, for both arts (and I do claim for teaching the honorific "art") require a willing suspension—not of disbelief but of *beliefs*. For if we cannot suspend, or at least temper, our prejudice against, say, murderers, the odds are that we won't be able to write convincingly about one. And if we can't suspend our aesthetic prejudices long enough to understand those of our students, there's little chance that we'll be able to teach them anything. The danger is not that we'll impose our aesthetics on our students—that's inevitable and even, to an extent, desirable—but that we won't provide them room to develop their own. In order to diminish this danger, I discuss some of my aesthetic prejudices with my students, stressing all the while that it's not necessary that they share them, only consider them. The best students will sift through the advice I offer and take only what serves their aims; the worst will attempt to write what they falsely think I want. Something Bum Phillips once said about coaching football players is equally true about teaching fiction writers: "There are two kinds of football players I can't work with—those who don't do anything I say and those who do everything I say." If I had to work with only of one of these kinds of "football players," however, I'd choose the former.

What follows are some of the aesthetic principles that I discuss with my students. Although they may sound like rules, they represent my private absolutes, my personal "articles of faith," and nothing more. For the purposes of this chapter, I've put them in the form of directives to students, but I would ask those students to remember that the only rule fiction writers are obligated to follow is, as Henry James said, "be interesting" (Edel 1956, 9).

- Your real teachers are the books of great writers. To learn to write well, you must read widely and deeply. Occasionally, a student will say, "I don't read because I don't want to be influenced." My answer? "You should try to be influenced by as many great writers as possible."

But reading won't help you much unless you learn how to read like a *writer*. You must look at a book the way a carpenter looks at a house someone else built, examining the details in order to see how it was made. A scholar reads the product; a writer, the process.

- There is nothing as dangerous as blank paper. Despite all the claims of religious fundamentalists about the danger of certain books (usually good ones), the absence of expression is more dangerous to humanity, individually and collectively, than any form of expression can be. Silence is not golden; expression is.

  Though we often think of talent as something innate, it is less a gift than it is something you earn. As Comtesse Diane facetiously said, "Only a born artist can endure the labour of becoming one" (Gross 1983, 282). The best definition of talent belongs to George-Louis Leclerc de Buffon. Talent, he said, "Is long patience."[1]

- You should write for the sake of the writing, not for anything external to it, including money, fame, or tenure. As Eudora Welty has said, "I don't write for my friends or myself, either; I write for *it*, for the pleasure of *it*" (Plimpton 1976, 275). If your focus is on your art and how you can improve it, you will be impervious to what John Berryman considered the only two things that could destroy a writer: criticism and praise (298). Criticism can destroy you only if you are writing for praise, and praise can destroy you only if it blinds you to criticism. If you are writing for *it*, criticism and praise are your teachers.

- To adapt a comment that Philip Dacey, who was speaking about poetry, once made, "Fiction writing is too important to be taken seriously." Let me clarify this paradox with another: as Friedrich Nietzsche said, "Man's maturity" consists in recapturing "the seriousness he had as a child at play" (Nietzsche [1885] 1955, 78). This, I think, is especially true of a writer, for writing is not work but serious play. (Let me stress that phrase: *serious play*. And remember, the noun is, as always, more important than the adjective.)

  Work can be defined as expending the minimum amount of effort for the maximum about of return. Play, on the other hand, involves expending a maximum amount of effort for a minimum amount of return. Gabriel García Márquez, who tells of using up five hundred pieces of paper in the process of writing a fifteen-page story, is a good example of a writer engaged in serious play (Simons 1985, 18).

Attitude is all-important. Sir Laurence Olivier once said that an actor needs to achieve "the difficult equation" between "the proper initial humility toward the work and . . . the necessary confidence to carry it out" (Kalem 1975, 59). Too much humility and the writer will dissolve into silence; too much confidence and the writer will arrogantly inflict reams of ill-chosen words on the reader.

A few students are overconfident, but most are underconfident. This comes from failing to recognize that they've been telling stories all their lives and have a wealth of knowledge about how to do it. Gossip is a form of fiction, perhaps the root of all fiction, and we are all, like it or not, inveterate gossips. Fiction is nothing more (or less) than gossip about imagined characters. We all have years of practice gossiping and telling stories. We all know how to select certain details, omit others; how to pace the release of information to build suspense; how to exaggerate and alter facts for effect. People may be born tone-deaf, but as Leonard Michaels has said, "Nobody is born story-deaf." Just as we possess an unconscious knowledge of grammar that is far more sophisticated than our conscious knowledge of it, so too we have an unconscious knowledge of storytelling. Trust that knowledge.

- The best attitude toward writing is what Keats described as "negative capability"—the ability to persist despite uncertainty and doubt (Bush 1959, 261). You must make friends with doubt. It is the imagination's greatest ally, for it forces you to consider possibilities—different word choices, rhythms, character traits, events, and so forth—you would never consider if you moved too abruptly to closure and certainty. Although we often associate genius with confidence and certainty, great writers are almost always those whose doubts about themselves and their art are extreme. Witness Flaubert, who said "I doubt everything, even my doubt" (Steegmuller 1980, 52).

Doubt and mystery are related. The more certain we are as writers, the less mystery our stories will contain. It is a mistake to want to exile uncertainty from the writing process. As Flaubert said, "Stupidity consists in wanting to reach conclusions"

(Steegmuller 1980, 128). If we strive too hard to reach clear conclusions, we might deny the mystery that impelled us to write the story in the first place. As Donald Barthelme has noted, a good work of art both "invites and resists interpretation" (Barthelme 1986, 33). And Karl Kraus stressed the importance of mystery and uncertainty for art when he said "Only he is an artist who can make a riddle out of a solution" (Kraus 1976, 51).

The way to create mystery, however, is not to write vaguely or obscurely. "Make your poems as clear as you can," Robert Bly once advised students in a poetry writing class. "Let others find the mystery in them." As Bly's statement suggests, the world and its inhabitants are innately mysterious. A straightforward, clear presentation of any subject—say, a mother's relationship to her daughter—will inevitably be mysterious because such relationships are. Mystery and confusion are two very different things, and good art has no room for the latter.

- The common understanding of inspiration is a sham, and it puts a false burden on the writer. Inspiration is not some lightning bolt of wisdom and insight sent down from the gods; it is something eminently mundane and ordinary. Whatever compels your attention—be it a phrase you overhear in a cafeteria or the smell of the lilacs near your doorstep—is an inspiration. The very fact that we feel compelled to tell someone—in speech or writing—about such everyday occurrences shows they are inspirations to communication. Most people are inspired a dozen times a day, but few do anything with these gifts. I suggest you follow James's advice: "Try to be one of the people on whom nothing is lost!" (Edel 1956, 13).

  To keep from "losing things," keep a journal. Any detail that arrests your attention may one day spin a story around it or find a home in a story inspired by other details. Eudora Welty tells us that "Wherever you go, you meet a part of your story" (Plimpton 1976, 277). A journal should serve as a record of such meetings.

- What inspires a work of fiction is usually an insigificant part of the fiction that results. If the story or novel doesn't develop beyond the original inspiration, if it exists only to communicate that inspiration, then the form of the story has become subservient to its function, and the art suffers.

But writing is, to adapt Edison's comment about genius, only "one percent inspiration and ninety-nine percent perspiration" (Carville 1931, 78). And the perspiration almost always precedes the inspiration.

- There are two kinds of writer's block and only one truly deserves the name. There are some writers who are so self-critical that they edit their every thought back into the silence it came from and never put a word onto paper. Such premature editing stems from an honorable and necessary impulse—the impulse for perfection—gone amok. Approximations of perfection are possible only through active engagement in the imperfect writing process. Writers who wish to bypass the slow and messy process by which the product is achieved are trying to treat writing as if it were speech, which follows almost instantaneously upon thought and cannot be revised. The glory of writing, however, is precisely its ability to do what speech cannot: delay expression until thoughts and language have been carefully tested and formed. If you're afflicted with this type of writer's block, you need to recognize that you're demanding the impossible of yourself, and that such demands are a form of vanity you must overcome. If you want to succeed as a writer, you must first learn to accept the embarrassment of failure.

  The other kind of writer's block is more common and is in fact a part of the writing process, not its enemy. Often, we have something to say but just can't get the words on paper. When that happens, it's generally a sign that we're not approaching our subject appropriately. Our inability to write is telling us to reconsider some technique, some aim. Therefore, not-writing can be an integral part of writing, not something opposed to writing, as we often assume it to be. The only way to cure this sort of "writer's block" is to keep working at the problem—be it style, character, plot, whatever—until you solve it. Waiting until you're in the mood to write doesn't work; it just confirms the silence. As Collin Brooks has said, "The art of writing is the art of applying the seat of the pants to the seat of the chair" (Brooks 1950, 72).

  Not all silences are evidence of writer's block. Sometimes you simply have nothing to say—and that is not only understandable but inevitable. The notion that writers should be able to write brilliantly at will is misguided. Sometimes you should write, and sometimes you should take out the garbage.

- The common advice that fiction writers should write from their own experience is both valuable and misleading. It is valuable because it reminds us that our experience is the source of the emotions and ideas that constitute our vision of ourselves and the world and because it advises us to root our fictions in the experiences that have impelled us to write in the first place, but it is misleading because it often leads writers toward what James called "the fatal futility of fact" ("Preface," 122). Facts are futile because they cannot explain our experience to us; if they could, who would need to write or read fiction? The truth is, fiction—which revises and reconstitutes experience—can explain reality better than reality itself can. Therefore, when a writer remains too faithful to fact, it is fatal to the art and, ultimately, the reality that is its subject. George Santayana once remarked that "sometimes we have to change the truth in order to remember it" (Santayana 1937, 601). I second that opinion, though when we're talking about art I'd remove the word "sometimes." If fiction is to be memorable, if it is to be *art*, then it *must* change the truth.

    But before you can change the truth, you must know it. As Miller Williams's poem "Let Me Tell You" advises, we should "notice everything" and "memorize it" because "you cannot twist the fact you do not know" (Williams 1971, 13). Fiction—even science fiction—is composed almost solely of facts, though the facts are "twisted." If the facts are too twisted—if they are not taken out of their natural sequence and rearranged so as to alter their significance and effect—they restrict the imagination and inhibit the creation of art. To quote Eudora Welty, "if you write about an actual event, you can't shape it the way you can an imaginary one" (Plimpton 1976, 284). To shape it, you have to introduce other, unrelated facts. Say, for example, that you want to write a story about your divorce. If you stick to the facts as you know them, you will produce an expository essay, albeit a very personal one; the justification for the details included will be *truth*, not *art*. But if you change even one fact—make the main character your best friend instead of you, for example—you would still be dealing with facts—events and people you know—but you will have created something that never happened: *fiction*.

    Fiction isn't only the careful recombination of facts, however. To write well, you must be willing to *extrapolate* from facts, to exaggerate upon your experience. If you have ever lost something you loved—be it a pet or a favorite toy—you have experienced all that is necessary to write about the death of a parent. So when someone tells you to "write from your experience," realize that does not mean "write only about what has literally happened to you." Your experience is more than just the facts of your life; it is everything that your life has prepared you to understand, feel, and imagine. And writing fiction is a way of discovering just how broad and deep your experience truly is.

- Another reason writing about actual events without "twisting" the facts hinders the creation of art is that we know beforehand everything that will happen in the story. Fiction writers can never know too many facts, but they must be unsure about how to combine, revise, and order them. If you restrict yourself to a Joe Friday approach to fiction—"Just the facts, ma'am"—you deny yourself the chance to consider the alternate possibilities that doubt and uncertainty could supply your imagination. For fiction writers, knowing too much can be dangerous. As Donald Barthelme has written, "not-knowing is crucial to art, is what permits art to be made. Without the scanning process engendered by not-knowing, without the possibility of having the mind move in unanticipated directions, there would be no invention" (Barthelme 1986, 24).

  Writing is a higher form of reading. Because not-knowing is essential to the production of art, it is best to enter a story "open-handed," with perhaps only a few details—a character or two, a situation, an image—and then discover, through the hard labor of trial and error, the story. Just as the reader discovers the story as it progresses, so should the writer. In the words of an old lady quoted by E. M. Forster, "How can I know what I think till I see what I say?" (Auden 1962, 22). And as Frost said, "No surprise for the writer, no surprise for the reader" (Frost 1966, 19). The process of writing must be one of discovery or the story will seem flat, outlined, prefabricated.

- Outlines are helpful only insofar as you consider them something as tentative as any other part of the creative process. To adapt the advice of every Little League coach who ever lived, "Don't let the outline play you; you play the outline." If you don't revise, or even abandon, your outline at some point in the composition, you're not really writing, and all you can hope for is the literary equivalent of a connect-the-dots picture.

Though the author of a story is its god, that author must be careful not to restrict the freedom of will of the story's characters. Outlining is a form of predestination that destroys the characters' ability to develop and change beyond the author's original conception—in other words, their ability to behave as if they were truly human.

• The human mind always strives toward order. If you recognize this fact, you will find it much easier to approach fiction writing as a process of discovering a story rather than a process of connecting the dots of an outline. When we look at the night sky, we see randomly scattered stars, but we won't allow our senses to stop there: we must connect the stars in some way, create hunters and dippers and twins. We do the same thing with fiction. To prove this, give yourself any situation (for example, a man meeting his ex-wife by chance at a bus stop) and write a page of dialogue. But before the man speaks, choose a word at random from any book, and make him use that word. Then, before the woman answers, select another word at random for her to use. If you continue in this manner, before long you will have created from these random and discordant elements both a rational dialogue and a scene with a clearly defined beginning, middle, and end.

• The senses are all. Often, students write stories that are in fact essays or vignettes or anecdotes that illustrate a point (prejudice is bad, people see the world differently, and so on). But fiction should *embody* ideas, give them sensory form. As Federico García Lorca said, "A poet is a professor of the five bodily senses" (Nims 1974, 7). If you concentrate on capturing the senses in your fiction, ideas will arise naturally from them.

Sense deprivation is a form of death. If we can't see, hear, feel, taste, and smell, we're dead. Too often, beginning writers avoid the senses so strenuously that they wind up torturing their readers to death. Keep your readers alive.

• Content is less important than technique. To quote Karl Kraus, "In art the important thing is not that one has eggs and fat, but that one has a fire and a pan" (Kraus 1976, 47). All of us have enough eggs and fat—enough experience—to cook up a hundred stories, provided we have the necessary equipment. As Pascal said, "There are no dull subjects, only dull points of view" (1956, 37). All subjects are legitimate, and all can be fascinating, depending upon how they are approached.

Without technique, a writer cannot discover the meaning of content, much less manipulate that meaning to achieve the effect he or she desires. After all, technique consists largely of strategies for arranging words and meanings, and as Pascal said, "Words differently arranged have a different meaning, and meanings differently arranged have different effects" (1956, 7).

When a writer thinks too much about what is being said and not enough about *how* it is said, content defeats art.

- What you leave out of a story is as important to the story's success as what you put in, for good fiction derives much of its effect from careful omission. To quote a character in Ann Beattie's story "Snow," "Any life will seem dramatic if you omit mention of most of it" (Beattie 1986, 22). But writers not only omit the undramatic aspects of a life, at times they also omit—at least on the surface—the drama. In Hemingway's "Hills Like White Elephants," for example, what the characters don't say is more important than what they do say, and the story's drama arises out of the conflict between their implied thoughts and their narrated words. Hemingway believed that "you could omit anything if you knew that you omitted and the omitted part would strengthen the story and make people feel something more than they understood" (Hemingway 1964, 75). The good fiction writer, then, has to select not only what to include, but what to exclude. "Tell almost the whole story," Anne Sexton tells us (Plimpton 1976, 422). If you tell it all, the reader is left with the minor pleasure of passive learning, not the greater joy of active discovery.

One thing that novice writers frequently include but should omit is an explanation of the story's meaning. To explain your story to the reader is a form of condescension, and all such explanations cheapen the experience conveyed in the story by making it seem secondary to the theme—a means to an end. Even worse than explaining your meaning is commenting overtly on your characters' morality. To do so makes the story veer toward allegory or parable—in short, it denies the characters their primacy as human beings and makes them ideas. At times, students believe that laminating a story with moral commentary somehow "elevates" it to a higher purpose. But, as Chekhov said, morals purify literature as "flies purify the air" (Friedland 1964, 170).

- A good writer must be "schizophrenic"—he must write with enthusiasm from every word, and revise with disdain for the same.

  A writer who is not interested in revision is not interested in art. Art is not spontaneous; it is just supposed to *seem* spontaneous. In the words of Richard Brinsley Sheridan, "easy writing's curst hard reading" (Rhodes 1929, 117). And hard writing makes blessed easy reading.

- Ernest Gaines once said in a speech that every story should begin with a man standing in the middle of a freeway during rush hour; that way, he either had to move or the story was over. All too often, students' stories begin passively, with a character remembering the events of recent days, weeks, or even years. This is a too-convenient way to introduce exposition and doesn't involve the reader sufficiently. Put your characters into a situation requiring action.

- Endings do not necessarily have to answer the obvious questions in the reader's mind—will X marry Y? will Z mend his ways?—but they should always answer the questions he didn't know they were thinking. For example, in "Signs and Symbols," Vladimir Nabokov's extraordinary story of a couple whose institutionalized son has attempted suicide several times, the obvious question remains as unanswered as the phone that rings at the end of the story. By not answering our question about who is calling—it could be someone from the poorly run and understaffed hospital calling to inform them that their son has finally managed to kill himself, or it could be the girl who has twice before reached their number accidentally—Nabokov puts us forever into the hell in which they live, the hell of not knowing whether the next moment will destroy their lives or merely prolong the terrible expectation of that destruction. And by putting us into this hell, Nabokov answers questions his readers may not have even realized they were asking, the questions "How does the possibility of imminent death affect love? What is the relationship of love and terror? Of terror and uncertainty? Of the banal and the tragic? What happens to hope after years of suffering? And what happens to grief after it becomes your daily condition, after it becomes 'ordinary'?" And ultimately, Nabokov answers the simplest yet deepest question any reader can ask: "What does it feel like to be someone else?"

Writers who focus too much on answering their readers' obvious questions generally wind up focusing on plot gimmicks, especially the "surprise" ending. But surprise endings rarely surprise, and even when they do, they do irreparable damage to the fiction. For a surprise ending is a surprise only once, and a story that relies on one does not pass the all-important test of re-readability.

Murder and suicide, two of the most popular ways novice writers end their stories, almost always make for bad endings because the typical story's ten to twenty-five pages don't provide enough room either to motivate such acts or to make us care about the fate of those who commit them. As a result, such stories succumb to melodrama and ask more emotion of a reader than they have earned.

- Although few things damage fiction more than melodrama, the best stories and novels "play chicken" with it—coming as close to crashing as possible but veering away at the last minute. They deal with people who are on the edge in some literal or metaphorical way, where what matters is most dangerously apparent. The greatest fiction writers, then, are the ones who risk the greatest failures: Dostoevsky, inhabiting the mind of a murderer in *Crime and Punishment*; Nabokov, pursuing a sexual obsession in *Lolita*; Faulkner, explicating the anguish of an idiot in *The Sound and the Fury*; Melville, taking on themes as huge and dangerous as a white whale in *Moby Dick*. Remember, you can only be as good as you dare to be bad.

- There are several kinds of suspense besides that of "what happens next." The kinds that focus on character or motive are superior, for they are the only forms of suspense that can carry us through a second—or third, or fourth—reading.

- We hear a lot about the importance of "finding one's voice" these days. But realize, once you find your voice, you're stuck with it—and with the limited range of characters and situations for which it is appropriate. Fiction writers should concentrate not on finding their own voices but on finding their *characters'* voices.

- Though we often hear that believable characters are those who are "consistent," neither in fact nor in fiction do we believe in them. As Melville said, "Is it not a fact that, in real life, a consistent character is a *rara avis*?" (Franklin 1976, 94). The strongest characters are those who behave inconsistently—because they are drawn by conflicting desires and purposes. They may be "consistently inconsistent," as Aristotle would have it (Butcher 1961, 81), but nonetheless they are developed fully enough to surprise us, and themselves, with their behavior.

- "Brevity," Chekhov said, "is the sister of talent" (Friedland 1964, 170). Without economy, there is no art. Even if a novel is grand, panoramic, and encyclopedic, it still must be *economically* grand, panoramic, and encyclopedic.

  Economical writing doesn't result from economical effort, a fact Pascal acknowledged when he apologized for writing a long letter by saying he could have made it shorter if only he'd had more time (1941, 571).

- Finally, always remember John Barth's admonition to creative writing students: "Of the two thieves crucified along with Jesus, St. Augustine writes, 'Do not despair; one thief was saved. Do not presume; one thief was damned'" (Barth 1962, 36).

Notes

[1]Various versions of this statement are attributed to Buffon by Matthew Arnold (*Essays in Criticism*, 284), Flaubert (Steegmuller 1980, 65), and other writers.

Works Cited

Arnold, Matthew. *Essays in Criticism: First Series.* London: Macmillan and Co., 1921.

Auden, W. H. *The Dyer's Hand and Other Essays.* New York: Random House, 1962.

Barth, John. *Writing: Can It Be Taught?* New York: Random House, 1962.

Barthelme, Donald. "Not-Knowing." In *The Pushcart Prize XI: Best of the Small Presses,* edited by Bill Henderson, 23–37. Wainscott, N.Y.: Pushcart Press, 1986.

Beattie, Ann. *Where You'll Find Me.* New York: Linden Press/Simon & Schuster, 1986.

Bly, Robert. Comment to a poetry writing class at Southwest State University in Marshall, Minnesota, Spring 1970.

Brooks, Collin. *Tavern Talk.* London: J. Barrie, 1950.

Bush, Douglas, ed. *Selected Poems and Letters,* by John Keats. Boston: Houghton Mifflin, 1959.

Butcher, S. H., trans. *Aristotle's Poetics.* New York: Hill and Wang, 1961.

Carville, Robert. "Thomas A. Edison: Philosopher." Excerpts from an interview with Edison. In *The Golden Book*, April 1931: 13, 78–79.

Dacey, Philip. From a 1985 conversation with the author.

Franklin, H. Bruce, ed. *The Confidence-Man*, by Herman Melville. Indianapolis: Bobbs-Merrill, 1967.

Friedland, Louis S., ed. *Letters on the Short Story, the Drama and Other Literary Topics*, by Anton Chekov. New York: Benjamin Blom, 1964.

Frost, Robert. "The Figure a Poem Makes." In *Selected Prose of Robert Frost*, edited by Hyde Cox and Edward Connery Lathem, 17–20. New York: Holt, Rinehart and Winston, 1966.

Gaines, Ernest. Speech delivered at the Associated Writing Programs annual conference in Seattle, Washington, April 4, 1981.

Gross, John, ed. *The Oxford Book of Aphorisms*. Oxford: Oxford University Press, 1983.

Hemingway, Ernest. *A Moveable Feast*. New York: Scribner's, 1964.

James, Henry. "The Art of Fiction." In *The Future of the Novel*, edited by Leon Edel, 3–27. New York: Random House, 1956.

———. "Preface to The Spoils of Poynton." [1909.] In *The Art of the Novel* [1934], 119–39. New York: Scribner's, 1962.

Kalem, T. E. "Lord of Craft and Valor." *Time* 106 (December 29, 1975): 59.

Kraus, Karl. *Half-Truths and One-and-a-Half Truths: Selected Aphorisms*, edited by Harry Zohn. Montreal: Engendra Press, 1976.

Michaels, Leonard. From a flyer advertising a creative writing conference at the University of California, Berkeley, Summer 1981.

Nietzsche, Friedrich. [1885.] *Beyond Good and Evil*. Chicago: Henry Regnery Co., 1955.

Nims, John Frederick. *Western Wind: An Introduction to Poetry*. New York: Random House, 1974.

Pascal, Blaise. *Pascal's Pensees*. New York: E. P. Dutton, 1956.

———. *The Provincial Letters*. New York: Random House, 1941.

Phillips, Bum. Comment to TV sportscaster during the 1974 football season.

Plimpton, George, ed. *Writers at Work: The* Paris Review *Interviews, Fourth Series*. New York: Viking, 1976.

Santayana, George. *The Last Puritan: A Memoir in the Form of a Novel*. New York: Scribner's, 1937.

Sheridan, Richard Brinsley. "Clio's Protest." In *The Plays and Poems of Richard Brinsley Sheridan*, vol. 3, edited by R. Crompton Rhodes, 107–18. New York: Russell and Russell, 1929.

Simons, Marlise. "Love and Age: A Talk with García Márquez." *New York Times Book Review*, April 7, 1985: 1, 18–19.

Steegmuller, Francis, trans. and ed. *The Letters of Gustave Flaubert, 1830–1857*. Cambridge, Mass.: Harvard University Press, 1980.

Williams, Miller. *The Only World There Is*. New York: E. P. Dutton, 1971.

II Craft and the Creative Process

Interviewer: Can one, indeed, teach writing?

Malamud: You teach writers—assuming a talent. At the beginning young writers pour it out without much knowing the nature of their talent. What you try to do is hold a mirror up to their fiction so, in a sense, they can see what they're showing. Not all who come forth are fully armed. Some are gifted in narrative, some shun it. Some show a richness of metaphor, some have to dig for it. Some writers think language is all they need; they mistake it for subject matter. Some rely on whimsy. Some on gut feeling. Some of them don't make the effort to create a significant form. They do automatic writing and think they're probing themselves.

—Bernard Malamud, "Interview with Daniel Stern,"
Writers at Work, Sixth Series, 1984

5 Assignment

Ron Carlson
Arizona State University

There is an old saying about rolling newspapers for delivery: "start tight, stay tight," which is worth keeping in mind at the beginning of a semester of a creative writing course. Students enter with a general (vague) expectation of something creative, which up to this point in their lives has meant something loose, a course they can lean back into like an old lounge chair in the frat house basement, something easier, for God's sake, than chemistry. They expect to write periodically and to meet in our sessions and talk about their work the way they talk about movies afterward in a genial, general way, bringing to bear their natural expertise and understanding of narrative (from thousands of hours studying television programs) and chronology (from having already skillfully survived twenty, even twenty-two years) and dramatic tension (from having lived with their parents) and climactic epiphany (from having loved and lost). This course should be a cinch, a walk through. Maybe it should.

But I'm going to start a little differently this semester, a little "tighter." After all, we've been off for six weeks, plenty of time to talk about writing (in fact, this whole approach may be the result of the hours I'd spent on the phone with an editor), and: let's write. After I've introduced myself and announced my office hours and passed out the reading schedule and let everyone know the approximate expenses they will probably have for photocopying for the semester, I read the class "Araby."

There are fifteen students in English 594 this semester and though most of them know the Joyce story, and though many of them know it well, they listen to the story carefully. I've introduced it as part of an assignment. Just the word *assignment* on this first day of the graduate seminar has earned me new attention. I read the story straight through with only one interruption, to pause and appreciate that sentence: "Through one of the broken panes I heard the rain impinge upon the earth, the fine incessant needles of water playing in the sodden beds." When I have finished I simply state the obvious assignment: everyone will write a one-thousand-word story for next week, a story that somehow deals with disappointment. It can be drawn from personal experience. They can use my reading of "Araby" any way they choose. I read that last two-line paragraph again, and taunt them: use the story as a model or don't. Reach into childhood or last week. Any point of view. Good luck. And I send them off with a deadline, like journalists. We all know it's a gift, but it still feels odd.

The most important thing in writing is to finish. The rest, and there is plenty, is gravy. The semester starts, shiny as new shoes, and everybody wants to talk. Not this semester. We'll dive in and see what happens. If we meet on the other shore, we'll talk.

There is a little buzzing through the week. My independent study students have heard something. What's going on in 594? Someone's griping about this deadline. What's this deadline about? Am I treating them like they're in junior high? My independent study students, who have taken 594 before when it was different, I come to see, are jealous.

The day of class I see two women who are in the workshop sitting together on a secluded bench reading each other's story. I buy a cup of coffee from the kiosk and wander over until the women see me. They look at me. I say hello. They do not ask me to join them.

In class, I lecture about creating character in a story, about finding the small thing that will distinguish your character from every other housewife or bachelor father in the world. And I go on with my favorite recent examples and digressions and suggestions, and the talk lasts forty minutes. I can see the bulging satchels all around the classroom.

There are some special moments teaching writing, some moments that are warmer than others. Making an assignment is a warm moment and asking students to pass copies of their stories around is a warm moment, a moment of risk. Writing suggestions on student stories is good for me, but I think it is cooler than any of the links in the chain. The hottest moments come, of course, between the writer and the paper, when the writer lets go and launches into a story and bears down through the story, even the soft parts, and then types the last word. A lot happens right there that is beyond the teacher's admonition, beyond regulation and suggestion, beyond final, analytical definition. The heat of creation—it is not always a comfortable place, but it is that place which we are talking about when we talk about writing, and I know that my role as teacher is to send students there, not simply to have the fun of talking about having written.

Writing is a creative not a reactive activity; and the purpose of class discussion should be to repair old or to gather new equipment for the next story. We are talking about the next story at all times, and when the discussion becomes most mired in the story before us, it becomes many times least useful. Process, not product—the next story. The next story.

Suddenly before us on the table, we have fifteen stories. This is a novelty of sorts. I've never had more than four before for a week's reading (maybe five, after a break), and here are all these reams of paper.

I make the next assignment. We will all read the fifteen stories this week, fair enough. A short book of stories by our colleagues in a week. Reading, in large part, is a reactive activity, passive to an extent. Any ordinary week, we read our stories twice, once with a pencil, and students know we'll start our discussion with a few simple statements of the things that actually happened in the piece. The plot points we can all agree on. Just the task of establishing common ground can be revealing and fruitful. But this week the assignment (how I'm coming to find a new affection for that word) is different.

After reading the stories, we will select the five we like the most and write a one-page essay on why we chose those five. We read Ray Carver's introduction to *Best American Stories 1986,* and Ann Beattie's introduction to her selections for 1987. (Ann Beattie refers to "surprise" and its relationship to the real complexity of human problems.) We can use these two examples as models or not. We must be guided by what matters to us, so the task is to identify what matters to us in stories and set that down.

Oh, it's a harsh order: choose some over others. The graduate students pick up their packets of stories and, eyes narrowed, saunter out of the room.

When we meet again, I look around the table into the faces of the students and it is hard to believe this is *only our third meeting.* They look like veterans already. And they talk like veterans: there is a lot of work before us and all of them have done their homework so we won't waste words today. We will not fall into jargon; we are armed—none of "this doesn't work for me . . ." or "I'm not certain about this. . . ." We're willing to say we're certain. I hand out my homework: four pages which list and summarize each of the fifteen stories.

I ask them how they felt about the assignment, and I learn: the students were not exactly comfortable picking some stories over others; they felt they were picking *people* over other people. I'm glad this has come up and it takes about two minutes to say what they've all seen clearly this week: the stories speak for themselves. They explain that the initial selection process wasn't that difficult. Writing the short essay was.

Our workshop discussion covers only about half of the stories in the remaining two hours, and we break up to cover the other half next week—along with the essays, which I will read. I make a quick tally of selections and note that every story was included in at least one "Best Five." It is the third week and we have all written a story and a version of our credo. It was a lot to bite off, but the semester, now, is a given. We have a strong tone, and tone is crucial to fiction classes, and we are taking each other seriously. We will fall into workshop rotation easily, happily, ready for the good work ahead. We have "started tight."

6 Guidelines and Exercises for Teaching Creative Writing

John D. MacDonald

My experience in the teaching of writing is limited. In 1947 I sat in on a few of Howard Nemerov's seminars in creative writing at Hamilton College in Clinton, New York. A few years later I was one-third of a teaching faculty at a two-week summer conference at Putney, Vermont. The other two were John Aldridge and Vance Bourjailie. Nine years ago I taught a semester of creative writing at New College in Sarasota. I attended no such courses during my learning years. From time to time I have read student work produced in creative writing courses, and I have, of course, heard many opinions about the merits and faults of such courses.

I have formed a few opinions over the years. These might better be classified as prejudices rather than opinions. I will list them here and number them in a loose order of importance:

1. First, more than anything else, I believe that writers must be readers. The only students who belong in advanced undergraduate or graduate creative writing courses are those who have been compulsive and omnivorous readers all their lives, and who have thereby acquired some sense of the excruciating complexity of the history and the existence of humanity. They will have a sense of geological time, of the sweep of political, social, philosophical, economic, and scientific thought and history. They will have a sense of geography, mental images of the continents and hemispheres, the nations and oceans. In contrast, nonreaders, by reading nothing except the daily paper and whatever else is required to pass other courses, have established inside their skulls huge areas of smoke, nonsense, and sterile space where knowledge and awareness should reside. The nonreaders are, on average, rotten spellers. That is because they do not see the printed words often enough to even know when they look wrong. I am not trying to say that spelling is all that important, merely that this non-

recognition of error carries over into phrases and sentence structure. There will be no equivalent familiarity with cliches, tired analogies, shopworn metaphors, and plain clumsiness. The nonreaders, when forced to write, will repeat tired nonsense without knowing they are repeating the sins of a few hundred years of bad writing.

2. Now we have a class composed of readers, bright, eager, and misinformed. They have the idea that creative writing is their chance to expose to the world the ineffable delicacy of their perceptions, the sweet harmony of their awareness of their own unique existence. Also, they have come up through a school system which has convinced them that learning should be fun, as well as relevant. They must be disabused of all three concepts as quickly as possible. They have all been writing for years, of course. All truly literate young people write down their dreams. *But they have been, in effect, standing inside themselves, looking out at only what they wish to see.*

Start with an assignment that will require hours of brute labor. They will not like it. As they take notes, you describe an automobile accident at a familiar intersection. Tell them that each one of them is to invent ten different people who saw the accident, each from a different vantage point and a different direction. They are to write a first-person account of the accident for each witness, using the style of presentation to give us some idea of what that witness is like, what he or she is doing in the midst of life. There can be no deviation from the first person. Ten people, ten pages. And let them know that this is going to foreshadow the pace and pattern of the course. They are going to write and write and write. And a lot of it is going to be drill rather than a lot of beautiful self-expression. You will lose a few, the ones who wanted to learn to write without learning to work.

Maybe the first two or three can be fun, of a kind. But ten accounts become brute labor. As a general rule, young people who are forced into doing dull work tend to whine and mutter. And they often speak of whether or not what they are doing is "relevant." If MIT finds it relevant to make students spend a semester devising an extraterrestrial creature and then creating the language, architecture, science, religion, and politics which will fit that physical structure they have invented, and fit the gravity of the planet on which the creatures live, then I suspect that writing ten eyewitness accounts of anything at all can be thought "relevant."

This exercise accelerates learning. Most of them gradually discover that there is a mysterious something known as "viewpoint." This exercise begins to detach them from their previous ego-image of writing and takes them rudely into a world of character, or different voices, of different rhythms of speech. And in so doing they will begin to get a whiff of plot design from the way the ten views of the accident differ, one from another.

Assign a few more in the same pattern. For example, have them take ten people in ten different parts of the country and have them give a first-person account of their reaction to the Challenger disaster and ten first-person accounts of the death and burial of a loved one. These are hard to do. They require thought and empathy. They make the student step out of his or her own skull and into another's.

The next step is dialogue. Make two strangers talk to each other. Make them reveal who they are, what they think, what they believe, how they live, through conversation. Tell them to get these two people into a hot dispute about a matter that the student does not feel strongly about.

Slowly, slowly you are easing them into an awareness of the true shape of a story. A story is not an obscurantist celebration of wry mystery of existence. *A story is something happening to somebody.* They are learning to make things happen, and learning how to build the character to which the things will happen. In the shallowest of stories the happening is entirely physical. In the most significant fiction things happen on all possible levels—physical, spiritual, intellectual, moral. They will learn that the "quality" of the fiction is a function of the quality of intellect of the writer, his or her perception, sensitivity, and the quantity and quality of the storehouse of knowledge behind the writing, to the rewards of long reading.

3. Demand production. Five thousand words of fiction per week is a meager minimum. Do not fret if you don't have time to read and appraise it. They will learn more by writing than through anything you can say to them. Select students at random to read specified portions of their work in class, for open criticism by all. In this way you guarantee the writing will be done. Collect it and put it away. In the next seminar refer to what you have read.

4. Be aware of exactly what *you* are doing. The most motivated of these students would have acquired adequate skills with you or without you. You are there to save them time and effort. You are there to point out the shortcuts to competent work. You are not teaching nuclear physics or quantum mechanics or any kind of hard discipline. You are taking heads stuffed with the odds and ends of our culture, taking young people who want to turn the odds and ends and the dreams and yearnings into an acceptable, accessible form. They want to speak in their own voice, and the best of them will do so despite your teaching.

So we give them a taste of the hard work involved, a good dose of discipline, and a framework of procedures. I think it is impossible to try to codify the teaching of creative writing, but we can teach a few useful shortcuts.

Do not let them *tell* you about their characters. Do not let them say, "She was a nervous and troubled woman." Make them show you the woman sitting there, sweaty, wringing her hands, rattling her spoon on her coffee cup, pinching her under lip. Don't let them say, "He was a fool." Make them show you the fellow doing a fool thing. They will learn this by themselves, of course. But at what a cost in wasted stories.

Another time-saver involves movement. Do not let them take the character out into the hall, down in the elevator to the garage, across town in traffic, into a parking lot, up in another elevator, down a hall to knock at a door. This is laborious and dumb. Let the character walk into the hall and then one skips two spaces and shows him knocking at her doorway across the city. Trust the reader. The reader is not a fool. He does not have to be led across the city by hand. She knows how to get across a city. Don't try to teach the reader. As a corollary to this concept, do not let the student describe everything in a room. Make the student pick out two or three objects that are unique to this *type* of room and describe them with care. By drawing on one's own life experience the reader can build the rest of the room in a fractional part of a second, be it downgrade motel or IBM office.

Description can be a chronic waste of energy and space. Give students one simple rule to go by. If they finish a portion of a manuscript and they have a feeling of pride and pleasure, and that portion is involved with action and the interaction of people, leave it alone. If that portion is involved with the description of a landscape, a cityscape, a bosky dell, a grove of pines, cut it to the bone. This bad habit is called, "Look, Mom! I'm writing lovely!"

All in all, you will have saved them a Godawful amount of time. You will have saved them from committing a plethora of dying, blind musicians, and boxes of bad poetry, and thousands of yards of excruciatingly beautiful writing about beaches and sunrises and suicides.

And you can't do it while being "nice." You have to put them under stress because that's where the learning happens. Lots of luck.

7 How a Writer Reads

Stephen Minot

John D. MacDonald's initial point in chapter 6 deserves to be repeated at the opening meeting of every writing seminar: "The only students who belong in advanced undergraduate or graduate creative writing courses are those who have been compulsive and omnivorous readers all their lives."

This is, of course, an ideal. We are not always so lucky as to have a class made up entirely of students who are truly qualified. Indeed, some of us who fought over the years for a separation between the literary and the creative writing wings of English departments have found to our chagrin a tendency for nonreaders to drift toward the writing program. There is a good reason for this. The motive for writing fiction or poetry is part artistic and part therapeutic. When a student's need for therapy outweighs a fascination with the art form, there is no need to read what others have written. The act of writing—often without revision—becomes an end in itself. Therapeutic writing has its function, but teachers of writing are neither trained to deal with it nor paid for the hours of consultation required. For these reasons it is essential to stress at the first class meeting that literary writing is an art form no matter how rooted a work may be in personal experience.

Omnivorous reading is certainly the best possible preparation for a student writer. It counters the notion that writing fiction or poetry is a purely personal and private act like daydreaming. More positively, it places a student in the context of a literary heritage. Even rebels need to know what they are rebelling against. This is why I prefer to select students for an introductory writing course on the basis of what they have been reading rather than what they have written. I have found this to be the best way to distinguish students whose primary concern is literary creativity from those who—often with great sincerity—wish to use the course and me to untangle personal problems.

Omnivorous and compulsive reading, however, is only a base. Once the course begins, I make a point of stressing the differences between reading simply for pleasure and reading as a writer. This is not to suggest that writers must renounce pleasure—far from it! It is simply that the committed professional usually looks for and draws pleasure from different aspects of literature more readily than do recreational readers. By way of analogy, a professional violinist listens to a symphony orchestra differently than does even an avid music lover, and a ballet dancer who attends a performance sees a different dance than does the rest of the audience.

Put in most general terms, most readers—even compulsive ones—tend to be passive. If there is no exam looming in the distance, they allow plot and characters to flow by in flickering images. Dramatic scenes linger, but subtle scenes are soon forgotten, including those that were essential. Even highly perceptive, well-trained readers tend to forget within a day whether a story was written in the past tense or the present and whether it was presented from the wife's point of view or the husband's. This passivity and rapid loss of recall has undoubtedly become more prevalent as a result of film and television, but it would be a mistake to believe that the average nineteenth-century reader of *War and Peace* retained more than what we would now call a cinematic impression.

This passivity is particularly prevalent among adults who have been out of an academic setting for a while. When one takes a turn teaching an extension course—a valuable experience for any teacher—one is struck by what is best described as a tilt toward subjectivity. "I have cousin just like that," and the discussion lurches into gossip. You get it back on course only to be shunted off once again with, "Well, I never would have let *my* children talk like that." In all fairness, these individuals are paying literature a high tribute: they are treating fiction as an extension of their own lives. Because they have not been reading actively and often have had little occasion to use the vocabulary needed to describe literature, it is entirely natural for them to keep veering toward more familiar subjects—themselves. But to allow that kind of discussion to run on in class for more than a sentence is to transform a writing seminar into a coffee klatch without pastries. It does not take more than one or two class meetings for students to see this distinction and shift their attention to the work at hand.

Active reading focuses on the writing itself. Students who are in the middle of their academic programs and who have done well in traditional literature courses remember this. But they tend to place a heavy emphasis on theme and characterization. Those two concerns dominate most literature courses from the seventh grade on. I have no quarrel with that since it places the emphasis where it should be, on the work at hand. Looking closely and objectively at theme and characterization are steps one and two on the route to active reading. But relying on them excessively can turn out to be a dead end with some fiction. It's a sad day when a class tries with furrow-browed seriousness to analyze the theme of Eudora Welty's "Why I Live at the P.O." or a Tolkien fantasy. It is equally futile to try defining character in one of Donald Barthelme's flights of whimsy or in Italo Calvino's wry parables. We tell secondary-school students that every work of fiction *must* have an intellectually definable theme and well-developed characterization for the same reason we tell them that every sentence must always have a subject and a verb: it's a convenient myth. But when serious writing students in college or graduate school cling to such myths, their range of fictional innovation is sadly reduced.

Theme and characterization are certainly important in most works, but they are not necessarily what writers look for first, and they are not always the best topics to initiate a student discussion in a writing seminar. What topics are? Every writer has somewhat different sets of interests, of course, and every literary work has different characteristics. The following list, however, represents some of the concerns that particularly interest me and that keep turning up in my classes. They seem to lend themselves to the kind of active reading which is important to writers at any stage. The list represents a range of concerns certainly not shared by passive readers and rarely stressed in traditional literature courses.

- *The means of perception.* I prefer this term to *point of view* because it can't be confused with the more general use of the phrase, as in "From a French point of view." But no matter which term you use, the concept is central. Through whose eyes are we seeing this? How consistently? What are the tactical advantages of presenting the story through this character rather than that one?

    I am constantly surprised at how many well-read and conscientious students have never noticed that most short stories are limited to a single means of perception. Novels, of course, are less restrictive; but I have recently gone through three anthologies to find a single example of a story that entered the mind of more than one character. Appreciating this important aspect of short fiction clearly requires more than omnivorous and compulsive reading; it requires a close examination of literary techniques.

From a writer's point of view (using that phrase in its broad sense), the means of perception is something one notices right from the first page—before characterization is developed and long before the theme takes shape. It's the operating principle. It is as basic to all fiction—even the most innovative—as the metrical scheme is to a metered poem. Yet for all this, it is largely ignored by the recreational reader.

- *Voice* is in a sense the flavor of the means of perception. Are we hearing someone talk to an actual audience? Is it a monologue without an identified audience? If it is a third-person voice, are we hearing echoes of how the protagonist talks? Or does it frequently echo the thoughts of that character rather than spoken words? Or is it neutral? Even if it is apparently neutral, how close does this make us feel to the protagonist? Are we sharing his or her world (verisimilitude), or are we looking down with amused disdain (satire), or with a greater understanding than the character will ever have (irony). While the passive reader is flipping ahead, impatient to get a rush from a dramatic plot, the writer is savoring those subtle distinctions of voice right from the beginning.

- *Scene construction* is another concern for the active reader. "That scene down by the lake," we may say, "is so vivid it makes the rest of my story seem flat." Scenes, then, have contours—some seem flat or they sag, others reach a peak, a few are best described as the pits. Occasionally it's "all downhill from that scene." Scenes also have tonal qualities, both good and bad—dramatic or melodramatic, moving or sentimental. Some are crucial, others needless. All but the microscopic, one-celled story are actually segmental, a series of related units. If you have ever bicycled over a route you had previously known only by driving, you will remember how an apparently straight and level road turns into a series of uphill climbs and downhill sweeps. Every curve becomes distinct. In the same way, those who have never written a story tend to see a work of fiction as one single, seamless unit, while writers who are also active readers are acutely aware of the many contours.

- *Risk.* Every basketball fan admires the player who tries the unorthodox approach and gets away with it; every aviation fan is impressed by flights made with hot air balloons or human-powered flying machines when we know perfectly well that there are easier, quicker, and cheaper ways of getting from A to B. We tend to admire the risk-takers in our own field. Only sailors admire the person who sails alone around Antarctica; for the rest, that person is a show-off at best and perhaps a bit bonkers as well.

Every writer has his or her favorite show-offs. One reader's notion of innovation is another's example of obtrusive obscurity. And daring tricks are subject to fashion. Donald Barthelme's remaking of the short story form—moving it in the direction of the fable and the slightly stoned standup comic—was astonishing when it first appeared, but it has become a kind of subgenre in the course of the past decade. Robert Coover's dizzying leaps are dazzling to some and simply too tricky for others.

Although risk-taking is a literary quality writers often admire, I don't encourage beginning students to strive for special effects too early. I remind them that there are good reasons student aerialists don't start on the high wire. It's wise, I think, to recommend caution; but at the same time it is only fair to share one's enthusiasms. For example, I urge my beginning students not to try the "you" form in fiction because the chances are they will echo bad detective fiction, yet I encourage them to study Jay McInerney's masterful use of it in "It's Six A.M. Do You Know Where You Are?"

Active reading, then, depends on a fascination for the technique of fiction. Good teachers of creative writing don't just teach the techniques; they infect the students with certain enthusiasms simply by being in a closed room with them long enough for the virus to catch.

By extension, active reading also involves active selection of new fiction—knowing where to find it and actually buying it. I once asked a class of twenty freshmen in a composition course to write down the names of their two favorite authors and their two favorite musicians. Of the thirty-odd different musicians named, all but one was alive. Of the authors, all but one was dead. As a live writer of novels and stories, I brooded about that for some time.

When I tried a similar test with my graduate students at The Johns Hopkins Writing Seminars, my faith was somewhat restored. Some of these students were introducing me to writers I had not read. A heady experience! The point is that entering freshmen have rarely bought a book that has not been assigned. Some have never spent their own money for a work of fiction in their lives. They have been passive receptors, accepting whatever authors teachers force on them—though these same students have strong feelings about music and often spend a great deal of money collecting their favorites and memorizing the lyrics.

Except in the large cities, most undergraduates wouldn't know how to find contemporary fiction even if they wanted to. And it's not their fault. Most college bookstores offer a great variety of college-logo ashtrays and beer mugs but not a single literary quarterly, and courses in literature rarely refer to little magazines. For these reasons, it is essential for creative writing courses to stress the various ways writers find new material—keeping up with the literary journals in the library, actually subscribing to one or two (less expensive than a single rock concert), finding collections of stories by writers one admires.

The process of finding new fiction is so important that every writing instructor should make a point of luring his or her students into the library as a start. My approach is to ask all of my students to read two copies of a literary quarterly in the library and report to the class on what kind of fiction they found there. I also urge them to use *Books in Print* to find out if any of the authors represented there have collections available. I have often assigned special fiction issues of little magazines so that they will actually own their own copy. The same could and should be done with poetry issues for student poets. My point is that active reading is not merely a matter of studying what a teacher has assigned. It requires the know-how and the effort to seek out good fiction on one's own.

Finally, there is the matter of recall. Word processors are good at that, but human memory is forever leaking data. It also has other items to store—historical dates, chemical formulas, and song lyrics. It is unrealistic to recommend taking extensive notes on everything one reads. Not even the most conscientious writers do that. But the sad fact remains that one can read, say, *The New Yorker* and *The North American Review* religiously for a year and only recall perhaps six stories and the names of five authors. Active reading requires some method of retaining what one has read.

The system I use and recommend to those student writers who are really serious is to keep a notebook in which one writes down a three-sentence factual description of each story that is read. It takes no more than a few minutes each time, but it is extraordinary how a brief memo like that will bring back the entire story. It is similar to the way a single snapshot in an album can bring back an entire vacation.

It is well worth going over notebooks like this every couple of weeks. These periodic reviews have to be motivated not by the prospect of an exam but by a real desire to retain what one has read. As one recalls each story, some rather basic questions come to mind: "How on earth did that get published?" "How come I remember that one when I thought it was lousy when I first read it?" "Oh yes, that's the one with the long flashback. Maybe I should try that." This is not profound literary criticism; it's the sound of a writer contending with other writers.

A teacher of creative writing can speed a student's development by explaining concepts like the means of perception, voice, the illusion of dialogue, and techniques like how to reveal character without resorting to exposition. On this level a good textbook may be of help too. All this should not be underrated. But there is a deep structure to a writing seminar that is just as important for students. A good teacher serves as a model for an aspiring writer. The teacher shares his or her enthusiasms, sense of wonder, and spirit of inquiry. One of the core lessons—one that is transmitted by osmosis, not directly—is that writers are active readers who are constantly learning from other writers. In short, that writers are perpetual students.

8 Writing for All Ages

Elizabeth Winthrop

William Matthews said once, "Writers are not born nor made, but written." I believe that absolutely. The best way to learn to write well is to write all the time.

I must have learned this lesson firsthand because I was born into a writing family. Both my uncle and my father worked as journalists in Washington, D.C. Every afternoon when I got home from school, the first sound I heard was the distant banging of my father's old Underwood keys. He interviewed people, he read books and magazines and newspapers, he scribbled notes in his small notebook, but most of all, he wrote. Every day. From my father, I learned lessons about the simplicity of language and the importance of clear writing, but most of all, I learned about perseverance and endurance, about sticking with it.

As far as my formal education goes, I was lucky enough to end up at Sarah Lawrence College where I studied with Grace Paley and Jane Cooper. This was in the early 1970s, in the days before most graduate writing programs even existed, but in its own enlightened way, Sarah Lawrence took its undergraduate students seriously when they said they wanted to write. Most teachers expected us to deliver a new or revised short story at the end of each week of the term. So, for four straight years, I wrote. When I left college, I was carrying a suitcase bursting with short stories, and held the conviction that I was a writer. Although I didn't publish for two more years, I felt like a writer because I had written. And that feeling has persevered. As long as I am writing, whether I am publishing or not, I feel like a writer. And that, to me, is half the battle.

In the last year, I have managed to finish a seven-hundred-page "adult" novel and two picture books for ages three to five. When people hear that, they often ask me how I do it? How do I write picture books for two-year-olds and fantasies for ten-year-olds and young adult novels and fiction for seventy-year-olds.

I assume people are asking about my writing schedule. How do I produce so much? Is there some secret formula? The answer is simple. I am at my desk four to six hours every day. If I am not working on a book, I am writing articles like this or speeches or letters to friends or entries in my journal. I am communicating on paper with words. I am using all my writing muscles. The more I use those muscles, the better writer I become, the more I produce, and the more I publish.

But people also ask me *why* I write for so many different audiences, and in a way, the answer is the same. Each kind of book I write exercises a different one of those muscles. The language I use, the plot I create, the characters I give birth to all have to be different depending on the audience I am writing for. Just like an athlete who puts in a better performance because she has stretched out her shoulders as well as her hamstrings, I am a better writer, I believe, if I have stretched out all my writing muscles, so I write for all ages.

Now what do I mean by writing muscles and how do I stretch them? Let me start at the beginning with the books for the youngest readers, the picture books for two-year-olds. The "youngest" book I've ever written is called *Shoes*. When I wrote it, it had no specific characters, no plot, but yes, it had a theme, if a catalogue of different kinds of footwear could be called a theme. It had structure, if poetry and the necessity for rhyme could be called structure. It starts this way: "There are shoes to buckle, shoes to tie, shoes too low and shoes too high. Shoes to run in, shoes for sliding, high-topped shoes for horseback riding." William Joyce, the artist, added the characters, the four floppy-haired moppets who dance across the pages. He even put in a little plot on every page. For example, when I wrote, "shoes to turn a double flip in," he put the character in flippers doing a fancy flip off a diving board while the other children watch.

I've never met William Joyce, which is typical of my relationship with my picture book artists. He lives in Louisiana and I live in New York City. We've produced a book together but we wouldn't know each other if we stood side by side in a railroad station. I did not even write Mr. Joyce a letter about what the pictures should look like. After many years in this business, including a three-year apprenticeship as an editor, I've learned to give half the book away to the artist. After all, the artist is the master of the visuals and I gratefully hand that job over so I can concentrate on the language. "Shoes to skate in, shoes to skip in, shoes to turn a double flip in." I was listening to the beat. To the bounce and jump of the words. To the music. Joyce was seeing the pictures. And together with the help of our "midwife," the editor in New York, our baby, the book, was born.

Even when picture books don't rhyme, I think they are the closest thing to poetry. They are designed to be read aloud after all, so the ear must listen for the peaks and valleys of the sentences, the rolls and slides of the words. Writing picture books fine-tunes my ears and stretches my language muscles.

Moving up the age ladder, we meet the eight- to twelve-year-olds, the age group that spans everything from "first chapter books" to the beginning of young adult fiction, and the readers you're dealing with range all up and down that "ability" scale.

In form, the book for the middle-grade reader is very close to the short story in adult fiction and the same rules apply. When I'm writing with this group in mind, I know I've got to get into the story quickly, tell it from one point of view, move the action along in short swift scenes and get out at the right moment. This is not to say that character is unimportant. The readers in this age group must be able to identify with the protagonist, jeer at the villain, rejoice at the defeat of the dark forces. But action and the quickly sketched visual picture are just as important. As the reader gets older the balance between character and action can lean more towards character.

So writing for the youngest members of this group forces me to stretch one of my stiffest and most unresponsive muscles—plot. I don't like to think about plot. I like plot to take care of itself, to evolve naturally on the page. When I'm working with this kind of shorter book where, because of the limitations of space, the characters will be more one-dimensional than in a longer novel, the first plot twists that occur to me are often tired and overdone. The plot does not naturally develop from the characters. In the beginning, I have to apply it to the characters and, because I work better the other way around, I find I have to work harder, dig deeper. Creating the story that breathes life into the characters stretches the hamstrings of my brain to the breaking point.

The process I go through to create the novels for ten-, eleven-, twelve-year-olds and even the teenagers resembles the creative working out of my "adult" fiction. In both cases, the book starts with character development. As I've said, I like to write from character but there are pitfalls here too. I have been accused of lingering too long and lovingly over a special description, of not moving the story along fast enough, of letting a character develop as slowly as a flower opening. Children don't take the time these days to watch a flower open. Nor do adults for that matter.

When I was writing *The Castle in the Attic,* I had gotten to the point where William had been made small and was living in the castle with Mrs. Phillips and the Silver Knight. He was in training for the quest he had to undertake to save them all. I knew unconsciously that the next section of the book would require a great deal of plotting. Quests mean action, one incident after another. Plot again. So in order to avoid it, I put William through months of unnecessary training, deceiving myself into thinking that while the readers watched William train, they were learning a great deal about William as a person. Every week, when my editor called me up to check on my progress, I would say cheerily, "Oh, I'm doing just fine. William's learning how to handle a sword" or "William's cleaning the shields." "Enough," she finally said. "Get him out of the training and into the quest." And she was right. In the final manuscript, the training scenes were cut way down in order to move the story along faster. I had to get out of the safe castle of character development and on to my own quest for plot.

Possibly I'll admit to one important difference between writing for adults and writing for children and it's best summed up in that old adage, *show don't tell.* Here again I learned to stretch out another muscle, how to build a story scene by scene instead of explaining it to the reader. Telling is a very important tool for writers to learn how to use but it's best picked up only after you've learned to create effective, immediate scenes. Telling comes to us from fairy tales and the nineteenth century when God was firmly ensconced in his heaven—"Once upon a time. . . . Dear Reader"—and of course it belongs in children's books and in my opinion, nobody uses it with more effectiveness than Natalie Babbitt. But for my development as a writer, I needed to learn how to *show* first and foremost. As a result, none of my children's novels span more than a year in time, and the narrative voice is limited to an occasional transitional line. The action begins immediately. Listen to the difference (first Natalie Babbitt from the beginning of *Tuck Everlasting*): "The first week of August hangs at the very top of summer, the top of the live-long year, like the highest seat of a ferris wheel when it pauses in its turning." And Winthrop, from *The Castle in the Attic*: "On Monday afternoon, Mrs. Phillips was waiting for William at the kitchen door. He came in shaking like a dog and blowing the raindrops off the tip of his nose."

Babbitt stands back, the all-seeing narrator. I have to leap into the fray of the scene immediately and show every feeling as the character feels it. I tend to jump from peak to peak in the story, or from scene to scene. The hardest adjustment I made when I started writing adult fiction was moving from scene to summary, from showing everything to telling at least some of it.

I write for all ages because it allows me to stretch all my writing muscles: the scene versus the narrative voice, character development, the creation of plot, and the use of language. But there's another part to the answer. I write for so many different audiences because, frankly, it keeps me writing.

Every writer has a deep fear of drying up. We all have different systems for avoiding that catastrophe. One writer I know uses this system: she writes a young adult novel, ten pages a day until she's done. When it's finished, she allows herself to read fiction for a month, nonfiction for another month, and then she starts on an adult novel, ten pages a day. Some writers work in bookstores because it inspires them. Some writers won't have anything to do with the written word in their everyday jobs because it dries them up. They sell shoes or repair televisions or trade stocks. One poet I know programs computers because it pays the rent but also because the work is so different from his writing that one doesn't drain energy from the other. So we all work out our own peculiar systems for protecting that underground stream, that source of the stories. Mine is to write for different ages.

For example, my picture books are what a friend calls my "tweenies": they come in the middle of or between longer books. I am never just working on picture books. Often I put a novel aside for a week because a picture book idea has bubbled to the surface and the first line has come to me, and no writer can wander around for too long haunted by a first line. *Lizzie and Harold* starts this way: "More than anything else, Lizzie wanted a best friend." Just like the reader, the writer is wondering, does she get one? At some point, I've got to sit down with Lizzie and find out.

Or I put one book aside because it isn't going well. *In My Mother's House,* my long novel, has been in the works for seven years. In 1984, when I had handed in yet another version that didn't please me or the editor very much, I asked for an extension on my contract so that I could go back to children's books. I needed to build up confidence again much like the mountain climber who returns to base camp to repair equipment and rest up before the next assault on the mountain.

During that extension, which stretched from one year to two, I wrote three or four picture books as well as *Belinda's Hurricane* and *The Castle in the Attic*. None of that time was "wasted" as far as my adult novel was concerned. First, I was stretching out those muscles I spoke about earlier. Second, my confidence in my abilities as a writer was slowly returning. And finally, in the case of *Castle*, I was digging deeper. The story of William and the Silver Knight is really the story of entrapment, of an egotistical love that binds a person too close. I had been trying to work out that same theme in the adult novel but with totally different characters. Writing *Castle* allowed me to break through to a deeper level in the adult novel. I had written the entrapment story out of my system so that I could now see that *In My Mother's House* was really about a river of women, about the ways that seepage upstream pollutes the waters below. Writing a children's novel had taught me what the adult book was really all about.

So writing for all ages helps me to stay limber, to keep the lines of communication open not only between me and my readers but also between Elizabeth Winthrop, the person, and Elizabeth Winthrop, the writer. But most of all, writing for all ages helps me to keep writing. And, as I said in the beginning, as long as I keep writing, I feel like a writer. For me, that's the real magic in it.

Works Cited

Babbitt, Natalie. *Tuck Everlasting*. New York: Farrar, Straus and Giroux, 1975.

Winthrop, Elizabeth. *Belinda's Hurricane*. New York: E. P. Dutton, 1984.

———. *The Castle in the Attic*. New York: Holiday, 1985.

———. *Lizzie and Harold*. New York: Lothrop, Lee and Shepard, 1986.

———. *In My Mother's House*. New York: Doubleday, 1988.

———. *Shoes*. New York: Harper and Row, 1985.

9 Unlearning to Write

Donald M. Murray

When students sign up for a fiction course they are usually experienced writers—too experienced. They have done well at introductory writing courses and literature courses. Many are skillful writers of nonfiction. Some have published nonfiction or earn their living writing. All have enough interest and confidence to dare to study fiction. They want to be fiction writers or, for a few hours a week, to imagine themselves short story writers or novelists.

The problem is not motivation; the problem is that the students have learned to write. They bring with them knowledge which may be true for some of the writing they have done but which makes the writing of fiction difficult. The better educated the student, the harder it is to return to the natural, magical art of narrative—the mother of all forms of significant discourse.

> But what do beginners know? Too much. It is what they think they know that makes them beginners.
>
> —William Gass

A process of unlearning has to take place. This is painful and frightening for students and for an antique nonfiction writer tutoring himself through a period of unlearning when he returns to fiction.

Old rules become comforting to us all. Skills—and the attitudes behind them—become beliefs raised to the power of Truth. I am used to unlearning, but most of my students have come to learn new truths, not to have old ones stripped away; they have come to construct a system of higher skills on the foundation of old ones, not have the cathedral of their learning razed so that the wondrous and essential mists of unknowing can take their place.

> You write—and find you have something to say.
>
> —Wright Morris

I write out of ignorance. I write about the things I don't have
any resolutions for, and when I'm finished, I think I know a little bit more about it. I don't write out of what I know. It's what I
don't know that stimulates me.

—Toni Morrison

Producing constructive unlearning is a challenge for the teacher.
To replace rules with rules, an old theology with a new one, inappropriate formulas with appropriate-appearing formulas, is easy
compared to replacing knowing with doubting, answers with questions, dependency with independency. Yet this is what has to be
done if students are to learn to seek, respect, and make use of
doubt, questions, wonder, surprise, failure, accident, and discovery
to explore the uncomfortable, exciting territory of the fiction writer.

Most students arrive in the fiction class with a dangerous assumption: they believe in the precedence of theme. They have the
misconception that idea always precedes story. They see fiction as
propaganda, the illustration of a preconceived concept.

Think before you speak, is criticism's motto; speak before you
think is creation's.

—E. M. Forster

One is not free to write this or that. One does not choose one's
subject. That is what the public and the critics do not understand.

—Gustave Flaubert

Oddly enough, the ideas that seem vague and useless—"love is
complicated," "people need love," "outsiders (parents) don't know
how love feels"—are often the ideas that *may* develop into a piece of
fiction. It is easy for teachers to dismiss such ideas as banal, but the
"idea" of a Shakespearean play or a novel by Tolstoy can also be
reduced to such a statement. Often they are banal, but they also
may be code words for the deep-running experiences, fears, concerns, and needs of the student writer. "I worry about an unhappy
married woman" can become pure flapdoodle or *Madame Bovary.*

The beginning of every short story is ridiculous at first. There
seems no hope that this newborn thing, still incomplete and
tender in every joint, will be able to keep alive in the complicated organization of the world, which, like every completed organization, strives to close itself off. However, one should not
forget that the story, if it has any justification to exist, bears its
complete organization within itself even before it has been fully
formed; for this reason despair over the beginning of a story is

unwarranted; in a like case parents should have to despair of
their suckling infant, for they had no intention of bringing this
pathetic and ridiculous being into the world.

—Franz Kafka

The idea for fiction is a question to be answered, a feeling or a
place to be explored, a "what if" to be observed. It is private, an obsession that has an importance for the writer which cannot be seen
by others until it is written (when it will be seen far differently by
the writer). The idea is just that—a hint, a clue, something overheard from the next book, a reflection in a store window caught in
the corner of an eye.

> All I have to go on is something I caught a glimpse of out of the
> corner of my eye.
>
> —John Updike

> I start my work by asking a question and then try . . . to answer it.
>
> —Mary Lee Settle

> What if? What if? My mind raced, and my emotions kept pace at
> the sidelines, the way it always happens when a story idea ar-
> rives, like a small explosion of thought and feeling. What if?
> What if an incident like that in the park had been crucial to the
> relationship between father and daughter? What would make it
> crucial? Well, what if the father, say, was divorced from the
> child's mother and the incident happened during one of his vis-
> iting days? And what if . . . ?
>
> —Robert Cormier

But students have been taught to write thesis statements, sentences
that contain the conclusion that will be reached after the writing is
done. Writers write to explore, to discover, to know. The writer has
to keep the idea open so there is room for the story to happen.

> I write because I don't know what I think until I read what I
> have to say . . . . The more you write, the more you will realize
> that the form is organic, that it is something that grows out of
> the material, that the form of each story is unique . . . a story is
> good when you can continue to see more and more in it, and
> when it continues to escape you. In fiction two and two is al-
> ways more than four.
>
> —Flannery O'Connor

> Let the story arise of itself. Let it speak for itself. Let it reveal it-
> self as it goes along.
>
> —Eudora Welty

The greatest joy in writing fiction is surprise, but students have been taught that they should know what they want to say before they say it. If I did that, I would have no need to write. I would seek a craft in which I could not predict the product before it was begun.

> That's not what writing is—writing what you know. You write in order to find things out.
>
> —Garrison Keillor

> We write out what we don't know about what we know.
>
> —Grace Paley

Students who seek literary fame have often been taught literature in such a way that they do not understand that the writer was conducting an experiment in meaning; the writer usually finds the theme after reading with surprise what has been written. The fiction writer doesn't intend, but observes and records. Yet the literary writer thinks the story rather than writing it—choosing subject matter, actions, the author's voice, the theme, the background from literary history—the way the student shops for the back-to-school wardrobe, selecting what is in, rejecting what is out. Their work is clever, imitative, and as pointless as wearing a fake Reebok—or even a real one, as I am at this moment.

And, as I am carried away with these beliefs of mine, I have to remember to temper what I am telling my students with contradictory information: that Steinbeck often wrote a sentence or two on a 3 × 5 card saying what the book was about, and kept it in front of him as he wrote the book (and I may do that too); that many writers know the end before they begin; that planning is part of preparing to write. The secret is balance, and the balance may be different for the experienced and inexperienced writer, may change with the writing task, may vary according to the personality and thinking style of the writer.

> I don't know how far away the end is—only *what* it is. I know the last sentence, but I am very much in the dark concerning how to get to it.
>
> —John Irving

> If I didn't know the ending of a story, I wouldn't begin. I always write my last line, my last paragraphs, my last page first.
>
> —Katherine Anne Porter

Writers who scorn "literary" writing and seek an immediate cash return on their talent revere plot above all else. They design their stories the way you design a supermarket. The book is constructed to appeal to each reader: sex, violence, laughter, a behind-the-scenes background that reveals the world of toilet bowl manufacture or summer waitressing, characters who can be ordered off the TV shelf—one urbane, one crude, one pretty, one plain, one a user, one used.

> I have no regular system for writing. . . . I sit down at the typewriter when I feel like it. Something—an image or phrase—from five years earlier may suddenly come out as I type. I try to follow it. I never think to myself, "Boy, would such-and-such make a good story." I don't have any preconceived ideas of plot. When I start writing it is a process of discovery.
>
> —Ann Beattie

> Plot might seem to be a matter of choice. It is not. The particular plot for this particular novel is something the novelist is driven to. . . . It is what is left after the whittling-away of alternatives.
>
> —Elizabeth Bowen

> When I start a book I have no idea of how it's going to end. I really don't know what's going to happen more than a chapter or two ahead. The characters audition in their opening scene—I listen to them, see how they sound. The plots develop on their own. If I'm curious enough to turn the pages, I figure it will have the same effect on readers.
>
> —Elmore Leonard

Some students want both literary fame and the large cash advance; they want the in's reputation and the out's best-seller status. And they suffer writer's whiplash as they try to be all things to all readers. It is hard for any of these students who have been asked "What did the writer mean when. . . ?" and been given a precise answer to be patient with a teacher who says that the writer was probably dumb before such questions, that the writer may not have known where the story was headed until it got there.

> . . . creation must take place between the pen and the paper, not before in a thought or afterwards in a recasting.
>
> —Gertrude Stein

> Any man who knows in advance what he's going to write about would be so bored that he'll bore his readers, or he won't finish it.
>
> —Paul Theroux

My teacherly task is to make my students uncomfortable, to lead them into unknowing, but not to abandon them there, but to be an effective Maine guide, paddling them towards the salmon but allowing them to make their own catch.

I encourage my students to start with a character or, if they have an idea, to populate it with a character, an individual who is seen and heard and felt, who can hurt and be hurt, who can act when it would be wiser not to and not act when it is important to act—a person, who is complicated, probably drawn from those we know, but not too consciously, and not drawn in a sketch but in dramatic action.

Character meets character. There is action and reaction, push and pull, cause and effect. The scene in which characters act and react is the engine of the story, the energy produced from this dramatic interaction between characters drives the narrative forward—not meaning, idea, theme, or thesis; not literary style or voice; not background or setting; but character against character. All else comes from that—the language, the place, the meaning are revealed by the scene and the sequence of scenes.

> I begin to get pre-conscious intimations of what the work is going to be like, even before I awaken. I see faces and scenes, floors, walls, landscapes. I hear lines of dialogue.
>
> —Saul Bellow

Dialogue, as Elizabeth Bowen taught me in her fine "Notes on Writing a Novel" is action. Dialogue isn't talk. It is what people do to each other. It is what they say and do not say. It is how they speak and how they are silent, turning away or moving close.

> Dialogue has to show not only something about the speaker that is its own revelation, but also maybe something about the speaker that he doesn't know but the other character does know. You've got to show a two-way revelation between speaker and listener, which is the fascination of writing dialogue. Dialogue is action.
>
> —Eudora Welty

Dialogue, as much as anything else, reveals the character to the writer and, ultimately, to the reader.

> I don't have a very clear idea of who the characters are until they start talking.
>
> —Joan Didion

My students and I share our drafts and our *written* commentaries about how we have written that day or that week, how we have felt, failed, attempted; what problems we have defined and solved or failed to solve, what questions we have answered—or not answered.

Our breakthroughs to fiction come as we participate in the central experience of writing fiction: the characters begin to act on their own and the story is not told but observed and recorded. The writer doesn't make up the story but receives it.

> If you're silent for a long time, people just arrive in your mind.
>
> —Alice Walker

> The bad novelist constructs his characters; he directs them and makes them speak. The true novelist listens to them and watches them act; he hears their voices even before he knows them.
>
> —André Gide

> It's the characters who direct me. That is, I see a character, he's there, and I recognize someone I knew, or occasionally two who are a bit mixed together, but then that stops. Afterwards, the character acts on his own account. He says things. . . . I never know *what* any of them are going to say when I'm writing dialogue. . . . I'm very visual when I write. I see it all, I see everything.
>
> —Julio Cortazar

> It begins with a character, usually, and once he stands up on his feet and begins to move, all I do is trot along behind him with a paper and pencil trying to keep up long enough to put down what he says and does.
>
> —William Faulkner

> When I construct a scene, I don't describe the hundredth part of what I see; I see the characters scratching their noses, walking about, tilting back in their chairs—even after I've finished writing—so much so that after a while I feel a weariness which does not derive all that much from my effort of imagination but is more like a visual fatigue: my eyes are tired from watching my characters.
>
> —Graham Greene

> My characters really dictate themselves to me. I am not free of them, really, and I can't force them into situations they haven't themselves willed. They have the autonomy of characters in a dream. . . . It's a mysterious process. The character on the page determines the prose—its music, its rhythms, the range and limit of its vocabulary—yet, at the onset at least, I determine the characters. It usually happens that the fictitious character, once released, requires a life and will of his or her own.
>
> —Joyce Carol Oates

Of course there are writers such as Nabokov who say this is nonsense, and it may well be for him. But the evidence is overwhelming that most fiction writers are in a constant state of tension with their characters, that these writers battle with their characters for control of the story. And most writers learn how to accept defeat gracefully, to give the characters room, to allow them to break free and tell the story.

This is difficult for students, and especially for many literature teachers, to accept. (I am battling it this week as the father in my novel is behaving in such a way that he's taking the story where I do not want it to go. The battle is not over, but he will win.)

This process doesn't feel like thinking; it is irrational, disorderly, at best a dumb kind of thinking. My students, as if they did not have natural cognitive styles, have all been taught to think in a different way, a more logical, more controlled and directed way. Now they find themselves not knowing what they are going to say before they say it. Writing to them is not a matter of discovery, but a matter of presenting thoughts that have already been thunk.

> I'm working on something, I don't know exactly what.
>
> —Eudora Welty

> Writing and rewriting are a constant search for what one is saying.
>
> —John Updike

> Every short story, at least for me, is a little act of discovery. A cluster of details presents itself to my scrutiny, like a mystery that I will understand in the course of writing or sometimes not fully until afterward. . . . A story that you do not learn something from while you are writing it, that does not illuminate something for you, is dead, finished before you started it.
>
> —Mary McCarthy

To unlearn most of us have to write fast. We have to push ourselves to describe what is taking place before our mind's eye, because the velocity of the writing seems to cause the actions we record. The energy of the writing causes the energy of the vision.

> There are some kinds of writing that you have to do very fast, like riding a bicycle on a tightrope.
>
> —William Faulkner

There are other good reasons for speed in drafting. Acceleration of prose causes those accidental connections between what is known and what is suddenly remembered; it causes the interaction of information we would have thought inappropriate but which brings a crucial insight when it occurs on the page. Speed puts a spin on language, causing those phrases and tiny surprises that mark an interesting style.

> Follow the accident, fear the fixed plan—that is the rule.
>
> —John Fowles

> It tells you. You don't tell it.
>
> —Joan Didion

> Inch by inch, the words surprised me.
>
> —William Kennedy

And perhaps most important, speed allows us to outrun the rational mind and its busy chorus of censors—parents, teachers, editors, associates—who tell us what can be done, what we can't do, what is certain to fail. If we write fast enough we enter into the text, and are so busy getting down what we are seeing and hearing and observing and, yes, experiencing that we may forget—unlearn—what we know.

> All my life I've been frightened at the moment I sit down to write.
>
> —Gabriel García Márquez

We may, by writing fast, achieve the gift of concentration. We may be able, for the moment, to lose ourselves in our text, so that the world on the paper and behind it, is more real than the world in which we sit writing.

> If it is winter in the book, spring surprises me when I look up.
>
> —Bernard Malamud

But, of course, we will return to read and revise, read and rewrite, read and edit. The writing act has its intellectual and rational elements. But once we have a text, we can learn from the text. We have been taught that the answers are in the handbook or writing text (perhaps even one by Don Murray), but if we listen to our emerging text it will teach us to write. It will tell us what the text needs and what it cannot take. The text will establish its directions, its voice, its own meaning.

> The writer himself studies intensely how to do it while he is in the thick of doing it; then when the particular novel or story is done, he is likely to forget how; he does well to. Each work is

new. Mercifully, the question of *how* abides less in the abstract, and less in the past, than in the specific, in the work at hand.

—Eudora Welty

Students who have come to class full of external rules and laws and theories and standards and skills that they have been taught to apply to a text will begin to see that the writer's craft comes from within a text that the writer has learned how to receive. It is a matter of acceptance and cultivation and harvesting what is not what was hoped for; it is not a matter of making but accepting.

An artist observes, selects, guesses, and combines.

—Anton Chekhov

[Writing] is sort of like when you've got no electricity and you've gotten up in the middle of the night to find the bathroom, feeling your way along in the dark. I can't hardly tell you what I do because I really don't know.

—Carolyn Chute

The material itself dictates how it should be written.

—William Faulkner

In the academy, we separate the writing of fiction and poetry from the serious writing of the essay, the thesis, the term paper. We seem to fear the creative and want to fence it off as if it would contaminate other forms of writing. But the students who have the experience of characters who take over their story often discover they have learned a new and powerful way of thinking that will help them in scholarly, research, and vocational pursuits. They have found how to use written language not just as a method of recording thought but as a way of thinking.

How do I know what I think until I see what I say?

—E. M. Forster

I write both fiction and nonfiction, "creative" (a term fiction writers hate) and, I suppose, "noncreative" work, and find that my articles on composition theory and pedagogy, my textbooks, my newspaper columns, all work best when the ideas take off like characters and surprise me during the act of writing. In fact, I, like most writers in all genres, find out what I have to say as I say it. Writing is an act of discovery, and it may be just as important in the Freshman English class, in the advanced composition class, in the courses in nonfiction writing, that we help our students unlearn to write and encourage the experience of allowing characters—or ideas—to take off in the draft with the writer racing after them, at top speed, to discover what the text is thinking.

10 Getting Started: Planning and Plotting the Novel

Marion Zimmer Bradley

The important thing in all writing is to get in the habit of doing it; and that is as true of manuscripts produced in class as anywhere else. I spend a lot of time in workshops trying to keep my students writing instead of listening—and to keep from talking too much. The important thing is to keep them thinking not about what I'm saying, but about what they're going to be doing, because the best tool for a workshop is the student's own writing. Keep the focus, always, on what they are doing. After a few words about the importance of hooking the first reader and getting past the instant rejection slip, I get them writing right away. I never work with old manuscripts; I have them start a new one, *using* the techniques they're learning. The first exercise is to write a *first sentence* that will lead to a story which will hook the editor and be rejection-proof. (The old manuscript? If it were any good it would have sold. Put it away, and if it's a good story, use it later when you've learned what was wrong with it.)

It's easier to do that, perhaps, in a short story workshop; everybody knows you can't come to class and write a whole novel, even at night between class sessions—leaving out prodigies like Erle Stanley Gardner who could write a whole novel over a weekend. But there is no reason one shouldn't decide what one is *going to write* over the course of a workshop. And if the important work of a novel can be worked out then, the rest is just a typing job, which can be done as fast as you can type it. Why not? You don't have to conclude that a book's quality is decided by how long it takes to write it. A book that takes three years may very well be better than one that takes, say, three weeks, but not necessarily. When I was putting myself through college by writing novels for Monarch, I had to write papers, and, not least, run a house and take care of my child at the same time. How did I do it and never miss a deadline?

The answer was *planning*—getting the work, essentially, all done at once, so I only had to sit down and write it. I did the same thing

115

with *The Mists of Avalon;* people say they were astonished that it took
me a mere eight months to write after I had finished the research,
but basically, the hard part was already done—the actual work of
putting it on paper should be the fun part. (If it isn't the fun part, if
you don't actually enjoy that part, you're in the wrong business.
Why not walk dogs, or clean apartments, and get some fun out of
life? Nobody said you had to be a writer. I keep a sign that says
"Nobody Told You Not To Be A Plumber" over my desk, to remind
me of that whenever my chosen work gets tough.)

But in order to get to the fun part, and to let it be the fun part,
you need to work hard at planning what comes next. That's the part
where you sweat blood. That's what makes writing hard work; and
you can, of course, skip it. You can just start writing, with no idea
where you are going, or why, and some day you'll have a novel.
You can do it that way—if you have a well-trained subconscious
which does all that work for you. But it's easier to learn how to do it
consciously.

This is the way all too many writers do their work. Why not? You
can skip all this part—and it will eventually be done by the subconscious. This works, usually, if you don't mind writer's block,
waiting a year or two while your subconscious grapples with something else, or having your deepest darkest secrets become obvious
in your novels. But why not do it the easy way? Plan it all out
ahead.

What is the most important thing in writing your novel? Just to sit
down and get started—if you don't write the first page you'll never
write the second. So how do you get started? The answer is *planning*. And there's no reason it can't all be done in a workshop.

I like to think of the little sign they used to have in so many offices, which illustrates this point: it says "Plan Ahead." But while
the *plan* looks very nice, the word *ahead* is squashed-looking, with
the final two letters crowded into a corner. That can happen to your
novel; and sometimes it does. You'll find that you've created a situation where there's no way to end the story—you've painted yourself
into a corner. There's no way for the hero to escape—and so you'd
better plan ahead. That's what plotting is—just planning, figuring
out what happens next—in short, figuring out which leg moves
after which, or making sure that when the invitation is sent out to
the third child's christening, you don't suddenly find out that you
didn't hold the wedding first. (This is the way it's done in the best-
regulated families.)

Does this mean an outline—you know, those things they taught us to make in fifth grade, with a topic sentence and subheadings A, a, b, B, a, b, and all that? Of course not. I know a fairly promising writer who gave up on a fascinating project because someone told her she should outline it first, and she couldn't face doing that. Frankly, I don't blame her. How dull, how uncreative, though I must admit that for nonfiction pieces like this one, I still make fifth-grade outlines; it seems to me the easiest way to keep the whole project straight in my mind. But that isn't the kind of outline I mean. I remember once selling a novel on the basis of a half-page description of my plot that went like this: "Callista is kidnapped by the catmen. After many adventures she is rescued." Of course at that time I had about twelve published novels to my credit, and my editor knew he could trust me to do all the other things to keep the story straight. But after he bought it I had to figure out just what the "adventures" were, write them down, and figure out *what order they came in.* That's plotting.

But, you ask, why *plot?* Why not just—I'm sure you've heard the advice—take a character, start writing about that character, and let him or her generate the plot? Why? Because planning ahead is easier, that's why; it keeps you from going from Los Angeles to San Francisco by way of Phoenix, Arizona—or by way of Kazakhstan. If you don't plot your novel, it's likely to go off on a tangent, and you'll find that instead of going by way of Bakersfield—or by way of Santa Barbara, either of which routes would make sense—you're going by way of Chicago. There is an old limerick I use in my classes to demonstrate the importance of plotting:

> A centipede was happy quite
> Until a frog in fun
> said 'pray, which leg moves after which?'
> Which raised his thoughts to such a pitch
> He lay exhausted in a ditch,
> Forgetting how to run.

If you don't plan the whole thing out in advance you may forget which leg moves after which, and the whole thing may turn out to be too much work.

I am convinced that a historical novel is one of the simplest forms of the novel to write, because you have your plot all figured out and you don't have to make up nearly as much. Say you want to write a novel about Bonnie Prince Charlie. You have the raising of the standard at Glenfinnan, the battle of Falkirk, the battle of Preston Pans, the battle of Culloden, the escape to Skye, and so forth. Your climaxes are determined by history; your only choice is to decide whether he was a gallant adventurer, working to restore the important principle of the "Divine Right of Kings," or whether he was a lowlife fighting the mainstream of history. (You also have to decide that for his supporters, but that's unimportant.) Once you've made the main decision everything else follows. Think, for instance, of the different views taken in Robert Louis Stevenson's *Kidnapped*, or— which bothered me dreadfully when I was a kid—Cormack and Alexander's *Last Clash of Claymores*. One takes the unabashed view of Jacobite heroism; the other treats Charles Edward as, basically, an intrusion into history as irrelevant as that of the Emperor Norton— an amiable lunatic who proclaimed himself "Emperor" of America.

How do you plot? The answer is to simplify; relentlessly simplify. Keep simplifying your material until you can tell somebody "what's it about?" in a sentence. Does that sound too simplistic? Let's try it. What's *Gone With the Wind* about? The Civil War, told through the point of view of a woman who is selfish and spoiled, thinks she wants one man, and can't have him. What's the *Odyssey* about? A man's struggles to get home despite weather, evil sorceresses, and the many dangers along the way; he finally gets home and runs off the bad guys. It's impossible to be too simple. When you're writing commercial fiction, remember that, as William Randolph Hearst said, "Nobody ever went broke underestimating human intelligence." "How cynical" you say. Well, you have to be a little cynical for commercial work, but not too cynical—that creates lots and lots of half-witted romances and Gothic heroines without sense enough to come out of the rain. You just need to be a little cynical— not starry-eyed, wanting to solve all the problems of humanity in one book—just realistic. Even for a historical novel, where your plot is predetermined by "what happened," you have to sort out your notes, and find out what happened *first*; and for any other kind of novel you have to figure out your plot line—what happened *when*— and to whom.

In teaching my own workshops, I immediately insist that the students start thinking of a story, not in terms of an *idea*, but in terms of *people*. Every story begins with a *character* . . . preferably a likable character with whom the reader can identify. From there on out, while planning out the story, I make them ask themselves, what does this character want? Does his character get it? And, most important of all, *what keeps the character from getting it?* Then I have them write down on a 3 × 5 card *who their story is about*, and *what does he/she want?*

Basically, that's what any story is about; to figure out what your main character wants: in the case of Bonnie Prince Charlie, the kingdom of his fathers; in the case of David Copperfield, to live and do well; in the case of Captain Ahab, revenge on the white whale, and so forth. Is this a worthwhile goal? It must be so, or at least it must seem so to the main character. (If Captain Ahab just liked to kill whales, he would be despicable.) Whatever your view of history, you cannot blame Charles Edward for wanting to restore the crown of his fathers, but he might well have had some qualms about a restoration many of his subjects did not want, so much so that they cut off Charles I's head and sent Charles Edward's father fleeing for fear of his life. As for David Copperfield, *everybody* wants to live and do well; it's only a question of deciding how David will do so. The obstacles to his success vary—his stepfather, the blacking factory, and so forth—but they are all *obstacles in the way of his getting what he wants;* just as for Bonnie Prince Charles the obstacles in the way of his getting what he wants are the British Army, the royal House of Hanover, his own bad judgment, incompetent advisors, and so forth. And Captain Ahab must fight against wind, weather, Starbuck, and so forth.

What happens then? That's up to you; it's your story. Does your character get it or not? One could write a story where David Copperfield does not do well at all—only then he would be Holden Caulfield—a story where Captain Ahab does not catch Moby Dick or even a science fiction story where Bonnie Prince Charlie *did* restore the Stuarts; and *then* what? It's your story; you figure it out.

The important thing is to figure it *all* out—preferably before you ever write *Chapter One* at the head of the first blank piece of paper; it saves a lot of trouble. Otherwise you may write and write and find out you've painted yourself into a corner, and the story won't go; you'll find yourself desperately wondering "what happens next?" and you'll have to sit down and figure it out.

Ideally your outline will look something like this. I don't care whether you do it on a 3 × 5 card or in an exercise book (though when I start out to plot a novel I usually use a spiral notebook).

Let's say you're about to write *Moby Dick*.

Write the name (or your name) on the cover so the kids won't find it and write their latest Dungeons and Dragons project in it. (You can see what conditions I write under.)

Figure out first *who the story is about* (Captain Ahab, Bonnie Prince Charlie, or whomever you're writing about). Only make sure it's a *person*, not an *idea*. Young writers are always writing about ideas. Professionals write about people. Stories—I can't say it too often—are not about ideas; they're about people. Now figure out what the main character *wants*.

Now—preferably no later—figure out, *does the main character get it?* If you're writing *Moby Dick*, you'd have to say "yes," but he sinks his ship trying, with only the first-person narrator, "left to tell the tale."

That's another decision to be made very early in the plotting—or planning—stage. *Moby Dick* is about Captain Ahab and the white whale, but it's told from the *viewpoint* of Ishmael, a sailor on his ship. One could tell the story from Ahab's point of view—but one could hardly have Ahab tell it, because he does not survive his quest.

If you choose a first person narrator, you compromise the suspense—that's what keeps the reader turning pages. You know, if it's first person, that the narrator survived whatever experience and "lived to tell the tale." This may or may not make any difference; if you were writing the story of a man who grows to manhood, you can assume that he survived. One does not tell a murder story from the viewpoint of the victim, or it would be a very short story indeed. While I'm thinking about it, I want to mention something else I'm always telling people in my workshops: don't write a story in which your protagonist gets killed off. In the interests of realism, young writers are always doing this, thus trying (probably) to confound the stereotype of "Nothing will happen to him; he's the hero," and trying to write unusual stories. Without getting into the ethics of the matter, I advise against it, for a number of reasons; the main one of which is you've spent however many pages building up sympathy for this character, and if you kill the character off, it's all wasted. Besides, why bother to tell the story of a failure? If you are going to kill off a character, tell the story from somebody else's point of view. (You see, I do recognize that you may have to kill off a main character, as I killed off Jaelle in my *City of Sorcery*, but I managed that because the main character was Magda, and Jaelle's death was one more obstacle Magda had to face.)

Once you have determined how the story will end—David Copperfield achieves life and prosperity, Captain Ahab gets revenge on Moby Dick, Charles Edward gets gallant (or ignominious, that's *your* choice) defeat at Culloden, Frodo gets the Ring to Mount Doom and destroys Sauron, or whatever your main character wants to achieve, and you've decided either that the character gets it or doesn't (and that can make a good story too, with Charles Edward gallantly defeated at Culloden, and fleeing into exile)—then you start figuring out *how* the main character gets it or doesn't.

There is a certain way every story *wants* to end. I am remembering Saturday kiddie matinees. Remember the bomb in the closet, and the way the audience yells every time the hero approaches it: "Don't go in there! Don't open it!" You want your reader—figuratively, if it is an adult audience—sitting on the edge of the chair, mentally crying out to your hero, "No, don't do that!" I saw *Return of the Jedi* at a kiddie matinee; I still remember the screams of joy from the audience when Darth Vader killed the Emperor. That's what I mean; Good had triumphed over Evil and the hero had won again. The audience was young and unsophisticated and this was what they wanted. You can be as subtle, or as unsubtle, as you like; your hero may get the beloved, or the kingdom, or may fail to get them both, in any way you like. It's, as I say, *your* story. You may want to tell a very different story; Bonnie Prince Charlie may be honorably defeated at Culloden (let's hope your reader greets this intelligence with floods of tears). If you do your job right, your readers, even if all their sympathies are rationally on the other side, are going to *want* your prince to win (at least while he or she is reading the story).

Now let's think about two other things: complications and climaxes.

Complications are simply what keeps your hero or heroine from getting what he or she wants. In a marriage story, it would be the Other Woman (or Other Man); in a quest story, the dragon the hero has to pass to get at the treasure. In my preceding example, it would be, say, one thing after another, in logical sequence. Bonnie Prince Charles goes out after his crown. First he has a few small successes—the battle of Preston Pans, for example, where the leader of the other side, Sir John Cope, ran like hell; he had raw untrained troops, and they all ran away rather than face half their number of berserk Highlanders. But sooner or later you realize that because of the superior force of arms on the other side, because of his own bad advisers, or whatever you stack up against him, there comes a moment when you realize that the Prince simply *isn't* going to make it; gallantry aside, there comes a moment when God is on the side of the bigger guns. This is a *climax*.

In every story there comes a moment when the story turns around; it may be the moment when you suddenly realize it's all over but the shouting, or it may be the moment of despair when the hero realizes that death is imminent. Maybe the main character will survive but thinks the chances are slim; and that is also a climax.

When you have reached that point—if you are wise—you wrap up the story as quickly as you can. (Remember the point where Errol Flynn, trapped in the old castle with fifty soldiers between him and exit, thinks that all is lost? What does he do? He whips out his trusty sword, and cuts his way out, of course, over all fifty of them, and especially the villain who has opposed him from the first.) Then, either the hero gets a medal, or the castle back, and maybe the lover, depending on the age of your audience, or maybe not. The hero may even decide to forego everything. As I say, it's your story. But anyhow, that's where the story *ends.* Anything more is an anti-climax.

No matter what you think of those old movies, you can learn a lot from them about plotting. And you should. They knew, at least, how to make things satisfactory to the audience. And this is the whole art of fiction.

11 The Dynamics of Character

Sheila Schwartz
State University College, New York

Where Do Characters Come From?

Where do characters come from in fiction? Do they come from exercises such as "The Most Unforgettable Person I've Ever Known," or "The Person I Most Admire"? I believe they do not, that there is no transference from abstract exercises such as these to the development of rounded, multidimensional characters in a work of fiction. That is not the way I write, and that is not the way I teach my students to write.

My experience has led me to believe that development of characters cannot be done in isolation, without a context. Character cannot precede situation. And where does situation begin?

Dorothea Brande, in her classic work on writing, *Becoming a Writer*, states:

> It is commonplace that every writer must turn to himself to find most of his material. . . . There is just one contribution which every one of us can make; we can give into the common pool of experience some comprehension of the world as it looks to each of us. There is one sense in which everyone is unique. No one else was born of your parents, at just that time of just that country's history; no one underwent just your experiences . . . or faces the world with the exact set of ideas you must have. If you can come to such friendly terms with yourself that you are able and willing to say precisely what you think of any given situation or character, if you can tell a story as it can appear only to you of all the people on earth, you will inevitably have a piece of work which is original. (1934, 119–121)

Such writers, she goes on to note, have "a vision of the world and set out to transcribe it, and their work has the forthrightness and vigor of all work that comes from the central core of the personality without deviation or distortion" (122).

In my opinion, all fictional writing stems from emotion; from the need and desire to communicate; from the need and desire to exorcise old wounds, to redress old grievances, to bring clarity to unresolved events of the past. Once the writer has found a situation based on one of these needs, the development of the characters can begin. This philosophy is the core of the method that I employ, both as an author of fiction and as a teacher of writing.

I would like to illustrate this process through my own first work of published fiction, a young adult book entitled, *Growing Up Guilty*, written during the course of a six-week summer session workshop in which my students were required to produce daily writing while I, as role model, did the same.

The Exorcism of Old Wounds

The process of working on *Growing Up Guilty* was a process of memory and of discovery. Each day characters and events emerged which surprised me in the same way that we are surprised when we open old trunks and drawers and find many things we've long since ceased to think about. We sit there looking through old letters, mementos, pictures, and a rush of nostalgia, of bittersweet emotion, sweeps over us. We remember the good things and the bad things of another time, and we want to share these feelings with others.

Growing Up Guilty is filled with these mementos. It is based on two major wounds that I had long since consigned to memory. Both of these wounds are what Joyce Carol Oates calls, "that obscure but vulnerable, and, once lost, precious life that [the writer] lived before becoming a writer . . ." (1983, 9).

The source of the first of these wounds was summer camp. When I was a child, all middle-class children went away to summer camp. I went to a traditional camp, where campers wore uniforms and most of the summer was devoted to preparation for "Color War," the climax of competition in which the entire camp was divided into two warring sides to compete against each other. Winning was the only thing that mattered. I didn't like camp. I didn't like competition. I didn't like wearing uniforms. I didn't like sports. I liked to read. I liked to listen to music. I liked to be let alone. But there was no place in the traditional camp for such children.

When I first read Glendon Swarthout's *Bless the Beasts and Children*, which deals with a group of misfits at a summer camp, I said to myself, had I been at that camp I, too, would have been one of the misfits.

A second wound went back to the 1950s, when I first became a teacher and joined the original Teachers Union in New York City. Sometimes it is difficult for us to remember the era before the 1960s, when the antiwar protest opened up the universities and the real world entered the halls of dear old ivy. Before that time, in many schools, there was still a great gap between town and gown, and it was possible to get through college with very little awareness of the real, political world.

To come from that setting to the Teachers Union was to be exposed to a whole new way of thinking, to a bombardment of new ideas, new literature, new politics, new values. To illustrate, before the Teachers Union, I had never known a black person who was not a domestic. But in the union, I met proud black teachers and a special breed of white teachers who cared about the dispossessed and oppressed peoples of the world. The Teachers Union was the first group to publish material for "Negro History Week," acquainting me for the first time with such names as Nat Turner and Crispus Attucks. In the Teachers Union I discovered a brave new world of labor dedication, left-wing politics, interracial friendship, and teaching that was placed in the context of the socioeconomic and political events of our society. I felt tremendous admiration and respect for my fellow teachers who were giving me this invaluable education.

And then, with the Cold War, the sky fell in. The witch hunts of the 1950s began, the Rosenbergs were executed, and many members of the Teachers Union were fired, becoming displaced professionals.

A dream and an era had ended. I got married, had children, moved to the suburbs, became a college teacher, and every year my memories of the Teachers Union dimmed and moved far back into the recesses of my mind.

And now back to the summer of *Growing Up Guilty*. When I sat down each day to write, twenty-six years later, I had no clear characters in mind. But as I worked, a character emerged, a wonderful woman named Millie: radical, poor, generous, intelligent, optimistic, and a little naive. This novel, set just before World War II, before the world knew of gulags, of charade trials, and of mass exterminations of the Kulaks, dealt with a period of romantic communism in which a good-hearted compassionate woman like Millie could say, "Some day Stalin will find a cure for cancer and cavities."

Who was this woman? I never knew someone exactly like her. But as I worked I realized that she was an amalgam of the best qualities of the Teachers Union women I had so admired. I liked her gypsy freedom from ritual and restraint, her willingness to break with tradition, her involvement with politics and intellectual ideas, her nonconformist Greenwich Village clothing, her dangling copper earrings, her undisciplined long curly hair and her sandals. She was just the kind of person who could help a poor, despised teenager grow into the right kind of adult. Susan, the heroine, says:

> Millie was the first grown woman who had ever been honest with me. To my amazement, she spoke openly about such things as sex, the problems of being a woman, about people in her cell she just couldn't bring herself to like, about the financial hardship of her contributions to the party, about the boredom of cell meetings, and about her concerns about getting older and losing her looks. I was glad that she had some superficial concerns, as I did. (1978, 153)

At the opposite pole from Millie is the girl's mother, a bitter, cruel, destructive, disappointed, unhappy, rigid human being who is well on her way to destroying the girl before Millie saves her. Again, I never knew a woman quite like this mother. My own mother was warm and constructive and loving. But I knew the kind of mother I'd hate to have, and Mrs. Green turned into this person.

I wanted to make another point with these two diametrically opposed women. Both of them were poor, as were most ordinary people before the WWII boom, but poverty had led one to generosity and a desire to embrace the world, and had led the other to cruelty and narrowness. I wanted to show through these women that financial poverty need not necessarily lead to poverty of the spirit. One grows by merging one's pain with that of the world.

Gradually two different sets of characters emerged, those who would push my heroine down and those who would help her up. Another negative character is Helen, a cruel camp counselor, based exactly on Helen R., a counselor I had at camp. The real Helen was my first experience with irrational hatred, based not on something I had done but simply on what I was. Helen has stayed in my memory since then, providing an initial scheme for all people who are cruel to defenseless children. I am grateful for having known her. The encounter with evil is essential for writers.

With *Growing Up Guilty*, I inadvertently followed Brande's stricture to give, "into the common pool of experience some comprehension of the world as it looks to each of us." When the book was published, some of my camp friends read it and said, "But you were never unhappy at camp," and "Helen really wasn't so bad." Their comprehension of our camp world was completely different from mine. Each one of them would have written a different book.

But I was unhappy at camp and Helen was cruel to me and this is the way the world looked to me at that time. This perception is expressed through Susan, the stubborn, feisty, honest, irreverent heroine of the book.

Is Susan me? Well, yes and no. Philip Roth, in discussing this subject, says that the black cleaning woman in *The Anatomy Lesson*, who commiserates with his protagonist, Zuckerman, about his mother's death, "is modeled on the housekeeper of old friends in Philadelphia, a woman I haven't seen for ten years and who never laid eyes on anybody in my family but me. I was always entranced by her tangy style of speech, and when the right moment came, I used it. But the words in her mouth I invented. Olivia, the eighty-three-year-old black Florida cleaning woman, *c'est moi*" (Roth 1986, 278). And in the same way, every character I depict is me. Either what I really am or what I really am not, what I long to be, or what I dislike and fear to be. Every character is me because every character is filtered through my perceptions and worldview. Every character is part of me because each has emerged from my mind and experience. However, I have found that at a certain point, freed from the initial wound and freed from the psyche and experience of the creator, the character takes on a life of its own. William Maxwell describes this process as follows:

> In *The Folded Leaf*, the man who owned the antique shop bore a considerable resemblance to John Mosher, who was the movie critic at *The New Yorker*. He was a terribly amusing man whom I was very fond of. Nothing that John ever said is in that book, but I felt a certain security at the beginning in the identification. Then I forgot about Mosher entirely, because the person in the book sprang to life. I knew what he would do in a given situation, and what he would say . . . that sudden confidence that makes the characters suddenly belong to you, and not just be borrowed from real life. Then you reach a further point where the character doesn't belong to you any longer, because he's taken off; there's nothing you can do but put down what he does and says. That's the best of all. (1986, 45)

Bernard Malamud, in answer to the question, "Do characters ever run away from you and take on identities you hadn't expected?" answers, "My characters run away but not far. Their guise is surprises" (1984, 163).

I would like to demonstrate the process of character development emerging from an initial wound in another one of my novels, *So-*

rority, a work of fiction for adults. I started this novel, as I had started *Growing Up Guilty*, with an old wound. The wound, which was at the heart of *Sorority*, was a burning old resentment from my college days, a resentment against my college's sorority system.

I went off to college thinking that the sorority system was a variant of innocuous pajama parties. Instead, I found that the sorority system was not a party and was certainly not innocuous. I also found that there were aspects of sorority with which I strongly disapproved. If you did not join sorority, you were denied significant participation in college events for the next four years. If you did join sorority, your social relationships for the next four years were strictly limited to the other members of your sorority. If you found you didn't have much in common with them, it was too bad—you were stuck. It was like making a hasty, bad marriage without the possibility of divorce.

Another disturbing aspect of the sorority system was that the girls were inexorably either Jewish or Gentile, and there was no crossing of lines. World War II was being fought in Europe and Jews were being incinerated in concentration camps, but there was no transfer of meaning to the sorority system, despite the warning of a world in flames.

I could not be party to such a system. Regretting my inability to control my iconoclastic spirit, I stayed out, then found, to my delight, that other girls like me had also stayed out. They became my friends and the basis of my novel. During the years after college these memories dimmed as I married and became a busy mother. And then, thirty-five years after graduation, I began to read articles, one notably in *The New York Times*, proclaiming the resurgence of fraternities and sororities at the very same time that the newspapers were reporting deaths from hazing. Very little had changed. It made me angry; it reawakened all of my old disapproval of the system.

I decided to write a novel about this. I wanted to tell the story of three nonaffiliated girls who become friends and affect each other for the rest of their lives. I wanted to say that a sorority based on affection, caring, and common interests is far more meaningful than an association based on three Greek letters.

I express my feelings about this in the last scene of *Sorority*. The plot goes from the 1940s to the 1980s. One of my heroines, Sarah, is remarrying in her fifties. She thinks:

> And what a valiant group they were. . . . Four women who had found each other and formed a sorority. Most sororities are based on a need to belong, Sarah thought. But we were a band of outsiders, and our sorority was based on love.

Sarah looked at her friends, and they seemed ringed in light. How beautiful they were! Her friends! Erect, strong, unbowed. In this room, suffused with sunlight and the fragrance of gardenias and plumerias, she could feel her soul expand and her senses roar, and she wanted to hold them all against her and tell them how she loved them. We are all survivors, she thought. We are all victorious. They'd held on, they'd come through, and she was proud to be one of them.

She held aloft her glass. 'To our sorority,' she said. 'And to tomorrow.' (473–74)

Once I had my basic idea for *Sorority*, the characters began to assume shape. One of them is Sarah, a political radical from a rich, conservative family, who has a legendary romance and marriage to a member of the Lincoln Brigade and becomes a college professor at New Paltz. She is obviously loosely based on me. Not exactly, of course. As Maxwell says, once she was conceived, she took on a life of her own. But her values and politics are mine. She is, to some extent, an adult version of Susan in *Growing Up Guilty*.

A second girl is Wendy, heiress to a vast West Indian hotel fortune, who, despite all taboos of that era, or perhaps because of them, falls in love for life with a black man. Wendy is a composite of several girls I knew. Physically, she resembles a girl at college of legendary wealth whose family did own a hotel in the West Indies. There were always exotic rumors about this girl: that her sister had a black baby, that she was of mixed blood. She is blended with other girls I knew at that time: one who emigrated to Mexico because she fell in love with a black man, and a third who was so conscience-stricken about the treatment of blacks that she went out of her way to sleep with as many black men as possible. All of these traits are blended in Wendy. She, too, took on a life of her own.

A third member of the sorority of outsiders is Charlotte, whose psychotic mother regularly abuses her. I knew of such a girl. I know of many such girls. The girl I knew had a well-meaning but weak father who committed suicide.

This is the basis for Charlotte. But as I worked I found, to my surprise, that she loved painting, that she found peace and comfort in depicting a world more beautiful and serene than her own. Anxious to escape from her mother and tired of being poor, she marries the first man who proposes and finds, to her amazement and mine, that she has married a man very much like her father.

The men in my book developed in similar ways. Maurice, the black man Wendy loves, is based on a man I knew at the University of Mexico. After I left Mexico, I lost track of this man, but given his anger, his intelligence, and his abilities, his life could have paralleled my fictional life of Maurice, who moves through the civil rights struggles of the sixties, through the assassination of Martin Luther King, Jr., to affiliation with the Black Panthers. Maurice is a composite of a number of optimistic young black men who came back after World War II, had their postwar hopes for equality dashed, and joined the struggle for the rights to which they were entitled.

Day after day, the characters became more real to me. I'd think, Sarah wouldn't say that, or why must Charlotte be so destructive, or Wendy would love the way Joe Turner sings "I've Got the World on a String." And every day new characters and new relationships between them took shape. By the time the novel was finished, it ran to seven hundred pages, and I had created a world full of my own people.

My Method of Writing

I have attempted thus far to describe my own method of writing. First comes my desire to redress old wounds, to say something to the world, and only after that does the plot emerge, and with the plot, the characters. After that, my method of work is *recursive*.

Each morning, when I begin to work, I go back over at least the past ten pages, scrolling through them for necessary changes. I am very grateful for the invention of the word processor because it makes the recursive method far less onerous. As I look back over what I have done the previous day, I am sometimes shocked at a poor phrase and sometimes equally pleased with a good one. "Not bad," I think, and that sets me up for the work ahead. Sometimes I have no recollection at all that I have said such a thing. Sometimes, away from my desk, I'll think of a new and relevant detail, and then I can easily go back to insert it where it fits. After a certain period of time, the novel is finished to the best of my ability.

And then it goes to an editor. If I'm lucky, I am assigned to one with high literary standards. After a while the manuscript comes back to me with little colored flags extending out on the sides. Ultimately, these flagged manuscripts are always returned to the author. I save them to show my students that the writing process for them is not all that different from that of a professional. Despite all of my revision, there remain items on almost every page that must be questioned or changed for one reason or another. I also show them these marked-up manuscripts to make them think about what they demand from their own students, to demonstrate that every writer needs editing, every work can be improved. With *Sorority,* for example, there were approximately two flags per page, which means that initially the editor questioned 1,400 items. I tell my students that I do not feel hurt when I receive a well-edited manuscript. On the contrary, I feel grateful to receive this tangible reminder that I am no longer as alone as I have been during the initial writing, that I have a third eye working with me, helping me to refine and improve my work, helping me to achieve excellence.

Of course, editors, in common with teachers of writing, are not infallible. Sometimes they make mistakes. But all good editors are willing to discuss areas of disagreement with the author. Sometimes the editor concedes and sometimes the author does. But it is all done without harshness, without rancor, with everyone pulling together for the best possible result.

The Translation into Teaching

With teaching, as with my own writing, I have students begin with something they want to say, something that is uniquely theirs. For this purpose, free writing and journal writing are indispensable. At each class session, before I teach whatever lesson I have planned for the evening, we read one or more journal entries to each other. The amount read depends on the time and the number of students in the class. If class registration exceeds eight or ten students, I divide the class into small groups for the initial reading. While they work in small groups, I confer with individuals. Then, when the groups have finished, I ask for a few volunteers to read their work to the entire class. Volunteers must be willing to accept comments from class members outside of their own small group and from me as well. As they comment and listen, students begin to gain insight into their own work.

At the beginning of each semester, we arrive at rules for discussion of the readings. Students are instructed not to praise or denigrate each other's work, but instead to ask questions of the author about purpose and meaning. It is more difficult for students to understand that "It's great" is as unacceptable as "It's awful." If a student provides such a comment, he or she is directed to follow it with an explanation. If required to explain such comments, the questioner soon finds it easier to ask questions such as, "What was the date?" or "Who was the man?" Gradually, students learn to base all queries on validity of communication.

During prewriting, we spend a good deal of time in oral discussion, telling each other stories that will reveal these old wounds. This oral discussion leads to journal entries and eventually to the finished pieces. At this period, journals will include not only entries that are individually devised at home, but also entries based on these oral exchanges in class.

One evening, the subject of our discussion was "the most frightening thing that had ever happened to us." One girl told us about a near rape. When she had finished, she said, "I never told anybody about this before."

In the discussion, elements of character began to emerge. "I called my parents to come and get me," she said, "because I was too weak to walk. But I didn't tell them what had happened. I told them I just didn't feel well because, in part, it was my own fault for always disregarding my mother's advice. She always told me not to go into deserted places to make telephone calls, but I never listened to her about anything." As she described a willful girl who was chastened by her experience, both the characters of the mother and the girl took on dimension.

"What was the man like," someone asked with a little shiver.

"A bear," she said instantly. "He didn't talk. He grunted. And he was all bundled up in a thick nubby brown coat and thick mittens and a dark brown balaclava covering his face. He came up from behind me and grabbed me, and at first, in my initial shock, I actually thought he was a bear."

Another student had already written a journal entry about the most frightening thing that had ever happened to her. It was an automobile accident, and she and her husband had been first to arrive at the scene. In the small car were a husband, wife, and child who were on their way to church. They were hit on the wife's side by a truck. Because of an early, sudden storm, the traffic light was out.

The wife, my student wrote, was crushed like a plum and red juice was running out of the smashed door. The husband was unconscious. The child in the back seat, conscious throughout, screamed for over an hour while a machine called "The Jaws of Life," attempted to extricate them. One "Jaws of Life" broke and another had to be obtained. They were on their way to church, my student wrote. She decided to call her small vignette, "Racing to God."

After she had finished reading, another student got violently angry at the plum description. "That's disgusting," she said. "Can't you just write that she was badly injured?" Others said it was an excellent description precisely because it was so upsetting. From there, we moved to the question of characterization.

"If you want us to care about this accident," one student said, "and not merely to be titillated or horrified, we have to know more about these people. If you intend to turn this into a short story, start just before the accident and show them getting ready for church. Help us to know them and care about them and then your description will be even more devastating."

After Finding the Characters

Once the students find the characters they want to write about, they make homes for them in their journals, adding more and more details, either through research, imagination, or class discussion. The group asks questions: "What do we know about the woman in the automobile accident?" "Why was she driving?" "Why wasn't she more careful?" "What does she look like?" "Is she fat, thin, short, tall?" "Is she always worried about putting on weight?" "How old is she?" "How old does she feel?" "Is she concerned about getting old?" "How old is the child?" "How old was she when she had the child?" "What is her relationship with the child?" "What does she do with her life?" "Perhaps she works in the local old folks' home and is the kindest attendant; the old folks wait for her cheery smile, not knowing that she will never come again." Similar questions are asked about the husband and the child.

The student who had written her initial vignette decided to do a little research. She discovered that the man in the car was the local minister. The wife was driving because he was going over his sermon. She was driving too fast because he was afraid of being late.

At that point, the journal entry turned into a short story with fear, plot, characters, and bitter irony, and the student was able to put it into final form.

In Summation

Writers have always examined the development of their characters; it's one aspect of their craft. Elizabeth Bowen, the noted British novelist, has written:

> One cannot 'make' characters, only marionettes. The term, 'creation of character (or characters)' is misleading. Characters

pre-exist. They are found. They reveal themselves slowly to the
novelist's perception—as might fellow-travellers seated opposite
one in a very dimly lit railway carriage. . . . (Allen 1949, 179)

And Anthony Trollope also writes about this process of growing
intimacy in the course of writing:

> The novelist has other aims than the elucidation of his plot. He
> desires to make his readers so intimately acquainted with his
> characters that the creatures of his brain should be to them
> speaking, moving, living, human creatures. This he can never
> do unless he knows those fictitious personages himself, and he
> can never know them unless he can live with them in the full re-
> ality of established intimacy. They must be with him as he lies
> down to sleep, and as he wakes from his dreams. He must learn
> to hate them and to love them. He must argue with them, quar-
> rel with them, forgive them, and even submit to them. He must
> know of them whether they be cold-blooded or passionate,
> whether true or false, and how far true, and how far false. . . .
> And, as here, in our outer world, we know that men and
> women change—become worse or better as temptation or con-
> science may guide them—so should these creations of his
> change, and every change should be noted by him. On the last
> day of each month recorded, every person in his novel should
> be a month older than on the first. If the would-be novelist has
> aptitudes that way, all this will come to him without much
> struggling—but if it does not come, I think he can only make
> novels of wood. (Allen 1949, 193–94)

Both Bowen and Trollope describe the development of characters
as a process of increasing intimacy. In the beginning is situation, the
wound to be healed, the feelings to be exorcised, the ideas to be
communicated. At this point, characters are little more than figures
on the landscape.

But as the writer works, writing daily about these characters in a
journal, living with them as Trollope describes, seeing them unfold
as in Bowen's metaphor of the fellow traveler, the characters begin
to take on dimension, begin to surprise their creator, and eventually
to take on lives of their own. At that point, the author has developed characters "whose response to the world feels necessary"
(Busch 1968, 20), and the development of multidimensional characters has been achieved. The act of creativity has reached its objective.

Works Cited

Allen, Walter E. *Writers on Writing.* New York: E. P. Dutton and Company,
    1949.

Brande, Dorothea. *Becoming a Writer*. New York: Harcourt, Brace and Company, 1934.

Busch, Frederick. *When People Publish*. Iowa City: University of Iowa Press, 1968.

Malamud, Bernard. "Interview with Daniel Stern." *Writers at Work: The* Paris Review *Interviews*, Sixth Series, edited by George Plimpton, 149–68. Harrisonburg, Va.: Penguin Books, 1984.

Maxwell, William. "Interview with John Seabrook and George Plimpton." *Writers at Work: The* Paris Review *Interviews*, Seventh Series, edited by George Plimpton, 41–70. New York: Viking Press, 1986.

Oates, Joyce Carol, comp. *First Person Singular*. Princeton, N.J.: Ontario Review Press, 1983.

Roth, Philip. "Interview with Hermione Lee." *Writers at Work: The* Paris Review *Interviews*, Seventh Series, edited by George Plimpton, 269–98. New York: Viking Press, 1986.

Schwartz, Sheila. *Growing Up Guilty*. New York: Pantheon Books, 1978.

Schwartz, Sheila. *Sorority*. New York: Warner Books, 1987.

12 Teaching Point of View

Wayne Ude
Old Dominion University

Readers don't care much about point of view; they're far more interested in character, plot, language, theme. The fiction writer cannot afford to share that disinterest; poor understanding of and control over point of view will almost always result in a dull, poorly told story, no matter how interesting the characters, plot, language, or theme. For that reason, I emphasize point of view with five hours— a full week and a half, assuming three one-hour meetings per week—of exercises in every beginning fiction writing class.

This set of exercises has at least two purposes. The first and most obvious purpose—and the one I emphasize most in talking to students—is to give beginning writers some understanding of and practice in using various points of view, and to allow them to discover what effect a change in point of view has on a story—to allow them to, as John D. MacDonald says in chapter 7, "begin to get a whiff of plot design from the way ten views of [an] accident differ." The second, less overtly discussed, purpose is to surprise beginning students into using material from their own experiences.

This second approach is necessary because too many beginning students are reluctant to use material from their own lives; they believe their lives are dull and therefore not material for fiction; they believe all fiction must be somehow exotic. An exercise that focuses their immediate attention on a matter of technique may—if the exercise is not announced in advance and they're given only a short period in which to perform—require them to use material from their own experiences. Once students have used such material successfully, I believe, they not only discover that their lives have contained more than they had assumed, but also that they are more capable than they had thought of communicating the material of those lives. (Eve Shelnutt attacks this problem in another way in chapter 14, and her exercises might very profitably follow this series of assignments.)

The exercise begins with a handout containing paragraph-length examples of various points of view; it has been passed out at the end of the previous class so students can read through it at home. Before they do any writing, we spend most of a class period discussing the various points of view as shown in our examples. (My actual examples, with some comments on each, conclude this chapter.)

First person central, in which the narrator uses "I" to refer to him- or herself as a character and is also the central character in the work, is illustrated by a passage from *Catcher in the Rye*. *First person peripheral*, in which the narrator still uses "I" and is a character, but not the central character, can be illustrated by a passage from Baldwin's "Sonny's Blues." *Third person limited*, with its narrator who is *not* a character in the story and who tells the story using "he" or "she" rather than "I," but limits him- or herself only to what one character in the story could know, is demonstrated nicely with a passage from Welty's "A Worn Path." *Third person shifting*, in which the narrator is still not a character, uses "he" and "she," and presents only what is known to characters in the story, but shifts from character to character, can be illustrated with a passage from Dinesen's "Sorrow-Acre." Editorial *Omniscient*, in which the narrator is not a character, is not limited to what characters might know, and is also free to comment on action, move around in space and time, move from character to character, and so on, is illustrated by a passage from William Faulkner's "Barn Burning." Neutral *Omniscient*, which maintains all the freedoms of editorial omniscience except the freedom to comment, is illustrated by a passage from Shirley Jackson's "The Lottery." The *objective* or *effaced* narrator, which attempts to be very scenic and dramatic so that there seems to be *no* narrator present to interpose him- or herself between the reader and the material, and who rarely or never goes into character's minds, and then only shallowly, can be illustrated by many of Hemingway's early stories, such as "Hills Like White Elephants." I also like to include a bit of *stream-of-consciousness writing*, in which, again, there seems to be no narrator: the reader seems to be listening in on the character's mind as it ranges, apparently artlessly, through the character's mind, from preconsciousness to the most rational level. A paragraph from Porter's "The Jilting of Granny Weatherall" works nicely.

First Person Central

The first writing portion of the exercise begins at the opening of the next class period:

> This exercise asks you to use *first person*. Here is the situation: two people have been close—perhaps they're parent and child, brothers and/or sisters, husband and wife, close friends, lovers—whatever you'd like. But they've grown estranged—they've lost that closeness, perhaps they've grown to dislike or even hate each other. In this scene, these two people are getting together again for the first time in a long while—months, at least, perhaps years. They're meeting in a fairly neutral setting, in a public place—a cafe, perhaps—but at a time of day when they'll be almost the only customers. Use the first person central point of view; write a couple of paragraphs about their meeting from one of their perspectives, as though you were that person. You have ten minutes."

By the time they reach high school or college, most students have experienced at least one of these situations, and can use it to fuel their writing. And if they do write about something that happened to them, or to someone they know, it will be natural for them to describe it in the first person, much as they saw things at that time. Most of them won't be particularly objective, neutral, or balanced in their presentations; they'll have almost no distance from the material.

A few of them read aloud what they've written, and the class and teacher comment on it: "Is it actually in first person central?" "Do we understand the situation, the character's feelings [and so on]?" This takes anywhere from ten to twenty minutes, and then the next phase of the exercise begins.

Third Person Limited

> Now tell of this meeting again. You're still limited to what one character sees and knows, but this time use *third person limited*—"he" or "she"—to tell what that character sees and feels. And you have to tell about things from the perspective of the *other* person involved in this meeting, not from that of your first narrator. You have ten minutes; try to write about two paragraphs.

This causes a little consternation; even those who have used an entirely fictitious framework will most likely have already identified with the first-person narrator to the degree that they feel uncomfortable telling the story of this conflict from the other party's perspective. Once they've settled down and written, several again read what they've come up with, and the class discusses the changes involved in moving from one character to another, and in moving from first person to third person. They're beginning to learn something about fiction, about the way that point of view shapes the story, about the inherent untrustworthiness of narrators.

By the time the next step has been explained, the class period will be nearly over, so this next portion becomes a take-home assignment.

First Person Peripheral

> I want you to tell about this meeting once again, this time using the *first person peripheral* point of view—the "I" narrator again, but an "I" who is not central to the story, who is not either of your original characters. In fact, this narrator should be a complete stranger to the two persons who are involved—perhaps a waitress or waiter, or another customer. If a customer, you probably should make her or him a "regular," someone who is in the place a lot and knows that these two haven't been here before.
>
> This new narrator can't hear their voices clearly, and therefore can't hear everything they're saying. This narrator can only hear isolated words and phrases, perhaps occasional sentences, and will hear the tones of their voices—angry, sad, accusing, resigned, whatever you choose. So this narrator has to work mostly through speculation and whatever concrete evidence you allow. Something else you might want to keep in mind: this narrator may well put together his or her observations and bits of overheard dialogue in a way that gives a mistaken impression of what's going on. This narrator may be wrong about everything, or only wrong about some things, or may even be correct about events but may interpret them incorrectly.
>
> One other thing: rather than retell the whole story over again, you may, if you prefer, go on from where you left off with either of the first two narrators. On the other hand, it might be fun to retell your story as this uninformed narrator tells it. That choice is up to you. Give me about four paragraphs, since this is a take-home assignment and you'll have a little more time for it. And, finally, bring your first two narrators to class with you next time so we can compare their versions of events with this narrator's.

The next meeting of the class will begin with several students reading aloud what they've done at home. In addition to reading from their latest narrators, they also read from either of the first two narrators (first person central or third person limited) for contrast; this will take a full twenty minutes, perhaps more if several students read. A number of them will have had some fun with an untrustworthy narrator, which will lead nicely into a discussion of that aspect of point of view. Most catch on immediately that the narrator has often been able to accurately describe individual events but has misinterpreted their meaning; untrustworthy narrators don't so much lie as misinterpret or misvalue what they see and hear.

In addition to learning about first person peripheral and about untrustworthy narrators, they're also beginning to see a little more about another way a writer works, which is from a position of both involvement with and distance from characters and situations. They're learning something about the objectivity that their first attempts (mostly) lacked.

The exercise builds on that developing awareness of distance by having them try the story yet one more time.

Omniscient

> This time we're going to use an *omniscient narrator*. This narrator uses the "she" or "he" form, and isn't a character in the story. Most important, this narrator isn't limited in any way. Up to now, your narrators have had to justify their knowledge; they've had to explain to us how they knew what they knew. An omniscient narrator knows everything, but doesn't have to tell the reader how he or she knows it. In addition, an omniscient narrator has complete freedom to move through time and space, and to jump from one character's mind to another's—so your omniscient narrator can see into the minds of each of your other narrators, and can jump back and forth among them at will. This narrator can also speak directly to the reader (an omniscient narrator always knows that he or she is telling a story and has an audience), and therefore can tell us for certain what is true. And this omniscient narrator can not only go into the past, but also predict the future relationship between our two characters. You have twenty minutes; try for at least two paragraphs.

When students read their latest material and we discuss how it has changed, I try to focus the discussion, in part, on distance and objectivity. I also suggest that students begin thinking consciously, if they haven't already, about how to convert biographical material into fiction, about escaping from "what really happened" to "what might happen." By now they've reworked the original material often enough to begin seeing additional possibilities—things that didn't happen, but might have—and are beginning to feel free enough to prefer some of those possibilities to what did happen.

The series of exercises extends a little further yet, probably as another take-home assignment, once again showing the reader the same situation with the same characters. (If time allows, students may begin this assignment in class and complete it at home.)

Objective or Effaced Narrator

> Now you've got to do it again, but have courage; we're within a day or so of being finished with these two people. This time I want you to work with a very *objective* and *effaced* narrator: you can't go into anyone's mind—no one's mind at all, not even for a sentence—and you can't give us any direct comment from the narrator. You want to make your readers believe that we are hearing what is said and seeing what is done as though we, the readers, were invisibly present. You cannot directly tell us the meaning of anything. Instead, you need to work by giving us details that push us toward a particular meaning or set of meanings. Since you'll have a little more time to work on this one at home, try for four paragraphs. And remember: your narrator can present only what we could see and hear for ourselves—we readers, if we were hiding invisibly in a corner.

This objective narrator, who can *only* show and isn't allowed to tell anything, is terribly difficult for most beginning students; almost none of them will create a completely objective narrator, but instead will slip in some commentary and evaluation. It's important that they've been allowed to use the omniscient narrator before starting the objective exercise, both for the contrast and for getting some of that commentary out of their systems.

When the next class meeting begins, it may be necessary to have half the class read their samples in order to find a convincing objective narrator, or even to have them revise their paragraphs to make them more objective. Then, they need to read them aloud a second time. Despite its difficulty, this part of the exercise is very important: students need to learn to condense, to find the significant action or dialogue that will communicate for them, to show rather than tell; they need to learn the difference between what happened, as event, and the value or meaning of that event.

Stream-of-Consciousness

The exercise logically goes a single step further, when they try stream-of-consciousness writing, though they don't handle it even as well as they did the objective narrator: when their work is read aloud, their first attempts are usually indistinguishable from the thoughts of a very emotional first-person narrator. However, every class I've ever taught has been fascinated by stream-of-consciousness writing, and eager to try it; usually someone brings stream-of-consciousness up as we're doing the first in this series of exercises, and I promise that we'll get to it. And we do:

> We're going to work with that couple of yours one last time—yes, I promise this is the last time. We're going to try stream-of-consciousness. Remember that stream-of-consciousness, like objective, attempts to convince the reader that there really isn't any narrator, that the reader is receiving all of this material directly. But in this case, we are directly in the character's mind—one of your two original characters. Remember that stream-of-consciousness is not just a very emotional first person narrator thinking. Stream-of-consciousness attempts to present *all* levels of consciousness: the verbal and organized, the verbal and disorganized, the preverbal, and even things which are perceived but not consciously thought about. Remember, too, that stream-of-consciousness tries to appear random, unselected, so you have to select details, but make them appear almost accidental. Let's take twenty minutes for this one.

As we discuss their first attempts at stream-of-consciousness, I remind them of the basic elements of the technique, and then I usually have them rewrite their stream-of-consciousness paragraphs, adding other levels of consciousness, and giving a more random surface. A few students read aloud once again, and the series of exercises is over. (They've already tried shifting third person—where we go from one mind to another—as part of the omniscient narrator.)

So, what have they learned after an exercise that has taken up a full five hours of class time? In terms of the exercise's primary purpose, they've not only expanded their theoretical awareness of point of view and of what different points of view can mean to a story, but have also put that awareness to work in practice. In terms of the secondary purpose of the exercise, they've begun to learn how to use material from their own experiences (because they keep reading aloud what they've written, even those who've used totally fictional material are hearing what others have done with material that is recognizable from their own lives); they've practiced achieving some distance from their material; they've had the experience of doing several revisions of the same incident; and they've been forced to stay with material for a few days.

This series of exercises also helps alleviate another problem faced by many beginning students: finding a subject for that first story—in fact, about half of the stories turned in for the first short story assignment come from this exercise. Most important, these exercises help young writers begin to learn that it's not the material that determines the quality of their writing; it's what they do with that material. They begin to learn the craft of writing.

Examples of Points of View

Because so much confusing and contradictory material exists about types of points-of-view and the definitions thereof, I've attempted to develop a set of definitions and examples that are both clear and useful to the writer, while avoiding such obvious contradictions as "limited omniscience," which seems simply an impossibility despite the term's wide-spread use. I've also insisted upon distinctions that seem clear in practice, such as that between third person shifting, in which every perception comes to us through one or another particular character, and neutral omniscience, in which some perceptions come from outside the story, or at any rate are not presented as coming to us through a character. The examples referred to in the essay, together with brief comments about the type of point-of-view which I believe each exemplifies, follow.

First Person Central

> After old Sunny was gone, I sat in the chair for a while and smoked a couple of cigarettes. It was getting daylight outside. Boy, I felt miserable. I felt so depressed, you can't imagine. What I did, I started talking, sort of out loud, to Allie. I do that sometimes when I get very depressed. I keep telling him to go home and get his bike and meet me in front of Bobby Fallon's house. Bobby Fallon used to live quite near us in Maine—this is years ago. Anyway, what happened was, one day Bobby and I were going over to Lake Sedebego on our bikes. We were going to take our lunches and all, and our BB guns—we were kids and all, and we thought we could shoot something with our BB guns. Anyway, Allie heard us talking about it, and he wanted to go, and I wouldn't let him. I told him he was a child. So once in a while, now, when I get very depressed, I keep saying to him, "Okay. Go home and get your bike and meet me in front of Bobby's house. Hurry up." It wasn't that I didn't used to take him with me when I went somewhere. I did. But that one day, I didn't. He didn't get sore about it—he never got sore about anything—but I keep thinking about it anyway, when I get very depressed. (Salinger 1951, 98–99)

This is clearly first person central; the narrator tells of events involving other people, but is most concerned over what those events mean to him; he is central to the story, it is his story.

First Person Peripheral

> All I know about music is that not many people ever really hear it. And even then, on the rare occasions when something opens within and the music enters, what we mainly hear, or hear corroborated, are personal, private, vanishing evocations. But the man who creates the music is hearing something else, is dealing with the roar rising from the void and imposing order on it as it hits the air. . . . I just watched Sonny's face. His face was troubled, he was working hard, but he wasn't with it. And I had the feeling that, in a way, everyone on the bandstand was waiting for him, both waiting for him and pushing him along. . . .
>
> Sonny moved, deep within, exactly like someone in torment. I had never before thought of how awful the relationship must be between the musician and his instrument. He has to fill it, this instrument, with the breath of life, his own. He has to make it do what he wants it to do. And a piano is just a piano. It's made out of so much wood and wires and little hammers and big ones, and ivory. While there's only so much you can do with it, the only way to find this out is to try; to try and make it do everything.
>
> And Sonny hadn't been near a piano for over a year. And he wasn't on much better terms with his life, not the life that stretched before him now. He and the piano stammered, started one way, got scared, stopped; started another way, panicked, marked time, started again; then seemed to have found a direction, panicked again, got stuck. And the face I saw on Sonny I'd never seen before. Everything had been burned out of it, and, at the same time, things usually hidden were being burned in, by the fire and fury of the battle which was occurring in him up there. (Baldwin 1957, 137–38)

Again we can see that this is a first person narrator, but with a difference. While he still uses "I" to refer to himself as a character in the story, and he does tell us something about himself, he is more concerned with telling us about Sonny, with enabling us to understand Sonny, and even more with understanding Sonny for himself. The narrator is in the action, but not at the center; Sonny is at that center.

Third Person Limited

> She passed through the old cotton and went into a field of dead corn. It whispered and shook and was taller than her head.

Then there was something tall, black, and skinny there, moving before her.

At first she took it for a man. It could have been a man dancing in the field. But she stood still and listened, and it did not
make sound. It was as silent as a ghost.

"Ghost," she said sharply, "who you be the ghost of? For I
have heard of nary death close by."

But there was no answer—only the ragged dancing in the
wind.

She shut her eyes, reached out her hand, and touched a
sleeve. She found a coat and inside that an emptiness, cold as
ice.

"You scarecrow," she said. Her face lighted. "I ought to be
shut up for good," she said with laughter. "My senses is gone. I
too old. I the oldest people I ever know. Dance, old scarecrow,"
she said, "while I dancing with you." (Welty 1941, 279)

This is third person because of the use of "she" rather than "I,"
and limited because we know nothing but what the character
knows. She is confused; she sees something and isn't sure what it
is—at first she thinks it is a ghost. We learn only when she learns
that what she sees is actually a scarecrow. We see, we have knowledge of, only what she sees and has knowledge of.

Third Person Shifting

"I shall go on now," said the old lord. "But there is no need for
you to follow me. I will tell you tomorrow how the matter has
ended."

"No," said Adam, "I shall come back by sunset, to see the
end of it myself."

All the same he did not come back. He kept the hour in his
mind, and all through the evening the consciousness of the
drama, and the profound concern with which, in his thoughts,
he followed it, gave to his speech, glance, and movements a
grave and pathetic substance. But he felt that he was, in the
rooms of the manor, and even by the harpsichord on which he
accompanied his aunt . . . as much in the center of things as if
he had stood in the rye field itself, and as near to those human
beings whose fate was now decided there. . . .

But the old lord stayed on. Late in the afternoon he even had
an idea: he called down his valet to the pavilion and made him
shift his clothes on him and dress him up in a brocaded suit that
he had worn at Court. He let a lace-trimmed shirt be drawn over
his head and stuck out his slim legs to have them put into thin
silk stockings and buckled shoes . . . as the sun neared the
earth, he straightened himself, and took the way down to the
field.

> The shadows were now lengthening, azure blue along all the eastern slopes. The lonely trees in the corn marked their site by narrow blue pools running out from their feet. . . . Once he stood still; he thought he heard a lark singing over his head, a spring-like sound; his tired head held no clear perception of the season; he seemed to be walking, and standing, in a kind of eternity. (Dinesen 1942, 65–66)

Note that the passage still uses third person—"he"—and goes into the mind and feelings of more than one character. However, it doesn't tell us anything that would not be known to one or both of those characters. We still have a narrator who is separate from either character, who tells the story from outside the action, but who tells us nothing but what is known to, or felt by, one or more of the characters.

Omniscient (Editorial Omniscient)

> At midnight he was sitting on the crest of a hill. He did not know it was midnight and he did not know how far he had come. But there was no glare behind him now and he sat now, his back toward what he had called home for four days anyhow, his face toward the dark woods which he would enter when breath was strong again, small, shaking steadily in the chill darkness, hugging himself into the remainder of his thin, rotten shirt, the grief and despair now no longer terror and fear but just grief and despair. *Father. My father,* he thought. "He was brave!" he cried suddenly, aloud but not loud, no more than a whisper: "He was! He was in the war! He was in Colonel Sartoris' cav'ry!" not knowing that his father had gone to that war a private in the fine old European sense, wearing no uniform, admitting the authority of and giving fidelity to no man or army or flag, going to war as Malbrouck himself did: for booty—it meant nothing and less than nothing to him if it were enemy booty or his own. (Faulkner 1955, 26–27)

Clearly, this narrator knows and is able to tell us much that is not known to the character. The narrator is able to go into the past, before the boy was born, and tell us things that the boy does not have any way of knowing—indeed, will probably never know. Further, the narrator is able to comment, to compare the father's actions to a "fine old European" tradition; that commenting makes this "editorial omniscient." Nor does the narrator have to explain to us how he knows all this. He has complete knowledge, and also complete freedom to use that knowledge. Hence, we call this narrator omniscient, one who knows all.

Omniscient (Neutral Omniscience)

> The morning of June 27th was clear and sunny, with the fresh
> warmth of a full summer day; the flowers were blossoming pro-
> fusely and the grass was richly green. The people of the village
> began to gather in the square, between the post office and the
> bank, around ten o'clock; in some towns there were so many
> people that the lottery took two days and had to be started on
> June 26th, but in this village, where there were only about three
> hundred people, the whole lottery took less than two hours, so
> it could begin at ten o'clock in the morning and still be through
> in time to allow the villagers to get home for noon dinner. (Jack-
> son 1948)

This is still omniscient—the narrator is not limited to such knowledge as might come through the mind of a character, and makes no
effort to reassure us that some character knows all this. But the narrator, while keeping the privileges of omniscience to see all and tell
all, has given up the privilege of commenting on the action—hence,
"neutral omniscience."

Objective

> The girl looked across at the hills.
> "They're lovely hills," she said. "They don't really look like
> white elephants. I just meant the coloring of their skin through
> the trees."
> "Should we have another drink?"
> "All right."
> The warm wind blew the bead curtain against the table.
> "It's really an awfully simple operation, Jig," the man said.
> "It's not really an operation at all."
> The girl looked at the ground the table legs rested on.
> "I know you wouldn't mind it, Jig. It's really not anything.
> It's just to let the air in."
> The girl did not say anything.
> "I'll go with you and I'll stay with you all the time. They just
> let the air in and then it's all perfectly natural."
> "Then what will we do afterward?"
> "We'll be fine afterward. Just like we were before."
> "What makes you think so?"
> "That's the only thing that bothers us. It's the only thing that
> makes us unhappy."
> The girl looked at the bead curtain, put her hand out and
> took hold of two of the strings of beads.
> "And you think then we'll be all right and be happy." (Hem-
> ingway 1938, 274–75)

Note how careful this narrator is to never go into any character's mind, but to show us only what we might see and hear if we were an invisible audience, crouching in a corner. And also note how careful this narrator is to never evaluate anything, never judge, never explain. The narrator is as objective as possible, leaving us to find the passage's meaning for ourselves (and yet clearly intending the meaning we do find). This extreme objectivity is very different from the omniscient narrator's ability to explain, to judge, to evaluate, though in many respects the two narrators appear similar.

Stream-of-Consciousness

> (Her daughter's) voice staggered and bumped like a cart in a bad road. It rounded corners and turned back again and arrived nowhere. Granny stepped up in the cart very lightly and reached for the reins, but a man sat beside her and she knew him by his hand, driving the cart. . . .
>
> Lightning flashed on her closed eyelids, and a deep roaring shook her. Cornelia, is that lightning? I hear thunder. There's going to be a storm. Close all the windows call the children in. . . . "Mother, here we are, all of us." "Is that you, Hapsy." "Oh, no, I'm Lydia. We drove as fast as we could." Their faces drifted above her, drifted away. The rosary fell out of her hands and Lydia put it back. Jimmy tried to help, their hands fumbled together, and Granny closed two fingers around Jimmy's thumb. Beads wouldn't do, it must be something alive. She was so amazed her thoughts ran round and round. So, my dear Lord, this is my death and I wasn't even thinking about it. My children have come to see me die. But I can't, it's not time. Oh, I always hated surprises. I wanted to give Cornelia the amethyst set—Cornelia, you're to have the amethyst set, but Hapsy's to wear it when she wants, and, Doctor Harry, do shut up. Nobody sent for you. Oh my dear Lord, do wait a minute. (Porter 1930, 134–35)

Though stream-of-consciousness writing often does use the "I" to identify the narrator, it differs from first person because it attempts to present a mind as it might sound if we could somehow listen in; it also attempts to present that mind as it rambles from one level of consciousness to another. As Granny Weatherall lies on her death-bed, we hear her mind move from thinking of her daughter's shaky voice as sounding like a cart on a rough road, to thinking of herself as being in a cart. Then she imagines that her adult children are still small and must be called in from a storm. We seem to be hearing her actual thoughts. Stream-of-consciousness is not simply a very emotional first person, as students often assume; in fact, as we can see from parts of this passage, it often isn't terribly emotional at all.

Works Cited

Baldwin, James. "Sonny's Blues." In *Going to Meet the Man*. New York: Dial Press, 1957.

Dinesen, Isak. "Sorrow-Acre." In *Winter's Tales*. New York: Random House, 1942.

Faulkner, William. "Barn Burning." In *The Short Stories of William Faulkner*. New York: Random House, 1955.

Hemingway, Ernest. "Hills Like White Elephants." In *The Short Stories of Ernest Hemingway*. New York: Charles Scribner's Sons, 1938.

Jackson, Shirley. "The Lottery." In *The Lottery and Other Stories*. New York: Farrar, Straus & Giroux, 1948.

Porter, Katherine Anne. "The Jilting of Granny Weatherall." In *Flowering Judas and Other Stories*. New York: Harcourt Brace Jovanovich, 1930.

Salinger, J. D. *Catcher in the Rye*. New York: Little, Brown, 1951.

Welty, Eudora. "A Worn Path." In *A Curtain of Green and Other Stories*. New York: Harcourt Brace Jovanovich, 1941.

13 Transforming Experience into Fiction: An Alternative to the Workshop

Eve Shelnutt
Ohio University

The "workshop method" of teaching creative writing was ostensibly born at the University of Iowa fifty years ago with the creation of The Iowa Writers Workshop. But the idea behind the workshop method—that of apprenticeship, the professional teaching the novice—is hardly a recent phenomenon. The forms apprenticeship takes among writers are as varied as the personalities involved. Due to the nature of art itself, the apprenticeship of the writer becomes a life-long process. It could also be said that every writer is his or her own apprentice, since an artist's raw experience, is, in itself, of little value until a personal "act of vision"—as Eudora Welty terms the transformance of raw experience into form—lifts the mundane into art. While a writer may choose not to write *about* personal experience, he or she must nonetheless study personal experience since there is no other point of departure.

Apprenticeship, as it is practiced in university writing programs, presumes a text—a student's story or poem that is "on the table" for analysis. Does the story or poem "work" and, if not, what might the writer change in order to make it work? And, of course, writing does improve when the writer is able to hear reader's responses to material that is still in draft form, a way of taking material "on the road" before playing in *The New Yorker* or *Ploughshares*.

But M.F.A. students complain about the workshop method, especially if they already went through it as undergraduates. Not only do students talk of developing a "tin ear" from so many workshops, they also speak of themselves developing a tendency to write stories and poems specifically "for workshop," ones that they know will be crowd-pleasers. And with the members of the workshop changing each semester, writing to please the crowd is something like playing in Poughkeepsie one night and Saratoga Springs the next.

In part, the workshop method is ubiguitous because it helps students improve first drafts, but it is also popular because the workshop structure is manageable, easily understood by students, and highly visible. Writing programs with less-structured forms are also recognized by the university. Students are encouraged to attend fiction and poetry readings sponsored by the writing programs; writers' conferences are annual events for many programs; and after-class gatherings are encouraged for students who want to continue the discussion of writing that began in their workshop sessions.

What I have not mentioned as part of the structure of writing programs is the student/teacher conference, and it is this aspect of the apprentice relationship that has led me to investigate an alternative to the workshop method.

What happens when the writing teacher and the writing student simply talk, with no text on the desk for discussion? These "chats" are so commonplace, so natural a part of a writing teacher's job, that it is difficult to step back from what appears as an informal process in order to examine it. Yet, I spend more time teaching students about writing outside of class than during workshop hours.

Several years ago I began to list the topics I discussed with students during private conferences when we were not focusing on a specific piece of writing. I made notes about formal, scheduled conferences as well as the frequent, informal chats we had in the halls, beside duplicating machines, over coffee, and by phone. What I discovered was that my fiction students were concerned most frequently about "material," that which is presumed to exist in the workshop. Indeed, there is often so much material to be discussed in workshops that the students with manuscripts are like planes waiting to land at O'Hare. On the whole, there is no paucity of material.

But students' imaginations lie fallow at times, and many students continue writing even when that happens. After all, the workshop method presumes material; the grading system presumes a piece of writing to be graded; and students are self-protective insofar as they know *how* to be.

By taking notes about the topics that arose during student/teacher conferences, I came to believe, perhaps unconsciously, that students were seeking protection *from* the workshop method because its singular focus on material implies, on the other hand, that raw experience *is* the transforming "act of vision," since *how* a writer needs to work in order to experience that transformation is not a primary focus in workshops. *Re*vision assumes an original vision. Students seeking a dialogue about material were, I discovered, reflecting Welty's belief that raw experience is the worst kind of emptiness, and this sense of emptiness can be experienced by a writer *despite* a positive response from the readers in the workshop.

I understood this clearly when a student, whose professionally written stories had been endlessly praised in workshop sessions, talked during a private conference about her despair over her writing. Clearly it did not matter to her that she had won praise in workshops from instructors, or that she had, in fact, won a national literary prize for a story. She felt empty as a writer; the workshop method had failed her.

As my data from private conferences accumulated, I began to understand that writing students have a difficult time articulating questions about the material of their fiction. Such questions are difficult because they are much more subtle than those which arise about a particular piece of writing, when the questions focus on craft. Those subtle questions, haltingly articulated, have to do with whether or not a writer can discover a way to use language that will not betray the writer's mind and feelings as being less than they are or can be, even as the writer's use of language and form, as acts of discovery, change that writer, who also responds to a changing environment. The *fluidity* of a writer's position in relationship to material and the meaning of that fluidity is a difficult subject to encompass within the workshop method, and it may, in fact, be subverted by it, thus subverting creativity itself. Writers must compete for entrance into M.F.A. writing programs by submitting, as one requirement, a portfolio of writing that is then judged by admission committees. M.F.A. students who encounter problems with material *can* write. They are, then, seeking to learn something that is far more elusive: "What *is* an act of vision" and "How does a writer come to have one?"

With the support of the Honors College at The University of Pittsburgh, I began to consider how to design a fiction writing course that would take the focus away from the product and redirect it toward the creative process, not merely of writing, but of discovering a "vision." My initial questions were, first, "How could such a course be devised so that students would produce as much writing as they do in workshops?"—an important consideration since some of the students would be completing M.F.A. theses. And second, "Do students really seek, for all their questions, to relinquish myths about the creative process when some of these myths are used to protect themselves?"—such as the "agony" of the "writer's block" and the over-protested "ecstasy" of success, which allows some students to repeat themselves.

My initial decisions in planning the course arose from these questions. First, I would assign the writing of three, full-length stories, to be completed on time, by each of the fifteen students. Second, I would open class enrollment to any interested student, regardless of his or her experience as a fiction writer. In other words, I would welcome the naive student questions as readily as the sophisticated ones, on the basis that, if creativity contains bottomless mysteries, no question which seeks to plumb those depths is without merit, and, moreover, on the basis that naive writers engaged in the writing process might help deflate obtrusive myths about writing.

These decisions led to another regarding my role in the class. If the course was to be an investigation into a process that does not yield procedures easily, might not the direction I choose, as an experienced writer—might not the questions I ask—bear only a superficial importance to my students' concerns? Instead, I decided that the students should lead all discussions and should occupy, in turn, the teacher's traditional place at the front of the class. My place would be at the side, as observer and resource person.

I then decided to divide the course into four types of activity, each of them equally weighted. Students' grades would not rest solely on evaluation of the quality of their writing, or even on the degree of improvement in the writing over the course as a whole. At best, evaluation of writing is problematic: students develop as writers at varying paces; it is therefore not necessarily beneficial to segregate the student writers on the basis of their demonstrated abilities, nor fair when they are not segregated so that they can be evaluated one against another. Teachers must always guard against the element of subjectivity when evaluating writing; and students who experiment with form and language, as others polish their work, often appear at a disadvantage, even though experimentation is often most suitable for continued development.

One of the activities in my class was a set of "memory exercises," which I chose to evaluate informally by asking students to talk with me about their thoughts and feelings as they did the exercises. I decided upon this type of evaluation in order to preserve students' privacy, as much as possible, while I also evaluated their involvement in the assignments. Students' responses to my questions were intricate, individualistic, and complex, assuring me that, even though I did not see the actual writing involved in the memory exercises, the students were doing the exercises and also gaining insight into themselves as writers who were seeking to understand raw material. I believe that, had I asked to read students' memory exercises (as a way of assuring myself that they were being performed), I would have destroyed their value, which suggests that the grading of work in writing courses especially requires a teacher to be sensitive to the situations where it is appropriate and inappropriate. Indeed, it is possible that the grading of student writing is appropriate only because teachers of writing most often work as teachers within academic structures that require it.

Before delineating the four activities, I should mention that several other strategies I planned appear, in retrospect, to have been crucial to the success of the course. First, I decided not to tell students beforehand who would lead each day's discussion on material from the text; rather, at the beginning of each class, I asked a student to lead the discussion. Since I announced this policy at the beginning of the course, what resulted was a roomful of students prepared to lead discussions. Most had notes on how they would proceed, should they be chosen. Initially, of course, students came prepared in order to protect their grades, but it quickly became evident, due to their interest in the discussions *they* were leading, that they had forgotten I would evaluate the class discussions and the student leadership. As discussion leaders, students appeared to prepare carefully, less from fear of a bad evaluation and more because a particular text elicited questions that they wanted to explore. They became protective of their interest in their questions instead of simply protective of a grade. During the first few weeks of the course, I asked the students who seemed more confident to lead discussions, while allowing the more reticent students to become comfortable with the class structure and personalities before I called on them.

Second, I decided that several of my own stories would appear in the text that I had assembled and duplicated. I was interested in investigating how students would respond to a piece of fiction by a teacher who was willing to discuss her understanding of the process by which it was produced. I had no preconceived notion of how the discussion would go, and, as I will explain later, students' handling of the assignment helped them to clarify a number of ideas they had grappled with during the semester.

Third, I decided to give students guidelines to follow when their own work was under discussion, in order to ensure students' privacy since the structure of the course and the work they would be doing could, in the absence of such guidelines, leave them overly exposed. I will mention the informal "rules" in the section about students' stories. Following are descriptions of the four activities that comprised the structure of the course.

Memory Exercises

The poet Dabney Stuart has written that a writer "begins to remember when he begins to grow away from his sources" (1971,
141). And Welty has written that "to a large extent a writer cannot
help the material of his fiction. That is," she adds, "he cannot help
where and when he happened to be born; then he had to live somewhere and somehow and with others, and survive through some
history or other if he is here to write at all" (1979, 141).

If, I reasoned, the students in our writing programs are generally
young, how much have they grown away from their sources, and
has it been enough to be useful in their fiction writing? If students
feel apprehensive about their material, might that be, in part, because their memories are insufficiently developed for use, which implies a need both for memory and a perspective of distance from it?

At the beginning of each class meeting, during the first ten to fifteen minutes, I gave students "memory exercises" to work on at
home, asking them to try to control a "floodgate" of memory in
order to deepen the memory of small segments of experience. This
might, in turn, give them emotional control over their memories—I
termed it "indifference"—so that what they remembered could, if
they chose, be used in fiction separately from the emotions that surround a memory or memories. A typical assignment was to ask students to remember all of the shoes they had worn and to list them
without recording the emotions associated with them. On another
day, I would ask students to write about the odors they associated
with one relative's or friend's home and, on another day, to describe
as fully as possible any kites they may have flown, including a description of the place where they flew the kites, the weather, and
their sensations during the activity. Perhaps weeks after asking the
students to remember the shoes they had worn, I asked them to
read the list again and write down the feelings they associated with
the various pairs of shoes. In a number of assignments, I asked students to return to previously recorded memories and to add to
them, on the assumption that they would have brought certain
memories closer to consciousness and that they would have been
"considering" those memories even when they weren't fully aware
that the memories were expanding. Each exercise was designed both
to broaden and deepen memory of familial life, on the basis that a
writer's subject, as Welty says, "may build up and build up inside
him until it's intolerable to him not to try to write it in terms he can
understand . . . " (1979, 141).

I asked students to take notes while daydreaming of past experiences or objects or people—in fact, to consider daydreaming as an active part of preparing to write—a part of a writer's task.

In discussing the memory exercises during the first weeks of the course, students revealed how little they had grown away from their sources—how little, that is, memory was of use to them as writers. As Wayne Ude accurately writes in chapter 12, students—especially younger students—undervalue their experiences as sources for writing, believing that experiences worthy of writing must be less mundane than theirs. I also discovered that students fear the unresolved emotional conflicts that can surface when memories are tapped. A few of the older students discovered that they had trouble separating specific memories from the habitual thoughts they had connected to those memories in order to "resolve" them as social interaction seemed to demand. They found this fact unsettling since it indicated that the use to which they, as social beings, had put those memories might not serve them well as writers. Occasionally, they expressed a fear of their memories, when those memories became separated from the conclusions used to resolve them. Several younger students expressed wonder at the changes that occurred in their feelings about family members as their memories deepened. All of them seemed gratified by assignments that honored their memories and by the possibility that they would learn more about their memories and the connections between memory and the work writers do.

Two exercises concluded the series of memory assignments. First, I asked students to spend several weeks drawing a map of their hometown or towns, filling it not only with indications of streets and buildings but people, animals, plans, refuse bins, and so on. "Leave nothing out," I said, "since you may need the memory one day in your writing."

When the students had "finished" their maps (some said they would never be finished since they kept remembering things to add each day), I asked that they construct a similar map, but this time to fill it with invented people and to give those people a world of their own. As students worked on the second maps, it became clear from their discussions that their invented people, bred in part by their own histories, directed their imaginations; or, as Welty has written, a writer and his or her fiction "were never strangers" (Welty 1979, 141).

Writing by Professional Writers

Since the course had as its goal the investigation of the fiction writer's creative process and, for more immediate, practical purposes to help students confront problems about material, I chose to have students read the work of writers who have written about the sources of their fiction. In narrowing down possible selections, I chose writers whose social and political backgrounds might be of special interest to the students: Nadine Gordimer, V. S. Naipaul, Shiva Naipaul, K. A. Porter, Eudora Welty, Flannery O'Connor, and myself—the Third World and the South, the backgrounds from which writers have written in the knowledge of great social and political change. In the text I created were stories, sections of novels, essays, interviews, newspaper and magazine articles, as well as biographical sketches of each writer.

It would require more space than I have here to provide an adequate picture of the class discussions about the material in the text, especially since each student who led a discussion had different interests in and questions about the material. But a few examples may indicate the range of topics. When discussing a review of Lelyveld's *Move Your Shadow*, by Nadine Gordimer, the class, surprisingly to me, began to take Gordimer to task for, what they perceived to be, the way she let her political opinions dominate the review, at the expense of providing the reader with information about the book. "What should a review do and be," they asked, thinking that they saw a relationship between how Gordimer handled the review and how she structured her short stories. When discussing Gordimer's stories, students had pointed to a similarity of structure in several, which they believed was demonstrating a writer at work who was more intent on her message than on allowing characters to discover what they termed "inevitable" events. "To what extent," students asked, "should the writer manipulate material until it exemplifies a theme or conveys a message?" There was vociferous argument, too, about whether or not Gordimer "forgives" her "poolside liberals," and there was fierce disagreement about how to read the ending of Gordimer's story "Something for the Time Being." The discussion of the story led to a discussion of the degrees of control a writer should exert over a particular reading of a story—any?—and how a writer who "intends" a particular reading of a story (*if*, they added, one can speak of a writer's intention at all) goes about getting control of the material. Ultimately the discussion led to the students' consideration of a reader's role, in society, in relation to the writer, and in relation to the form of the story as artifact, invention.

Discussion of the texts by V. S. Naipaul and Shiva Naipaul centered around the fact (surprising to me) that most students believed Shiva Naipaul to be better represented by his work, and therefore to be the more successful writer. This led the students to consider the part that readers' sentiments play in critiquing a work of fiction, and to the extent to which a writer should try to be aware of those sentiments when writing. When the students discussed the last chapter of *A House for Mr. Biswas*, they focused on V. S. Naipaul's restraint in depicting the son's emotions in relation to his father; and they considered whether a reader can use autobiographical material to augment a reading of fiction, as they had done when reading Naipaul's preface to the novel, a preface written thirteen years after the novel was first published. At this juncture in the discussion, students referred to their discussion of Porter's essay on the sources of "Noon Wine," recalling that, previously, they were unwilling to take the essay as fact, but, rather, they had read it as a fiction that *suggested* Porter's memory of the story's inception: *all* writing as approximation of vision, and with its own "life" apart from both the particular reader and the writer, including the writer as reader of his or her own work.

That students were making connections between ideas and that they were testing them as they read became obvious when my own stories were discussed. I had imagined answering students' questions about the sources of my stories. But this proved unsatisfactory to the students. They said, first, that whatever I might *say* was not in form similar to a piece of *writing* about my stories; since, as talk, my response did not have an autonomous life as did an essay, and second, it was possible that what I revealed would impede their reading of the story as artifact, separate from the author. *If* they had questions, they said, they would ask.

I will, at the end of this chapter, mention several adjustments to the course that I decided would be useful. Here, let me say that, in what turned out to be a genuine failure to fully allow the students to pursue their own interests, I gave a talk on the general sources of my fiction during the class meeting that followed discussion of one of my stories. That day, since I had also led a discussion of the day's memory exercises, *my* talking dominated the time, although students did ask questions. It was interesting for me to notice that students accustomed to participating in student-led discussion did not easily yield time to me and my unilateral decision about how to spend the class period. They were resisting a change in routine, my making a unilateral decision about what we as a class would do, and, I believe, they resisted experiencing students' inherent passivity in lecture situations.

The segment of time spent weekly on the work of professional writers was crucial to the success of the course; first, because reading was fully integrated into the study of writing, and second, because it demonstrated students' willingness to consider conflicting modes of criticism, to think of writers as separate from the text, regardless of how autobiographical the fiction under study appeared to be. As I had hoped, students responded to my choice of professional writing by asking important questions about writers' responsibilities in society and about their own vision as it related to socially conscious fiction. The discussion was probably more free because I had no position in regard to a writer's social responsibilities; instead, I shared my own questions on the topic as well as Welty's response to the pressure to "politicize" her writing and Gordimer's estimation of Welty's refusal to do so.

Student Stories

After an introductory lecture on the story form and an initial assignment of memory exercises, I asked the students to write a full-length story based, however loosely, on personal experience. In the second and third assignments, students were asked to write stories that were not based on the experience of an actual event, but which used material from the memory exercises to sharpen detail, provide imagery, and add emotional and intellectual "weight" to imagined material culled from a welter of memory. Students were asked, in other words, to "seed" their stories with experienced material, while avoiding expiation and case history. The second and third assignments were based on what students deemed to be the failures of their first stories, which they had discussed in class.

Each first story was studied at home by a student discussion leader who was not the author and who later read the story aloud as students took notes for discussion. I should mention here that it is my standard practice to have students' stories read aloud instead of being duplicated, read at home or in class, and then discussed, a method I have used after years of following the duplication method. By asking students to listen carefully to a verbal reading, I stress a reader's need for concentration; the story's traditional use of highly controlled language, including economy; rhythm, which a listener can sense as a story component in both individual paragraphs and in the whole story; I also separate the reader from his or her normal reading habits, whether they are strong or weak, which seems to help writers learn to reason *as* writers seeking to understand form. (I provide the student with a close reading of a text, either in conference or in written comments on a text.

During the discussions of student fiction, the writers of the stories were asked to maintain the writer's privacy and to help deflect defensive behavior by neither talking about nor revealing the personal experiences on which the stories had been based, even if loosely.

Since this segment of the course was shared, on alternating days, with discussions of the text, students were aware that this miniature workshop was only a small portion of the course. Most student discussion leaders chose, therefore, to focus on elements of form, primarily on what they generally described as "inadequate transformation of personal material," despite the fact that they were precluded from asking the writer if, indeed, a story contained a transcription of memory.

Students were critical of their own stories as seeming "pushy," sometimes wholly unbelievable, "embarrassing," and often tedious. They came to feel confident that they could recognize inadequately transformed use of memory, even though they lacked confidence that they could discover methods by which they could use personal experience to create "an act of vision" in form. They decided that fiction was not a form for expiation, for recounting personal experience in precise detail, for trying to win sympathy for the reader as a redress of grievances, or for crusading.

What was left? Students began to write their second and third stories with this question in mind, and I was surprised at how liberated they felt as writers.

Student Essays on the Sources of Their Stories

I asked that, just after completing a story, students write essays telling me where they thought the material in the stories came from and the methods by which they had incorporated memory into their fiction. I stressed that only I would read the essays, a decision I will soon comment on, and I stressed that if a student preferred to conceal any use of personal experience, he or she should feel free to do so. I did not suggest that the essays should follow any particular structure, style, or word limit, but I did suggest that the writer should study the small details in the work as well as the major plot strategies.

It was instructive, and frightening, to find how readily students reveal their deepest feelings and most traumatic experiences even when ways to conceal them are suggested. My students' first essays were difficult for me to read and required of me extra sensitivity since I wanted to honor students' trust, while also remaining solely a teacher of fiction writing whose job was not commiseration or counseling. It was necessary for me to respond to the essays, not as revelations which might make the writer vulnerable, but as material with which a writer of fiction could work. When writing on the essays, I suggested ways material could be transformed in order to give the writer sufficient distance from it for control, and, in some cases, I acknowledged simply that the writer's raw material would be especially powerful *if* it could be interpreted through a "sideways," oblique approach that could come with time. Perhaps I should say that I teach writing in the belief that one of my duties as a teacher is to encourage students to not depend on me as a teacher. It seems to me that such dependence, however slight, deters a writer from learning the responsibility inherent in the writing profession. This belief gave me pause as I planned this component of the course. I learned about aspects of my students' histories that were often most painful for me to know; and I had to be especially sensitive to each student's response to having revealed him- or herself willingly, in service to a pedagogy which was, after all, *my* experiment. Some writing teachers routinely encourage their students' revelations as a conscious way of helping those students to know the inner selves that will give rise to their work. However, I have never used that approach. I became, I believe, more businesslike after reading the students' first essays, and I have modified my assignments, which I will discuss shortly, as a response to that experience.

Since my readings of students' first stories and essays guided the directions I gave for writing second and third stories, I suggested that the second and third essays would, no doubt, change as well, probably focusing on memory as it surfaced in the small rather than large ways: in the selection of color, sound, snatches of dialogue, repetition of imagery, and so on. Since I use humor as often as possible when teaching, I suggested, in a hyperbolic tone, that I was sure the students had run out of familial chaos to relate and that now we would focus on the use of bits and pieces. This was, of course, a suggestion to students that I, as a teacher, could tolerate learning only so much of the pain they had experienced. Realizing this, I talked with them about form as liberating, as allowing a place for the expression of pain, turmoil, confusion, defiance, anger, joy, and love when form provides a reader sufficient "distance" to contemplate human nature without compensatory avoidance. Since the students had been highly critical of their first stories, they welcomed this "lecture" that connected a sense of hope to the use of form, and we were led, then, to discuss aspects of social history that might cause a writer to feel the futility of pursuing form as a stay against hopelessness. They talked, then, more enthusiastically about V. S. Naipaul and Nadine Gordimer, and they speculated about the effect upon art of the fact of nuclear weapons.

Students' second and third stories were a surprise to me, despite years of teaching about the expectation of surprise. Suddenly it seemed (although it was not really sudden at all) the students had, to a great degree, gained control of the use of autobiographical material in their fiction, for their stories seemed alive with scenes and detail within those scenes, which pointed to their being writers in service to form, characters, subtle changes in characters acting "inevitably," as we say.

Again, without reproducing their stories in full, it is difficult to convey a sense of the students' growing sophistication as writers. Two students have given me permission, however, to quote anonymously from their essays, which may indicate students' increasing understanding of the process of transforming personal experience into fiction.

The first student's initial story had been about her father—raw experience. In her second story, she wrote about a widower who suddenly finds himself attracted to a former friend of his deceased wife. In the essay about the sources of the material, the student wrote:

> At the beginning of the story Mitchell Smallwood's character was based on a minor memory I have of my father. He took us as kids to the beach for a vacation. It was the summer of my parent's 2nd or 3rd year of separation. Divorce was inevitable. My Dad was depressed. He sat on the porch of the beach house, watched the ocean, and drank beer after beer. I was depressed and angry watching him. I hated the way he was acting, and, initially, Mr. Smallwood's character was an extension of my father. However, the more I got into Mitchell's character, the more I sympathized with him. I found myself *becoming* Mitchell. For example, the way he thought about the neighbor women were my thoughts, the way be beat his head against the wall trying to get Pearl [the woman he was interested in romancing], and his dislike of Mrs. Smallwood were all things I shared with him. Mrs. Weston and Mrs. Smallwood were transformations of my mother. Mrs. Weston's character was like my mother's from

my point of view. . . . The parts of the story about the war were mostly fiction with a slight influence from my grandfather. [The name] "Devagovich" was embroidered on a real WW II navy sailor shirt that my grandfather gave me—origin unknown.

A student several years older than the one quoted above had been working during the course to control obsessional material, especially about her father. In an essay written in second-person, she confronted the obsession:

The setting of most of your stories: The South where your natural father was born and raised. By imagining the South, you imagine him; the feelings are easily transferred. You take the few arbitrary facts she's, the mother, given you—"very southern, very funny, and the bluest eyes you've ever seen"—and you re-invent him. It's easy; vacuity is readily filled with imagination. And so, subtlety, he works his way into most of your fiction. The repeated allusions to the celebrities in this particular story probably originated from a visit to your mother's house a month ago. Over lunch you ask (again) about your father, what he looked like, etc. He looked exactly like Steve McQueen in the movie "The Getaway," she tells you.

Later, on page thirteen of the essay, the student concludes:

If my father is to remain a myth, you want to say, then I'll imagine and invent him as I please. (And if we wanted to, here we could remember that the last stage in a mythical quest, before the hero can be transformed, is atonement with the father.)

But what of resolution?

And so it's all about honesty, isn't it? It's all too easy to sit giddy on a painted surface and follow the most accessible thread, but you realize now that to achieve any sort of distance from yourself or your fiction, you have to first fall into memory's dark hours to find a minute that glimmers.

By concentrating in the course primarily on the creative process itself and secondarily on how personal material is transformed into fiction, students were behaving differently as writers and readers than they would have in a typical workshop where the emphasis is first on the piece of writing itself. While critical analysis of writing occurred, students were learning how stories "work" by focusing on how the writer's personal act of vision transforms the emptiness of raw experience. Students were learning how to behave and think *as* writers even when they were not actively writing, so that the non-writing state became contiguous with the writing state. Students began to learn respect for the work writers can do when they are not actively writing. And they were learning respect for their own histories and themselves as creators bred from that history. Fear about a possible paucity of material became impatience to use all they had discovered that they owned.

Assessment of the Course

Due to the intricate design of the course, more preparation and evaluation time were required than for a typical workshop. As I considered the preparation and time I had spent on the course, I began to suspect that the workshop method's popularity with writing teachers is due, at least in part, to the fact that it requires little in the way of advance planning and little cause for apprehension because the pedagogy is "standard."

My preparation time, nevertheless, seemed to be time well spent, since the "informal" work in conference is a large part of a writing teacher's duties, and the design of the course shortened the time I usually spent in conference: many of the questions students normally ask in private were a formal part of the course. Moreover, students' excitement about the course enlivened me as a teacher. It was especially rewarding for me to discover that my students had begun to broaden their interests in literature in order to "cure," as they said, their ignorance about world politics and the literature of writers from other cultures. They began to question the *ennui* in much contemporary American writing in view of global politics, and they began to examine their roles as writers within a global context.

I will soon teach the course again, which requires that I replace some of the text material with more current information, commentary, and fiction. I have also decided to treat the students' final essays or the sources of their third stories as a formal piece of writing. I will ask them to write the essays in such a way that they would not mind having them read by the class, and not just by me.

This change resulted from a reading series I began soon after I taught the course I have described. As it turned out, interest in and excitement about the course were such that a number of graduate students who could not take the course began to ask that the methods used in it be incorporated into their writing workshops. Since scheduling constraints did not make this immediately possible, I asked two current graduate students and one who had graduated several years ago to consider writing essays about the sources in memory and experience of their fiction, choosing one story as a focus, for a public reading in the English department. As the writers worked, I also wrote about the sources of one of my own stories to discover firsthand how such an essay might change when written for an anticipated audience of graduate students in creative writing, literature, and composition. Part of my interest in the reading series was to provide a forum for an exchange of ideas about writing among all segments of the department (see chapter 1). As the four of us prepared for the reading series, we talked about the difficulties a writer faces when trying to describe one's methods of transforming personal experience into fiction, especially about the tension between wanting to reveal while also protecting one's privacy. We discovered, too, that our essays began to feel *like* fictions, even though we sought to convey what we apprehended as the truths about our writing processes. We became interested in what seemed to be a blurring of lines between the genres of fiction and nonfiction, and our essays began to reflect our discoveries. When the reading series began, each writer started by reading his or her story and followed by reading the essay about the process by which the story was written. A large number of students in creative writing, composition study, and literature, as well as faculty from the three areas, attended the readings, and, in a question-and-answer period that followed each reading, demonstrated by their questions a fervent interest in the strategies and problems of writing that writers in all forms have in common. The reading series was extended for a year to include twelve other writers (and it may continue further) as a result of the interest from both students and faculty. The format has broadened to include presentations by students not only in creative writing but also in composition and literature.

My observation about the interest in the reading series and an assessment of the value of the questions asked of the readers has led me to believe that the students in my course would benefit from making one of their three essays about the sources of their fiction into a formal piece of writing for presentation to the class. I am hoping that they will confront questions of strategy similar to the writers preparing for the reading series and be able to contrast the formal essay with the two intended only for my reading. I suspect, too, that by announcing, at the beginning of the course, that this formal essay will be assigned, students will, to some degree, begin to respond to the assignment even when writing the informal essays. I cannot, of course, report at this time what the benefits and losses may be as a result of this change.

I have also decided to include in the next material the essay I wrote as I planned the reading series, as well as the story that I wrote about. I will assign the two pieces of writing just as I would any other text material. A student, and not I, will lead the discussion of the two pieces. I will probably ask the students if they would prefer that I leave the room during the discussion, since, of course, students rarely, if ever, are able to avoid seeing a teacher as an authority figure, regardless of how a class is structured. I will, I trust, refrain from explaining my understanding of my own work in a lecture. I now understand that part of what I am investigating in the course is the role writing students want a writing teacher to play, especially in view of the fact that teachers of writing have, usually, published widely—a fact students are aware of even though most do not read their teachers' writings. In such a case, it is difficult to always know how much and what kind of interaction a writing teacher should have with writing students, especially since much apprenticeship now occurs within a traditional academic setting. During the reading series I have developed, I am "teaching," even though, during the program, I merely introduce the reader. My teaching is effaced and nontraditional in that context. I believe that it was valuable for my students to know that my course was an experiment, for me as a teacher. They observed me shifting strategies, some of which appeared to be failures. All felt, I believe, how genuinely I appreciated their participation and understood, I believe, that their work for the course had enlivened me as a teacher. It could be that, for these benefits alone, writing teachers should often design alternatives to the workshop method of teaching writing.

Works Cited

Stuart, Dabney. "Dabney Stuart Writes." In *Corgi Modern Poets in Focus*. Great Britain: Transworld Publishers Ltd, 1971.

Welty, Eudora. "Words in Fiction." In *The Eye of the Story*. New York: Vintage Books, Random House, 1979.

14 One Writer's Apprenticeship

Robert H. Abel
Mount Holyoke College

Formal academic training may not be necessary for the writer who can and does explore the world and the world of ideas out of a powerful personal curiosity. And it may even be true that if a writer is too immersed in the theories and methods of a particular academic discipline, the door to artistic creativity may be shut. But anthropology and physics need good writers, too—and often have them. The worst thing is for a writer to know nothing, to have nothing to write about, to be, or at least to feel, stupid about the affairs of the world and what matters in life. Study in pre-medicine did not hamper the creativity of John Irving or Walker Percy, starting out as an engineering student did not cap the creative well of Norman Mailer, and serious study in anthropology did not crush Peter Matthiessen or Saul Bellow. I suspect that if you met a Palestinian in a London pub and were told that person's life story, your understanding of it could differ depending on whether you were a historian, or a dock worker, or a computer programmer. Would the historian, however, be in a better position to understand the different points of view of all three listeners? Being formally trained as an academician does not have to shut you off from the rest of the world—and as a sometimes teacher myself, I sincerely hope that it doesn't. Education must be based on human realities, however disciplined the methods. And that is another thing which a good, formal education teaches a writer: you can't get away with half-truths and suppositions and good guesswork. You have to do your homework, too. A writer has to learn and to keep learning. Whether or not a college is the best place to begin this life-long activity is the question.

On the basis of my own experience, I would say that I might have floundered more without a college education, and that it has given me tools for satisfying and stimulating my curiosity; in addition, it certainly attacked my early pretensions about my ability to write, and then inspired me to improve. Would this have come "naturally?" I cannot possibly know the answer.

I may love ideas too much, as some critics have asserted, but that does not mean I love any less the facts of the case or the drama of our lives and fates. I don't believe, either, that my education deprived me of knowledge of the "real world," which for students of my generation would have meant service in the military or taking a job or bumming around the world. In fact, I worked while in college, and I dropped out for one year to hitchhike around Europe. I would not trade that year for another one in the classroom, but I also would not like to spend my life as a hitchhiker. What I was feeling, I suppose, were what I considered the awful strictures of small-town and college life of twenty-five years ago, where the women had to be in bed by ten o'clock and drinking a beer was considered a criminal act. Other writers have found plenty of mystery, drama, eccentricity, and character in limited environments—and if there is no formula for what an academic education provides a writer, there is certainly no formula for which life experiences prove beneficial. I have also seen many promising writers of my generation smash up on the rocks of their adventures. Their perpetual pursuit of experience becomes an excuse for never sitting down to the blank page; I have seen them become convinced they are gathering experience when, in fact, they are only repeating experiences again and again. And I have always felt that a writer who went into the world determined to seek out experiences to write about was rather like the clown with the big shoe who, when he tries to pick up his hat, ends up kicking it even farther away. What truth is there in manufactured experience? Surely, adventure is necessary in every life, not just a writer's. And who are we writing about? What makes us think we are any more interesting, essentially, than anyone else? What could possibly convince us that our experiences, even the most intense ones, are the sum total of what happens in the world? Education may even be a corrective to experience.

I believe there were experiences in my life—particularly deaths in the family and a boyhood awash in a crushing religious fundamentalism—that "compelled" me to write, or to discover in writing, a private, personal instrument for engaging the demons of my life. Only in recent years have I come to regard fiction as a way of knowing which is as legitimate in its pursuits—potentially—as chemistry, say, but I suppose my first efforts were really based on an attempt to imagine and understand other lives, and to create other possible worlds and futures. *This was something I apparently had to do.*

But in my education, I was never discouraged from writing. I remember a fourth-grade teacher who allowed me to stay in the classroom by myself to finish a story I was absorbed in—a rewrite of Rumpelstiltskin, I believe—while the rest of the class attended an assembly. In high school, no one ever said to me "and give up verse, my boy, there's nothing in it." And I was frequently selected to be an editor of literary enterprises because I not only wrote grammatically but could turn out poems that actually rhymed. I was aware that writers generally were not rich and famous, and even found some romance in the concept of the starving artist—Zola in his garret, eating the frozen birds gathered from the rooftop beyond his window—wow! But I did assume—wrongly, as it turns out in my case—that they eventually became solvent, at least. Since I grew up comparatively poor and lived among farming people and others without wealth, I was not intimidated by the financial prospects of a writing career. All the same, no one in my educational life, until I was in graduate school, ever put the facts before me clearly and strongly. I find them discouraging today, but I suppose it is too late to do much about it.

In college, my independent study advisor, Professor Raymond McCall, allowed me to write fiction during my senior year, in lieu of a research paper (which I had written the year before). His criticism of my work was, I now realize, so tactful, witty, true, kind, and helpful that I could take it to heart and continue to believe that I could, and should, make the effort to write fiction. Other professors who encouraged my creative efforts were David Moldstadt and Warren Anderson, who went out of their way to praise things of mine they had seen in campus literary magazines and to challenge me to think more seriously about literature's possibilities. They let me know, in other words, that I had a skill of some potential worth and that I had the potential to grow into it. In some ways, I am still trying to fulfill their expectations.

I now see also that, in education, a student needs to have a little faith in the long-term benefits. I am glad that I learned some Spanish and aesthetics, and if I hated economics and trigonometry at the time (and could not stay awake in most of my early morning Shakespeare classes), I am belatedly happy that these subjects were, in a manner of speaking, forced down my craw. I never would have imagined then how interested I have become in things zoological and botanical, after what seemed dismal hours in the laboratory dissecting sharks and frogs, years ago. When does learning and inspiration occur? For some of us, things take an awfully long time to sink in.

I never landed a job because of reading Shakespeare. So what? I never lost a job because of reading him either. Jobs are to education what a washing machine is to water. In a real education, you learn what needs to be done, what you can do about it, and you invent your own jobs.

Graduate school in English was another matter. There, I fought to find time to write fiction, and my strategy was to write a thesis on a subject, if possible, that I would both enjoy and potentially benefit from as a novelist. I chose to work on Laurence Sterne's *Tristram Shandy*, and fortunately was not sidetracked to some other grim subject. This opened the door to years of peripatetic teaching around the Midwest, and if the benefits to my fiction writing seem otherwise dubious, I have to admit that my first published novel was done in the eighteenth-century manner. I had taken a look at the Iowa writing program, meanwhile, and was quickly put off by the people I met there—for reasons which may have been idiosyncratic and a matter of time and place. Years later, after I had tired of being shunted from job to job because I could not receive tenure with an MA, and when I had published a few stories and had a novel in the drawer—and was determined to find out whether I could or could not write well enough to make something of it other than a hobby— I attended the University of Massachusetts' creative writing program. At first, my reasons for choosing this program were Massachusetts' relatively close proximity to New York City (the hive of publishers), two writers I admired on the faculty (Jay Neugeboren and Harvey Swados), and the offer of a flattering fellowship. Whatever this combination of variables—the fact I was ten years older than most students, was free of teaching responsibilities, was in some ways in the midst of a life crisis—this proved a period of intense productivity for me, of very rapid learning, of deep involvement with other writers, of great struggle and satisfaction. I thought the workshops very well handled, and encouraged tact and helpful criticism (as opposed to some of the gut-ripping and amateurish psychologizing I had witnessed at Iowa years before) without ever sacrificing adherence to the highest standards and expectations. The students I met were, over all, highly accomplished (at their young ages, I thought), and the mix contributed as much to my education there as the faculty itself. Most important of all, I want to emphasize, was that the workshops never seemed to me to be threatening places, where personalities clashed or criticism was offered in an aggressive manner. The emphasis was always on the words on the page and a reader's honest response to them. Never, in any instance, did a faculty member conducting a workshop encourage hostile exchanges, but always, when the potential seemed apparent, restored the criticism to the context of what a writer needed to know about improving the work that had been submitted, or to get a better grasp of whether the author's intentions were being realized in the reader's mind. There was no underlying assumption that part of the educational process was to toughen writers toward criticism, but to make them sensitive to good criticism. Similarly, it was not assumed that writers who couldn't stand the critical heat should get out of the creative kitchen. I found this atmosphere and these people invigorating.

In fact, it has been difficult during the ensuing years to maintain the same concentrated level of inquiry and productivity. The rewards, gratifying as they have been, seem comparatively few and far between, and the current state of the publishing industry, I think, frequently encourages a cynical product, so that the thrust of the writing is toward commercial work almost exclusively. Movie money sets the tone and the standards, and corporate concerns overwhelm those of even the most well-meaning editor. These complaints have been voiced so frequently by contemporary writers that they have taken on mythical proportions—even when, for a particular writer in a particular editorial relationship, they may not apply. It is just simply tougher to maintain the belief that writing well matters enough of the time to enough of the people so that they continue the effort. One can always open a video store, I suppose. One can always turn to the formula writing of screenplays. One does not really have to write, after all, for there are millions of ways to fail and succeed in America. One can give up trying to grow and to understand other people and other lives. Yes, one could go readily to sleep and be content with a sleepy culture.

If only we wouldn't dream!

15 Teaching Dialogue

William Holinger
University of Michigan

Why an article on dialogue, for teachers of writing? Although dialogue is a form of prose that is exclusively the province of narrative writing, we seldom teach our students very much about it. We read it in their manuscripts and criticize it, often superficially—but what substantive help do we give students? Or, to put it another way, "What do we, as writers and teachers of writing, know about dialogue and the writing of dialogue?" "How can we pass this along to our students?"

I first became deeply interested in dialogue when I realized that reading good dialogue was one of the great pleasures I got out of stories and novels. When I turn the page of a work of fiction and come upon a page of dialogue, I'm excited. I especially look forward to reading that page.

There's something simple and direct about dialogue. Simple because it's fewer words, less reading—it's condensed narrative. Direct because it's "real": there's no narrator between the action and the reader. Because written dialogue on the page represents an exact report of what happened, we take dialogue as fact, so dialogue carries an authority that straight narrative lacks, no matter how convincing the narrator might be. Yes, I know about untrustworthy narrators, and about voices that can carry a long narrative without dialogue—I know about those other pleasures of fiction. But I am talking about a gut reaction to dialogue, a reaction that's almost unconscious. "Ah, here's the real stuff," a quiet voice in my head says. "Now you're *talking!*"

Dialogue in fiction is a form of written language that is meant to represent spoken language, and is intended to be read silently. Those conditions are unique. Dialogue must appear to be spoken, yet it must satisfy the silent reader. What are the consequences of this? Unlike "real" conversation, which is often focus-less, in-

175

coherent, long-winded, and a syntactical nightmare, written dialogue must be organized and compact. It somehow has to appear spontaneous—"realistic"—and yet accomplish all the other things we ask it to do: entertain (it should be witty, crisp, engaging, clever, lively, and so on); move the plot along (you don't want your characters just standing around discussing the weather); and characterize the speaker (dialogue is a kind of action, and is significant in terms of character). Simple, eh? And we tell our students just to go off somewhere and write?

We also know that dialogue can be either direct (very frank) or indirect (contain veiled meaning). In other words, dialogue sometimes reports exactly what's on a character's mind, and sometimes it reports anything but. It might help students to know this. I'm thinking of the difference between a scene in which one character says to another, "I'm going to tell you something I've never told anyone before," then talks in a very direct and intimate way, and a scene in which all the drama (or conflict) is unstated and operates below the surface (the characters may very well be talking about the weather, but not really). Both sorts of dialogue—the sort that states meaning directly, and the sort that carries its meaning below the surface— have their own tensions, their own pleasures for the reader.

We also know some conventions of good dialogue that all students need to learn at some point. Here are a few:

1. Most speeches of dialogue are very brief—a few words or a couple of sentences—giving dialogue a short, "snappy" quality, with lots of "back and forth" and "give and take" among characters. I suggest to my students an approximate, almost visual yardstick: if a character's speech is over three lines long, it's a monologue—and it better have a purpose.

2. Phrases of saying are crucial, and are almost always problematic for beginning writers. My first creative writing teacher wrote these words on the blackboard: "Phrases of saying do not operate backwards over a full stop." Do you think I knew what he meant? Well, I do now. Among other things it means that in a speech of more than one sentence, the phrase of saying should be placed before, in, or after the first sentence. It's a convention that serves to identify the speaker for the reader as soon as possible.

3. Students might be well advised to keep phrases of saying simple: "he said," "she said." All that these phrases should be relied upon to do is identify the speaker. They should disappear,

and the reader should be practically unaware of them, as with proper punctuation. I've taught students who had previously been given this advice: "Give your phrases of saying variety, and use different verbs and adverbs to convey *how* something is said." (For example, "Get out of my kitchen," he yelled angrily.) This advice is plain wrong. The fancy verbs and modifiers draw attention to themselves and to the author, and away from the dialogue and the characters. Instead, the dialogue itself (including punctuation) should convey the tone of voice of the speaker.

4. You might tell your students that in order to do the kinds of things they may be tempted to do with a phrase of saying, especially in a longer bit of dialogue, they can break up dialogue with description. This is an effective technique because it can keep the reader firmly anchored in the scene, imagining (seeing) the characters as located in a concrete place and time. (For example, "Get out of my kitchen!" His hands kneaded the dishtowel like dough.)

5. See that your students' characters don't constantly refer to the last thing the previous speaker said or asked. In fiction, such overt references sound redundant and slow the pace of the scene, and besides, real conversation doesn't work that way. Students with this problem might be told to listen to real conversation with an ear to how each speaker refers to what the other person says. They'll discover that people sometimes seem to be delivering two unrelated monologues, seldom acknowledging a word the other speaker says; while one person is talking, the other is often thinking of what to say next and doesn't even hear, much less refer to, what was just said.

The preceding conventions of dialogue may seem obvious to the experienced writer, but the experienced teacher knows that every student has to learn these things in his or her own good time. Writing dialogue is often a matter of writing bad dialogue first, then revising it; a great deal of improvement in dialogue can occur late in the process of writing a story or a novel. Which brings me to the matter of the *process* of writing.

My own writing process varies considerably from one project to another. I never write the same way twice; each new story and novel grows differently. Nearly everything about the process of composition varies—perhaps because I and my life change every day, and each writing project is different and original, but who knows? The point is, one can't really talk about "the writing process"; there are infinite processes. A teacher of writing must be open to each individual student's needs, problems, and experience.

Of course, how one writes sometimes determines what one writes, and I've found that the best student writers are conscious of their own writing processes, and that most of them revise heavily. Thus, a few tips for your students about the process of writing dialogue:

1. One way to help students conceptualize what dialogue is and to learn how to write it is to send them out to listen to and record real conversation. Have them write down a conversation word-for-word, or tape one and transcribe it. Their analysis of a written version of spoken conversation will be illuminating. To complete the exercise, have them revise the transcription, making written dialogue out of it. Have them discuss what changes they made.

2. A writer I know said that she often just puts paper in the typewriter and writes down what she hears various voices in her head say. That is, as she writes dialogue the first time, she doesn't necessarily know to whom she will give the lines; she just writes stuff down. Later she ascribes characters to lines of dialogue, depending of course on what is said and how it's said.

3. A scene is an opportunity to get different combinations of characters together and see what sparks fly. That's kind of how I see dialogue: you take two characters (or more) with opposing viewpoints and let them talk to one another. Let them disagree. Just write the lines.

4. I love long monologues (if they're done well), and sometimes I ask a character to tell his/her life story, and then I write it down, as one might take dictation. Usually these extravaganzas don't show up in the final version of what I'm writing, but I learn a great deal about the character by letting him or her ramble along at will, as it were, independent of me.

5. Tell your students: "Read your dialogue aloud. Be sure to forewarn the occupants in the next room. During this reading, editorial opportunities will arise. Avail yourself of them."

6. Read through your manuscript a number of times, reading the dialogue of only one character at a time. Revise for consistency and distinctiveness of each character's voice. In the process,

give each character an idiosyncratic phrase or two in order to achieve more readily identifiable characters, and more characterization too. (Remember Jay Gatsby, old sport?)

7. Cut, cut, cut. Take out words, phrases, sentences. Good dialogue reduces to one-third to two-thirds the length of real conversation. Remember that dialogue in fiction is written to be read silently, so it must be condensed, and move at a fast pace (depending of course on the pace of the overall narrative and the demands of any particular scene).

8. Real dialogue, or conversation, is inductive; however, when we write dialogue, it usually comes out as deductive. (From particular to general = induction; from general to specific = deduction.) Students sometimes have to be told simply to reverse the sentence order of their dialogue. For example, "It was a horrible dinner party. The potatoes were lumpy. The soup was cold. Dinner was delayed for an hour and a half because half the guests were late." This example begins with the conclusion. Let's reverse the sentence order (and do some other minor tinkering): "Half the guests were late, so dinner was delayed two hours. The soup was cold. The potatoes were lumpy." She shuddered. "It was a horrible, horrible dinner party." Better?

So how do you pass all this along to your students? That depends to a large degree upon the level of the class you're teaching, but my general advice to teachers is this: don't get theoretical in the workshop. At least, not at first. I would never want to start off a class with a list of "conventions" to learn and obey. That would be preempting students, and might louse up a promising first draft. Besides, chances are they wouldn't know what you were talking about.

Go ahead and tell students just to go out and write, and then work with their writing. Fiction almost always involves human characters speaking, so there'll be plenty of dialogue in what they write. When you read that dialogue, and it doesn't work for you, you'll know what to tell them. You'll recognize problems, and sometimes you'll know what to tell them. You'll recognize problems, and sometimes you'll even be able to show them a better way. A good deal of teaching writing involves identifying problems and analyzing them; it's not often that we can find a solution that will work for the other writer.

But recognizing the problem and pointing it out—that's going a very long way.

16 Playing within Plays

David Kranes
University of Utah

Act I

Young writers can be ideal playwrights. Their lives are theatre. They are trying out various roles. They wear any number of masks. They dress in a range of costumes. They have remarkably unspoiled "ears" for the recording and playing back of real dialogue. Their world is intensely active and physical. They are closer, in general, to the "music" of their lives—the cadences and rhythms which are so important to the writing of plays.

Writing teachers might alert themselves to students who, while perhaps at times outrageous in creating a theatre of disruptive classroom "scenes," might, nevertheless, possess specific dramatic instincts and gifts. Though such "difficult" sensibilities often upstage lesson plans and call attention to themselves, they may represent personal storm centers; the students' public scenes are probably private as well. Something is usually "at stake" in the theatre of these younger lives, and that something is their unsure and emerging identities as "players." The scenes they throw, the scenes they create, are all pages toward some final scenario that we can only hope illuminates, that is cathartic, for them if not for us. These younger sensibilities are writing and rewriting themselves. They're confused, often by their own scripts. They don't know their own motivation. They're unsure who belongs in their scenes and who doesn't. They tear their pages as they speak them, rushing, without clear exposition, toward vague second and third acts. And we, as well as their parents and peers, are in the audience, reacting—watching, wondering, laughing, feeling tension, becoming anxious, becoming relieved, being saddened, being made glad.

Involving young writers in playwriting can be a way of tapping the behavior they are inescapably *in* and of helping them focus their "scripts," their "roles," their "plots." The experience can do what the best of theatre has always done: by framing and shaping a particular action (or "acting out") the action can be clarified, seen, understood. Thus, the actor's role can become focused. The way in which the actor/writer interacts with the other actors in his or her life can take on greater clarity and purpose.

Thornton Wilder spoke of theatre being an "agreed-upon pretense": we agree to pretend with one another. By pretending, we negotiate. By pretending, we explore. By exploring, we discover. Through discovery, our world grows. It is all play. Plays are play. Thus, we agree to pretend in order that we might explore and imagine and escape and survive in the most full and productive ways. Pretense is only bad when it isn't, finally, acknowledged or agreed upon. We should not "hide behind" pretense. We should not confuse pretense with the "real." "Pretense" is "imagination" embodied. Young writers, brimming with physical energy, may not yet have the patience or quietude necessary for "recollections in tranquility." But nine out of ten will jump at the opportunity to "pretend" actively.

Pretend with them. Become acquainted with the work of Viola Spolin. Use her "theatre games" in your classroom. Observe the contours such "play" takes on in individual students. What do those shapes tell you about the ways in which any of these students take their worlds into themselves, the ways in which they mirror their worlds, the ways in which they express them . . . or don't.

Great playwrights are masters of rendering the ways in which we *don't* talk to one another. They orchestrate the dialogues we have to *cover up*. *Real* communication, *true* communication takes too much, is too exhausting, leaves us feeling too exposed, emptied, vulnerable. More often, the conversations that we hold are conversations of agreed-upon-pretense. My son and I agree (without ever an actual contract) that we will talk about the cat because we both know that we would have a hard time talking about his feelings of tenderness for others or my feelings of love for him. Two twenty-year-olds agree, in the same way, to talk about how much this or that "sucks" because it is a much easier, passing conversation to have than a conversation in which they discuss their feelings of inadequacy.

The young are *masters* at nonconversation. They are extremely alert to all the ritual codes that both they and adults use. Ask your high-school students to write the dialogue between two sixteen-year-olds who *don't* want to talk about the report cards which came out that day. You'll be delighted with the results. "Write a dialogue between two people who both, more than anything, *don't* want to talk about "X." Try it. Or, "Write a dialogue between two people who both, more than anything, *want* to talk about "X" but are afraid to and so they talk *around* it." Have the rest of the class try to guess, in each instance, what the hidden agenda was, the *subtext*: what was it that *wasn't* talked about.

Most plays are progressions of nonconversations that move toward a final, no-longer-avoidable "Truth." Progressively, in most plays, the subtext percolates up until, much like the thermal phenomena in Yellowstone Park, it gushes into the otherwise lit and still air. And it is very possible that young writers, more than mature adults, are much closer, in awareness, to the cutting edges of all the various strategies of avoidance. We adults have embedded them, assimilated and incorporated them. The young are still trying them on—in the same way that they are trying on "cool" or "intellectual" or "rebel" or (perhaps especially) gender roles.

So . . . try the writing of plays with your students. Agree to pretend with them. Let them act out and throw scenes on paper. But be alert, as a member of the audience, to what is fragile and precarious in any of their scenarios, any of their scripts. It can be dangerous stuff. They need to trust you. It can be more dangerous than poetry or prose fiction. Playing a role that one does not feel supported in can be terrifying. Pretending to be cool when one does not feel cool can be very shaky and precarious. Be an appreciative audience member. Remember that what you are watching is always a "play in progress." At best, it's a "rehearsal." If you can help to structure the play or to ground any of the roles in reality, you will have provided an invaluable service.

Act II

Several words, then, about workshops and the "communities of trust" they necessarily assume.

Any writing workshop is, we know, charged with interpersonal dynamics. There is more vulnerability and power in equipoise in writing workshops than in other classrooms. And the creative writing "teacher" is empowered to a distressing degree. Sometimes, wrong people thrive. Other times, better people feel the burden too painfully. Writing workshops are teaching contexts which can almost invite the slipshod. They are also places where being slipshod may do the most personal damage.

Teaching *playwriting*, playing within plays, playing with the play of young imaginations, focuses this delicate "group awareness" aspect more, perhaps, than the overseeing of any other form of writing. If plays are about the power of roles—to mask, to destroy, to create—then probing discussions of roles, of layers of self, are inevitable. Any play seen or read "spotlights" such roles and their mechanisms dramatically before us. The personal interactions in the classroom will echo any number of personal "dramas." Good theatre presents "lies" that are "like truth." Discussions of guises and dissembling, unmasked and naked truths, are inevitable—and thrilling—when handled with proper care and delicacy. Playwriting is not simply talking about "second-act problems." Playwriting and its teaching are intimate; they center on the truths of being human and the fragile balance of personality. There isn't another way into it.

To both *use*, then, and *defuse* the preceding—to protect without ever denying—becomes a principal objective. As instructor in the play of this classroom, you are the messenger. You deliver the news. It's your job. It's your expertise. *When* you deliver it, though—*how* you deliver it—becomes all-important.

Imagine two playwriting workshops. In the first, students are told that their grade rests on a single play which they are to write that term. When they are ready, they should bring the play in and read it. Discussion will follow. If no one has a play on a given day, the writers talk generally about "problems" they're having with their scripts; and the instructor and the other playwrights comment and give suggestions. Prescription is anybody's prerogative. But some pigs, as we've all learned, are more equal than other pigs.

In a second imagined workshop, the instructor uses telling scenes from established plays to make specific dramaturgical points. The instructor may even (giving them independent credit) use actors from the school's acting or drama program to read the scenes. The instructor assigns exercises, three-to-five-page scenes, that are designed to solve problems the students are having with various areas of dramatic construction. At the same time, the instructor encourages in-depth characterization, "real" exploration of "real" people, and discourages vague science fiction and copies of episodic television. Three or four "solutions" to any given dramatic problem are photocopied, distributed, and studied each meeting, and the instructor delights in the number of solutions to a given problem and congratulates the students by describing, specifically, the best moves in any of the exercises. The exercises do not receive letter grades. They are, instead, given specific critiques—ideally, in writing. Often a small degree of on-the-spot rewriting by the student takes place *in* the workshop. The workshopping of *full scripts* takes place in the latter weeks of the term. Scripts are copied and distributed to everyone two days before they are to be discussed. Students write out critiques of all the scripts for their peers and then sign them.

Obviously, the first hypothetical workshop courts failure. Not only is it a one-shot, win-or-lose structure that makes writers maximally vulnerable—least prone to hearing balanced critiques, most liable to be safe, or cute, or sensational, or whatever—it also encourages the ad hoc and provides the least amount of teaching. The initiate has *one* chance to win the guru's approval, which the master will deliver off the cuff and as the mood strikes. The other students, being students, will of course leap onto whatever bandwagon. It's the sort of workshop in which discussion often begins with one of two sentences: "I loved it," or "I hated it." It is a workshop that is built on and proceeds by emotional recklessness and that most likely is reckless in its disregard for how such structures affect a student— not just on an "up day" but over time as well.

The second hypothetical workshop attempts to respect the innate fragility and power of the workshop situation. It proceeds carefully. It attempts to use small, shared (and thus less personally charged) exercises to encourage risk. In doing this, it never shies from pointing specifically to how the various dramaturgical points relate to issues of self. Since *all* the students may be working from the same situation, no one can slip into the presumption that, "Oh . . . this feels autobiographical." Members are responsible for their critiques. They write them down. Authors can call other writers up and ask, "When you said my character contradicted himself, did you mean. . . ?" In short, such a workshop attempts what much of the best theatre does: to nurture and strengthen a community, to attempt the condition of being more than alone.

Act III

What are the specific exercises one might use in shaping a productive workshop of playwrights?

Entertain a definition—*a play embodies the process of someone's attempting to do something*—and then work backwards through the key words: *do, attempting, process, embodies.*

Do. What gets forgotten too often is that plays are (imitations of) *actions.* They are "homecomings" and "revenges" and "last suppers" and "reunions" and "inquisitions" and "dreams" and "journeys." Over the course of a play we see a character *leave* the home he or she has lived in, *blind* himself, finally *embrace* a son, a daughter, a lover. Such actions start toward their completion when the curtain rises, and they resolve just before the curtain falls. These actions, these *doings*, are complex and ritual. Willy Loman *commits suicide.* He is in the process of doing that when the play starts; he completes his action in the final moments. The more a playwright can, almost as second nature, envision a play as an action, the stronger that work will be. In exercises, the instructor should, repeatedly, ask the playwrights to conjure up *actions* and then dialogue them. There are any number of small ritual actions: having a drink, getting ready for supper ("Write the dialogue of two parents and their eighteen-year-old youngster getting ready for dinner"), saying goodbye, cleaning up after a party, packing to go, giving a gift. If a given scene or play were a narrative dance, what might the dance be called? ("Watch two or more of your friends for fifteen minutes. Think of *what they're doing,* not in terms of words but in terms of an *action.* Give the action a *name.*") What is the import of the action? Does it serve to delay, simulate, bond, separate? Does it represent the necessary act of someone who needs something? Is it one of those rituals we perform because we are *afraid to act* out of our deepest needs and convictions? Is it a preparatory ritual, moving us into whatever state we need in order to ultimately *act?* If the protagonist of any play could act only in the arena of self—at whatever moment, seeing and acting upon personal truth—what would that character do? I ask questions here. But each question locates a dramatic issue. And each dramatic issue is a dramaturgical exercise. *Write a scene in which a character DOES something that—more than anything else the character could DO—represents who that character is.*

Attempt. Acts are not simple. Nor are they simply arrived at. We *attempt* to love. We *attempt* to communicate. We *attempt* suicide. We *attempt* to leave home—and then *attempt* to return to it. Wanting to *do* something is not to have it done. The pain and the joy are in the attempting. Tennessee Williams tells us that the human animal was born to struggle. And so we claw our way up the wall, *attempting* to escape. We try to make it through to the morning. We *try* to stop drinking: we struggle, we move forward, we slip back, we fail, we try again, we succeed for a while, we slip, we get desperate, we stop. To *attempt* to *do* something is powerfully, powerfully human.

And the power is considerably proportional to both *what* that something is—its value, its significance—and how *difficult* doing it might be. The "crippled" Laura *attempting* to *dance* with the Gentleman Caller moves us. It is courage embodied. It is a shy, physically impaired girl *trying* to rise above both limitations. The more seemingly impossible the *doing*, the "action," the more powerful its *attempt*.

Process. But even as we watch the *attempt* at *doing*, we are less interested in a one-shot stab than we are in an extended (ritual) *process:* a give and take, an ebb and flow. What culminates in the dance between Laura and the Gentleman Caller begins as a *process* some distance back. Laura refuses to go to the door at Jim's arrival, then goes to the door, then retreats, then goes to the table for dinner, then gets ill and leaves, then finds herself in the room alone with Jim, then moves to a dark corner, then ventures out of the dark corner, then initiates knowledge that they'd known each other in high school, then belittles herself, then takes some pride in herself, then disparages herself, then shares with Jim, then refuses to dance, then thinks about it, then attempts it. We claw up the wall; we slip down it. The act we attempt is unsure. It's not easy. It is a process. Almost always, in compelling plays, the process is dialectical. In a playwriting workshop, students might, then, be given the following assignment: *Write a scene in which character "A" attempts to break a relationship with character "B"—the central condition of such a scene/exercise being: that the attempt be a process.* What sorts of differing ebbs and flows might be found by a workshop of twelve? What are the cliches in the situation? Do we employ mimetic cliches in our attempts to act? What might constitute a "surprising" yet very human moment in such a process?

Embodies. Often, in talking about fiction, the question gets asked, "What does this character want?" It's a central, human question. Thus it becomes important in theatre as well. But then theatre asks, "What does this character *do* to effect what is *wanted?*" Theatre then asks, "How hard does the character *attempt* to do what is *wanted?*" followed by "What is the ritual/*process* of a given character's attempt to do that which he or she wants?" The *drama* is in the uncertainty, the reach and withdrawal, of that process. It's in the attempt being subject to both necessity and freedom. It seems unavoidable that Oedipus will discover his truth. But will he? What if . . . ? Yes, Willy Loman is going to kill himself—no, he isn't—of course, he is. But if Biff is able to show him the truth of . . . no—of course not! it's too late . . . but? . . . No! Even, it seems, in plays of "inevitable acts," where we, on one level, *know* that a dreaded act will ultimately occur, the writer gives us a process toward that act—gives us straws. Every other wave has a straw in it that we can clutch, that we might use to ward off the inevitable. In enactments of the most inevitable of tragedies, the most known and embedded of dramatic myths, audience members have always been known, in the final moments, to have shouted, "No! Don't do it!" toward the stage. Students might be given the following exercise: *Write a scene with no dialogue, in which your character, mimetically, through gesture/action, embodies the attempt to do something. This physicalization should have an ebb and flow to it, a push and pull, a movement toward accomplishing the goal and a retreat from it. Try to create a "rhythm" of this embodied attempt to do.*

A play embodies the process of someone attempting to do something. That person employs masks and pretense along the way. Sometimes the pretense moves the characters closer to their intended action. Sometimes the pretense is what stands in the way. The young writers you teach are living the most acute lives of transition. They are becoming. They are acting toward their futures— sometimes in breaktaking, sometimes in brutal, ways. They are all— in their use of a hundred masks and pretenses—in the process of attempting to *do* a life. They are playing within their own plays. Draw from that. Explore it with them. Be respectful. Be incredibly careful. You may uncover a remarkable play. You may assist an emerging self.

17 Teaching Poetry Writing Workshops for Undergraduates

David St. John
University of Southern California, Los Angeles

In the past ten years I have regularly taught poetry writing workshops for undergraduates. Many of my closest friends are poets who have taught similar workshops for as many as twenty years. From discussions with these friends and from my own experiences with undergraduates, I've come to believe that, though there are no formulas and no fail-safe exercises one might exploit in these classes, there are certain generalities that might be discussed.

As with all kinds of teaching, it is important that the poet who is leading or teaching the workshop be someone clearly engaged with and committed to the subject—in this case, poetry and the writing of poetry. This may seem an especially banal observation, but it is a tremendously important one since poetry workshops establish relationships between the students and the professor/poet that are basically apprenticeship relationships, similar to the situation in studio classes in the visual arts. It is crucial that the students sense their teacher's excitement and involvement not only with their writing but also with his or her *own* writing as well. In addition, it seems to me important that the students understand that their teacher's knowledge and love of poetry and literature includes a wide range of literary periods, not simply that of contemporary poetry.

I cannot emphasize enough the importance of making young writers read. Beginning writers have neither the reading experience nor the life experience to offer much more than the most trite poems about the most conventional subjects. As a teacher, one can't do much to change the equality of the students' life experiences; but one can certainly see to it that they begin to encounter a broad spectrum of poetic voices, voices both modern and contemporary. It is essential, in offering young writers a range of contemporary voices, to allow them to see that our poetry, American poetry, has a strong current of the colloquial in its dictions. Otherwise, the students often feel that it is perfectly all right to write with either an over-blown rhetorical grandeur (which they imagine or have been told is "poetry") or with the sing-song metrics of greeting cards, bad rock songs, and the like. Anyone who has taught even one class of poetry writing has experienced these kinds of poems. Yet, once students have been exposed to the manners and conventions and devices of modern and contemporary poetry, they begin to sense new avenues of response they might follow in dealing with whatever their prevailing subject matter might be—at this point, often episodes of childhood and events concerning their families. And, as they acquire the understanding that seemingly plain and colloquial diction is capable of being as lyrical and musical as a rigidly metrical poem, one can sense in their work a new confidence and conviction, a new immediacy and closeness to the emotions they wish to convey.

I have found it especially useful to encourage my students to acquire familiarity with Yeats, whose intimate, conversational ease and persuasive formal integrity make him a model one can fall back upon for years. A solid foundation in Yeats enables students to make increasingly successful forays into their own personal subject matter without sacrificing a sense of poetry's necessary music and composure. Next, I find Eliot a useful recommendation, though there is a tendency for students who are still beginners to be taken over by Eliot and his tone, which in student hands can become absolutely insufferable. However, Eliot provides students with a sense of scope and ambition that young writers seem to need and toward which they gravitate. Still, as a teacher, one may occasionally be required to yank stiffly on the reins the student has, ambitiously, let go of in his or her excitement. The obvious antidote to the rarity and grandeur inspired by an overconsumption of Eliot is a straight draught of William Carlos Williams, whose particularity is, for many students, positively illuminating. The last of the major twentieth century poets I initially suggest is Wallace Stevens, whose elegant melodies and iambic fluencies hit close to home with many, though certainly not all, young writers. Also, as an influence, Stevens tends to evaporate; that is, one rarely finds a student poem that feels over-bearingly freighted with Stevens's influence, even when the student has been immersed in Stevens's work. Instead, one finds residual melodies and a sense of beauty previously unknown to the student's poems, as students are almost never able to incorporate (that is, steal) those elements of Stevens that make him most unique—the capacity for dense colorations of diction and lyrical abstract figurations.

After I feel a student has absorbed this necessary background, my suggestions in regard to his or her reading take quite different forms. On the one hand, if I feel that a student is progressing well on his or her own, I'll make what seem to be casual recommendations about certain books and poets; however, these recommendations *always* are to read poets and books for which I feel students will have a real affinity, or by which I feel they will be challenged or provoked. The point of *seeming* casual about these secretly pointed suggestions is that this allows students a clearer, and necessary, sense of discovery and self-determination in their work. If, on the other hand, I believe a student is working lackadaisically or without sufficient self-direction, then I will be enormously specific and directive in my suggestions. Perhaps a better word is *prescriptive,* as I view these directive reading assignments as remedies for certain shortcomings in the student's work. The poets used in this fashion will range as widely—and wildly—as Wyatt, Campion, Adrienne Rich, Philip Levine, Donald Justice, and Norman Dubie, to those I may have just happened to read in some current periodicals. Again, I suggest poems that I believe will make a difference to the young writer, poems that will have a bearing upon the work and its growth.

Every class I teach has both a required and a recommended reading list. The titles on these lists vary according to the nature of the course, whether it is a workshop (and at what level) or a readings course, and whether the course concerns itself with a specific period or group of poets. If the course is a workshop course, as I see more and more of any given student's poetry, my suggestions for additional reading will grow more specific. With very beginning students, it is crucial to give them exposure to both traditional, formal models as well as to more conversational, colloquial, and contemporary models. I try to avoid using anthologies except as source books; if a poem in an anthology appeals to a student, I tell him or her to seek out an entire book or two by that poet in order to gain a wider dimension and truer sense of the poet's writing. Anthologies are classroom tools that help students save money; yet I rarely use them. My classes are indeed expensive, as I will often ask the students to buy between six and ten individual titles of poetry. Only when the diversity of work I wish to cover makes this impractical do I resort to anthologies, and then with the greatest reluctance.

I should say here that I don't wish to give the impression that I don't believe in teaching young writers traditional meters and forms. Quite to the contrary, I often teach a course, open to both graduate students and advanced undergraduates, entitled, "Poetic Forms." In this course, I alternate lectures on specific forms with workshops in which we discuss student work written in those forms. For graduate students and the most advanced undergraduates, I feel the course is terrifically successful; for intermediate and beginning undergraduate poets, the course is too difficult. Unless an undergraduate writer is a naturally lyrical young poet with a quite highly developed ear for metrics and for music in language, he or she will be frustrated and constrained—and dictated to—by the forms considered in the course. Let me say that I have had, however, students who were only sophomores do quite brilliantly in the "Poetic Forms" class, but they were the clear exceptions. Though I don't ask my beginning and intermediate writers to write in forms, I do ask them to read poems in traditional forms and meters as a way to help tune their ears to the music in language. As I've said, it is only after I feel that they have a more sophisticated sense of that music in language and a broader experience (by reading) of how English performs, traditionally and in contemporary poetry, that I ask them to begin writing in fixed meters and forms. I do not expect that these young writers will then write *only* in meters and forms; it is simply one more in a series of learning exercises that helps them to acquire a knowledge of craft in the language.

Though inspiration is not something that can be taught, attention to craft and to precision in language is something that can be demanded. It is necessary in working with young writers to allow them to *hear* what they have really said in particular poems, to consider for a moment that, often, what they *thought* they were saying is, in fact, a great deal different from what they have actually said or conveyed in the poems under discussion. One has to encourage young writers to show the *details* of experience to allow an experience to be recreated for the reader. The tendency in beginning writing is either to tell *about* the experience or to ruminate abstractly (and often highly romantically) about an emotional condition. Detail and specificity are the words with which I bludgeon my young poets. I tell them I want to be able to see, hear, smell, taste, and touch the individual elements of any experience in their poems, for it is those elements which will finally make that experience (or emotional state) in a poem seem real and convincing to a reader.

As young poets are helped to recognize the most successful moments in their poems, they are able to begin establishing for themselves criteria of judgment for future poems. Coupled with the growing ability, if they've been reading, to make distinctions about what they admire and would like to emulate in other, more accomplished writers, these young poets are able to forge a real beginning, however tentative, for themselves. They are able, in workshops, to begin to help each other clarify—for themselves and for the group as a whole—what qualities of tone seem unsuitable to certain circumstances or conditions of experience that they wish to speak of in their poems. Slowly, over a period of years, a real poetic identity emerges, a recognizable "voice" arises in the lines of the young writer's poems. It's been my experience that a young writer takes about six years to go from being a serious beginner to becoming a poet with a clear sense of his or her own voice. In those six years, influences are absorbed and rejected, styles are adopted and discarded. Yet finally there is a point at which the young poet begins to feel that the voice of the speaker within the poems at last approximates that voice he or she might wish to call one's own. This is an excruciating, exhilarating accomplishment.

Though I can offer no program and no precise sequence of exercises for helping young poets through their early years of writing, I hope that I've been able to offer a clear sense of my own orientation to the teaching of poetry writing to undergraduates. Because so much of the work with beginning and intermediate poets takes place in conference, in that one-to-one apprenticeship situation, the exact methods one uses are as various as the number of students one sees. Yet, a teacher of young poets should always remember (and continually convey to the students) that a belief in craft is crucial, and that if one never reads, one will never write.

18 Wearing the Shoe on the Other Foot

Mimi Schwartz
Stockton State College

Last year I became a student writer again—and a novice at that. For although I'd been teaching and writing nonfiction for years, both academic articles and feature stories, I had never written much fiction. And although I dabbled in poetry, even had a few poems published once, I never before took a course in poetry writing. Frankly, I didn't have the guts in college—never thought of myself as creative enough to risk such public exposure. The budding confidence I felt in fourth grade when my suspense thriller, "Thunderstorm," was published in a class booklet had been buried under too many years of exposition, both for school and for work. I didn't really recover it until long after graduation, when I received a fellowship that gave me released time from full-time teaching in order to take two creative writing courses at Princeton University: one in fiction writing with Russell Banks, author of the much acclaimed *Continental Drift*; the other in poetry writing, with Pulitzer-Prize winning poet, Carolyn Kizer. These were undergraduate courses incidently, because that's all Princeton offers, so except for three other "older" women (that is, over forty) in the poetry class, the rest of my "peers" were under twenty-two.

It was a remarkable experience—to wear the shoe on the other foot and be a student again. For one thing, I realized how much more I enjoy learning now than I did at twenty, when my future loomed before me like a huge, unmarked field. And how much more focused I am in energy once scattered over a million other concerns. For another thing, I've toughened up over the years. Twenty-five additional years of living and writing have helped me know and risk more, personally and intellectually, than I would ever have dared, even ten years ago. I have more of life to draw upon and more laurels to rest upon, as needed. These assets, I've found, are shared by other over-thirty adults—even if, like many of my returning students, their extra writing experiences are mainly in letter or report writing.

Life experience and writing success notwithstanding, I was surprised at my own vulnerabilities as a writer. Many of my fears, confusions, and needs were not as different as those of my younger counterparts. Remembering "what it was like" as a student writer—and recording in my journal what worked and didn't work for me and for my classmates—has altered my teaching as well as my writing. The experience also provided insight into some unexpected differences between "creative" and expository writing on the college campus. Let me share a few of these differences with you.

First was the astonishing power of response either to encourage or undermine creative risk-taking. There's a myth, which I half-shared, that experienced writers can quickly tell by themselves whether they are producing good work or garbage. This may be true when the territory is familiar and writers feel comfortable with their content and form. But when the material is experimental and new emotionally, intellectually, or schematically, then even seasoned writers can lose their ability to assess the value of their work. The greater the risk-taking, the greater the uncertainty—and the more vulnerable the ego to outside response.

Let me give you an example from my recent experience. Towards the end of the poetry course, I wrote a poem that was emotionally riskier than my others, so I showed it privately to a classmate, who was a seasoned poet and writing teacher for twenty years, rather than submit it for response by the whole workshop:

Elegy for Something or Other

Did you notice something died
around the house last week?
I'm sure of it:
Nothing obvious like goldfish
Or azaleas potted on the porch
Or the old refrigerator fan
Running nonstop for weeks.
So there was no funeral
And no one came to cart it away
But it was something just the same
Though I don't know its name.

You might even see it
In a closet somewhere
Or tucked in some old album,
But it's definitely not moving
So it's okay to touch it

> If that's what you're afraid of.
> You might even feel it
> Warm your morning cheek
> Or curl in your lap on cold nights,
> But it won't wrap around you
> Like a cloak you can wear forever
> Once the fire dies.

She said, "I don't know what this is about. It doesn't grab me," and went on to another poem, more quickly than she had in the past. I thought to myself "God, she's right! This is terrible," and groaned when I remembered that it was included in the portfolio I gave Carolyn Kizer, to be discussed in conference the next day. That night I was up at three a.m., figuring out how to cancel the conference, or at least how to sneak the poem out of the folder. But—good student that I am—I did neither and showed up, my stomach churning, in her office at nine a.m. The first thing she said was, "I like the informal tone of the poem; it's new for you—and it works." She pointed out some weak spots, recommended some changes, but thought the poem was promising. She even suggested that I try publishing a few poems. Naturally I left the office ecstatic, and with an entirely different self-image than when I went in. Suddenly I could write poetry again, and I was fired up to revise rather than burn it, as I had intended when I walked in.

The experience taught me several things about the nature of response. First, it made me realize its potency and its potential danger, especially when the writer feels insecure, which is the way most student writers feel—for most readers, even skilled ones, react only to what's on the page. Very few, like Carolyn Kizer and Russell Banks, can read what isn't there yet, that ideal, yet-to-be-named text which, to use Kizer's own metaphor, is still being born. At a "Conversation with Women Writers," held at Princeton University, she said, "I imagine poems as already existing whole inside me if I can find them and bring them out intact." She was talking about her own writing and revision, but the metaphor also explains her response to others, which is constructive, positive, and careful not to "damage the goods," so to speak, in delivery. She presents revision as the search for what's elusive, but out there somewhere, so it can be found, even if it's not yet on the page. Her attitude fosters optimism rather than depression in her students—that eventually, if you keep at it over time, the answers come, if not in one poem then in the next.

If I was feeling "Holier than thou" about my classmate's response—"you can do better than that"—it ended the next day in Russell Bank's fiction writing workshop. As always, we were to discuss three student stories that we all had picked up and read the night before. One, in particular, called "My Laundry Prostitute," seemed silly and sophomoric to me. Its premise—the woman who leans against washers and dryers selling her services to male customers (wash $5.00, starch a buck extra)—was clever for a few pages, but didn't go anywhere. Before anyone could speak, however, Banks said he loved it, thought it was the "most imaginative piece" this writer had done so far, and that if the second half were changed, he'd have a really "terrific piece." That night, I wrote in my journal:

> I was floored by Banks' reaction, realized that I missed the power of Steve's satire completely and thought it was just dumb. But then I'm not a big Monty Python fan or Saturday Night Live fan either. It shows how careful you need to be when reading outside of one's tastes. If this were my student, I would have given him bad feedback because of my preference for more emotionally serious work.

Banks, like Kizer, was viewing this work in a larger context, responding to more than what was just on the page. He was projecting what the story could be in terms of the writer's intention—independent of whether it pleased his personal tastes or not. And he was seeing this work on a continuum, not as an isolated piece of writing. Compared to earlier pieces, the writer was taking imaginative risks and Banks wanted to praise the effort more than he wanted to dwell on the problems.

Both Kizer and Banks valued inventiveness and experimentation more than safe, take-no-chances texts. And they looked for growth more than polish. That was evident not only from their comments—which praised risk-taking and criticized blandness, pretentiousness, and predictability—but also from the course structures as well. Unlike most expository writing courses, individual writings received no grades, only suggestions for revisions, which were expected on at least two pieces by the end of the term. Final grades were based on the whole body of work and the quality of revision. I wonder if it isn't this philosophy and structure, even more than genre, that distinguishes "creative" writing courses from other writing courses—for if my poems or stories were individually graded, even though, as a faculty member, these grades meant nothing, my imagination would have gone into a straight jacket, I'm sure of it. I would have given myself less permission to risk what might fail.

A second big surprise was the power of form to stimulate or inhibit creativity, depending on the circumstances. I have always been leery of assignments that stress form over meaning in my classroom. Too many essays fail, it seems to me, because form does not follow function, as Frank Lloyd Wright advises. The choice of short, simple sentences to avoid the danger of run-ons, and the lifeless, five-paragraph themes that give up voice to insert a thesis statement are by-products of what happens when the desire to follow rules over-powers natural expression.

As a nonfiction writer, this rarely happens to me anymore because I have internalized most of the forms. But as a novice fiction writer, unsure of the conventions, I experienced all the old pressures about "doing it right." I worried about whether I was writing dialogue correctly, which tense to tell my story in, how to move back and forth in time and point of view. The opening paragraph of one story, which you see in the following drafts, represents hours of anguish over the issue of tense. Like my ESL writers, I didn't *automatically* know when to use past, present, or a combination of the two. As you can see, I put the dream in past tense, the conversation with mother in present tense; but I became confused at the point when the speaker wakes up. Was the correct verb "rang" as in the dream, or "rings," as in the narrative that begins once she is awake?

I. Early Draft

> He appeared again last night . . . right at the edge of the pine forest; and I called him to wait, to come back. But I knew he wouldn't, that as soon as I made one move, let alone started running across the big lawn to reach him, he'd be gone again, into the woods like the last time. So I just stood there, frozen, for what seemed like hours, until the phone rang [or is it rings?], thank God, and my mother wakes me up for the third time this month. "Whatever happened to Valentine?" I ask her, once I figure out where I am and who is telling me that she can meet in town for lunch today. . . ."

My solution was this second version, a hopeless mix up of past and present, using a logic I have already forgotten. The back-and-forth tense shifting—"appeared," "call," "knew," "make," "start," "he'd," "stood," and so on—reflects my dilemma:

II. Middle Draft

> He appeared again last night . . . right at the edge of the pine

forest; and I call him to wait, to come back. But I knew he
wouldn't, that as soon as I make one move, let alone start running across the big lawn to reach him, he'd be gone again, into
the woods like the last time. So I just stood there, frozen, for
what seemed like hours, until the phone rings, thank God, and
my mother wakes me up for the third time this month. . . .

Finally I wrote the third version all in the present tense—to play it
safe, I even dropped the word "last" in "last night," in case that implied a past tense:

III. Later Draft

He appears again at night . . . right at the edge of the pine forest; and I call him to wait, to come back. But I know he won't,
that as soon as I make one move, let alone start running across
the big lawn to reach him, he'll be gone again, into the woods
like the last time. So I just stand there, frozen, for what seems
like hours, until the phone rings, thank God, and my mother
wakes me up for the third time this month. . . .

Like my students who shorten sentences in fear of run-ons, my
concern for correct form was making me simplify my expression and
use up an enormous amount of creative energy in the process. I
have more compassion now. What surprised me even more than
how form can undermine meaning, however, was how form can
also be a heuristic for meaning. One exercise, in particular, assigned
in Kizer's workshop, made this clear to me.

We were given a lyrical, four-stanza poem by Antonia Muchado
in which repetition of both full lines and half-phrases is a dominant
motif. To give you a sense of Muchado's rhythms, the first stanza is:

Your eyes remind me
of summer nights,
black nights that are moonless,
against the shores of the sea,
and the stars sparkling
in the low black sky.
Your eyes remind me
of summer nights.
And your dark flesh,
the sunburnt wheat,
and the fiery breath
of the ripened fields.

Our task was to imitate this poem by writing a four-stanza poem,
using couplets twice in each stanza and repeating half-phrases, too.
Everyone moaned and groaned, including me. This was not my
style: I never wrote lines like "and your dark flesh / the sunburnt

wheat / ." I didn't like repetition; this was just an empty exercise for the teacher; I couldn't possibly do it.

But again, as the good student, I tried . . . and with some interesting results. For the first time, I wrote on a new topic for me, one more political than domestic like my other poems. I also learned something about repetition. In prose writing, a strong rhetorical value of mine has always been "Don't be repetitive; cut the excess." Trained on Strunk and White, I automatically revise lines like "I went to the sea last week. . . . At the sea, I swam" into "I went to the sea last week and swam." But I realized that I was overdoing it. This exercise made me hear myself using a new voice that does repeat, and I liked the sound.

Other students also wrote on new topics and in new voices, not used before. Following are two examples of what happened. The first writer, who had consistently written ironic, hard-edged, prose poems such as,

> The therapist is watching her
> Sitting stiffly on his couch.
> The client is watching what he implies.
> This is not easy as behind her eyes in the
> darkened auditorium, there is a ring set up,
> Tiny, as if seen at a distance, complete with
> Ropes and mats and an overhead microphone.
> Gesticulating men adjust lights . . .

found a warm, nurturing, lyrical side to herself by doing the exercise:

> Your whinny reminds me
> Of the time of day,
> Time to throw down hay,
> Sweet-smelling of dried grass
> And the summer sun.
> And the rinsing rain.
> Your whinny reminds me
> Of the time of day,
> Time to measure out
> The gold corn,
> And the firm oats,
> And the dark molasses. . . .

The second writer, who had been writing detached, life-at-school poems, such as this opening stanza,

> The members of the Princeton University Band
> all have fun
> because they are there

for nothing and no one but themselves. . .

wrote a passionate poem about growing up in Iran with a stanza like this:

> . . . I was fifteen, a soldier,
> a thousand others like me
> were going to die;
> they bent low to kiss the Qu-uran.
> They were content, they were fifteen
> and destined for Heaven,
> they were doing Right
> they were doing Good—
> except for me, I knew it was a lie,
> I knew it was a dream:
> they were going to die for nothing.
> I was fifteen, a soldier,
> I bent low to kiss the Qu'uran. . . .

What's important here, I think, is not the success of these poems (many failed) or how well they followed the rules (many did not) but that the exercise pushed people beyond the comfortable limits of their composing patterns and themes. The new rhythms led writers into new expression they hadn't tried before. As I wrote in my journal, "It's like copying a Rembrandt in the museum or acting in different roles. You find something new in yourself by putting on someone else's shoes and walking around in them for awhile."

Not every form-based assignment does this, however, as we well know. What made this one stimulate rather than stifle creativity are three factors in particular. First, it was one of three, all semester. The rest of the time we were on our own; so, unlike the format of most expository writing courses, we had plenty of opportunity to develop our own forms out of our own themes. A few exercises, now and then, didn't interfere with this generally free framework. Second, the assigned structure had flexibility. Unlike the villanelle, which has a complex, precise formula for repetition, this assignment was open-ended: "repeat couplet anywhere and use some half-phrases" is very different from "repeat the first and third lines of an opening tercet alternately in a fixed pattern that must end together as the last two lines of the quatrain!" Third, we shared the results out loud, ungraded, so that everyone could see how others dealt with the task at hand and hear the new voices that emerged. And it was the new rhythms, not how well rules were followed, that were important.

Another surprise involved the beneficial effect that writing "literature" had on my reading of literature. Writing fiction and poetry has made me a more careful and appreciative reader. I study the craft far more than before, to see how others have solved my problems. I read Flannery O'Connor's "A Good Man's Hard to Find," for example, with a vested interest because one of *my* characters, like the ones in these stories, was a dangerous stranger on the road. I marveled at Gail Godwin's "A Sorrowful Woman," which succeeded as a contemporary fable, a genre I'd been trying unsuccessfully to write for months. And I envied Raymond Carver's economy of words, which had so much power in so few lines.

Writing "literature" also made me feel empowered as a reader. Instead of just liking or disliking a text, I began considering the options the writer chose to take or not to take. Did I agree with them? For example, when I read Gogol's "The Overcoat," I wondered not only what the ending meant but whether it worked. Was there another one I would have liked better? I felt less docile, more like an active partner in the text.

I've introduced this kind of reader response—that even published texts are not engraved in gold—into my own classes this year. We recently read Roger Rosenblatt's *Witness,* which has a lengthy digression near the end of one essay. Instead of asking, "What is the purpose of this digression?" I asked, "If Rosenblatt were in your writing group, would you advise him to leave this section in or take it out?" The consensus was, "leave it in!" and the reasons were far more insightful than if I had assumed a priori that the digression was good, and they had better figure out why.

One final surprise was the impact of fiction and poetry writing on my writing in general. Writing in one role definitely influenced my expression in other roles. Several poems became more conversational, with longer line lengths, as a result of the fiction writing. A few stories, on the other hand, became more lyrical, with richer imagery, as a result of writing poetry. Some of these innovations worked, some not; but either way, using new forms, experimenting with new genres, expanded my repertoire and confidence for expression; I took more risks, tried out more new options—both consciously and intuitively—than I had in years.

Even my nonfiction writing was affected. This paper, for example, is far more experimental than other academic articles that I've written over the years. Russell Banks' advice—that "you have to be willing to give up your initial ideas once the story takes on its own momentum"—seemed to carry over from short story to essay. I abandoned my initial plan after the first paragraph and let ideas from nine months of journal keeping take unexpected, yet pleasing, turns that were less traditional in presentation than I had anticipated.

I also found myself trying for a more individualistic, less generic voice than in most academic essays that I had read or had written. This need to challenge existing conventions—in this case, to be original yet still be accepted by one's readership—is the challenge that makes writing a "creative" act. It is recognized as essential in poetry and fiction writing, but too often, in academic discourse, this challenge is not valued enough. We are more focused on adhering to conventions than with pushing beyond them.

In conclusion, let me say that I wish I *had* taken these "creative writing" courses when I was twenty and in college. For what I gained from them—in addition to the time, encouragement, and craft of two master teachers and writers—are attitudes and skills that extend beyond poetry and fiction writing. To value self-investment, to avoid premature closure, to see revision as discovery, to go beyond the predictable, to risk experimentation, and, above all, to trust your own creative powers are necessary for all good writing, whether it is a freshman theme, a poem, a term paper, or a CCCC paper. Yet, in academic writing, except perhaps for the dissertation, these are not integral to the pedagogy. Few of us reward risk-taking that fails with a better grade than polished but pedestrian texts. We are more product-oriented, judging assignments as independent of one another rather than as part of a collective and ongoing body of work. No wonder that students interpret our message as "Be careful, not creative!"

It was only after graduation—partly by getting published, partly by a supportive writing group—that I gradually unlearned this message and developed some confidence in my own creative powers. I began to invest more in my writing, revise with more energy and patience, and be more optimistic during the chaos of composing that things would eventually come together. But I wish that had happened earlier—through school writing experiences that let me try out new voices and new forms which pushed me into new creative territory *and* made me feel I could handle it! We need more such opportunities in college—and not just in poetry and fiction writing workshops which many lack the time and courage to take. Composition courses, too, need to value originality, foster experimentation without fear of failure, and teach revision as an act of discovery, if we are to develop writers who believe, as Ann Berthoff does, that "all writing is creative," and have the attitudes and creative confidence to try for it.

III Editing and Publishing

A young author is tempted to leave anything he has written through fear of not having enough to say if he goes cutting out too freely. But it is easier to be long than short. . . . Think of and look at your work as though it were done by your enemy. If you look at it to admire it you are lost. . . . If we look at it to see where it is wrong, we shall see this and make it righter. If we look at it to see where it is right, we shall see this and not make it righter. . . . I always intend to read, and generally do read, what I write aloud to some one. . . . I feel weak places at once when I read aloud. . . .

—Samuel Butler

19 "Midwifing the Craft"— Teaching Revision and Editing

Alan Ziegler
Columbia University

Teaching writing is what you say to get students to write something authentic and interesting, and then what you say to get them to make it better. This chapter concentrates on the latter. Gertrude Stein said that "remarks are not literature." Maybe so, but remarks by teachers and editors help literature come into being. I will discuss the types of literary feedback, the roles of editors in publishing, the dynamics of feedback, and how the editing process can be applied to a creative writing program through the use of peer editors and the development of a course in literary editing.

The word *editing* often has a different definition in academic circles than it does in the publishing world. For example, in *The Confident Writer*, Constance J. Gefuert writes that "when you edit, you consider the surface features of writing –grammar, usage, spelling, and mechanics," and states that editing "should almost always come last" (1988, 17). But for publishing writers, this definition stands for a subdivision of editing called "copyediting."

"Editing," in the larger sense, refers to a variety of means by which one or more colleagues help to make a piece of writing as good as it can be; the editing process can begin before a word is written, and end with the final set of galleys. Editors can help writers to conceive, shape, and revise their work. One wouldn't call legendary editor Maxwell Perkins a "great corrector."

The Types of Literary Feedback

Literary feedback can be classified as reactive, descriptive, prescriptive, and collaborative. These categories overlap, and usually an

Brief portions of this chapter appeared, in different form, in "Editing: in Teaching and Writing," a special issue of *Teachers & Writers*, March/April 1986: 1–11, edited by Alan Ziegler.

editor or teacher will respond to a piece of writing with more than one type.

In *reactive* feedback, one gives only a general, unsubstantiated response: "This paragraph is great"; "I have some trouble with the dialogue." William Maxwell's novel *The Folded Leaf* started as a short story, which he showed to Louise Bogan, who suggested he expand it into a novel. He sent it to her chapter by chapter, "and she never said enough is enough. From time to time I got a penny postcard from her with 'v. good' or something like that on it" (1988, 64). Sometimes writers don't need *more* than this, but they do *need this*. Sometimes a negative reactive comment is helpful. Kurt Vonnegut wrote "reads junky" next to a paragraph in one of my stories. It did, and I did something about it.

Such comments as "This is terrific" or "This doesn't work" can be starting points for discussing why and how something is terrific or doesn't work. Sometimes, after a work is read in class, I ask every student to say *something*, even it it's just how the piece made them feel. This often evokes general comments that might not have been presented otherwise, and which suggest topics for discussion. It also gets everyone involved.

Not all reactive comments are received equally. I asked a class, "What's the worst thing anyone can say about your writing?" One student replied "Nice," and several students agreed. I've tried to rehabilitate the word, using it as an adjective followed by an exclamation point, as in, "Nice image!" Another word that can leave a writer cold is *interesting*, but I value any writing that maintains my interest. Like *nice*, I'm trying to enable *interesting* to lead a helpful editorial life. Reactive words I will continue to exile are *trite, sentimental,* and *cute*.

Reactive comments may be especially appropriate for surrealistic and experimental writings, which often either elude traditional criticisms or wilt when subjected to line-by-line scrutiny.

Descriptive feedback goes a step further and describes what the writer is doing, positively or negatively—"I can't figure out when the flashbacks are taking place, and the dialogue is too convoluted." It's up to the writer to figure out what to do about it. One of Louise Bogan's postcards to William Maxwell "objected to a physical description, on the ground that the writing wasn't very fresh, so I sweated over it" (Maxwell 1988, 64). Maxwell Perkins, in responding to a draft of Marcia Davenport's novel *East Side, West Side,* wrote to the author, "I do have some fear that the murder runs too far toward melodrama . . ." (Wheelock 1987, 293).

Prescriptive feedback offers concrete suggestions for change. In addition to the descriptive comment, "You have too many characters," you might add, "Get rid of the cousin and combine the two brothers into one character." If you feel a piece is overwritten, you might suggest specific words and sentences to be deleted.

Prescriptive feedback also includes suggestions for minor additions. In one story a student wrote, "I tried to stop him," and I suggested that the author show *how* he tried to stop him—with gestures, words, violence? In another story, the protagonist goes into a cold shower and emerges an hour later in the next sentence. I told the author that an hour in a cold shower might be worth a few lines of narration. I thought it was a problem in a student's play scene that a character just happens to drop by before eight a.m. and mediates an argument. I suggested that the character be a house guest who's been woken up by the argument.

Prescriptive feedback can be structural. An early draft of Mary Gordon's *Final Payments* was written in third person, and Elizabeth Hardwick suggested that she change it to first person (Evans 1985, 106). According to David Sacks (1987), editor Jonathan Galassi suggested to Scott Turow that he break down one early chapter of *Presumed Innocent* and distribute its material elsewhere, which speeded up the pace of the book (23).

Some prescriptive comments border on collaboration. I define *collaborative* feedback as occurring when editors or teachers actually contribute words to a text, often by rewriting sentences, or suggest substantive additions. Teachers and editors stick their heads into stories and say, "This is what I would do if I were you." Sometimes, a collaborative suggestion is more a reflection of the teacher's artistic sensibility than the student's, in which case you should say, "This is what you would do if *you* were *me*."

In editing *Final Payments,* Anne Freedgood suggested a scene in which the protagonist deals with birth control, and Gordon wrote Isabel's visit to a gynecologist (Evans 1985, 103–4). For *East Side, West Side,* Perkins suggested that Davenport put an orchestra on the Staten Island ferry to play "some old-time song" for Jessie and Mark (Wheelock 1987, 289). In the published novel, an accordion player performs a "wheezy" sounding "The Sidewalks of New York." William Maxwell got stuck while writing *The Folded Leaf,* and Louise Bogan sent him a collaborative postcard: "Get that boy up off the bed on the sleeping porch" (Maxwell 1988, 64).

As with other suggestions, collaborative feedback should be on a take-it-or-leave-it basis. *New Yorker* editor Harold Ross contributed the words *bucks* and the second *softly* in "softly, softly" to John Cheever's story, "The Enormous Radio," but Cheever rejected many other suggestions (Cheever 1981, 125).

One of my students wondered if she could "take credit" for a poem that had been vastly improved as a result of the workshop, and I replied that professional writers do it all the time. Ezra Pound's name doesn't appear on "The Waste Land." I've heard of writers who erase their editors' comments so there will be no trace of someone else's input. This might not have bothered Maxwell Perkins, who told his wife that he saw his role as "a little dwarf on the shoulder of a great general advising him what to do and what not to do, without anyone's noticing" (Berg 1979, 154).

Sometimes editors and teachers get "responder's block" so it is helpful to realize you have these four options. If you're not able to tell someone how to fix something, perhaps you can point out what's wrong; if you can't even pinpoint the problem, just referring to the troubled area can be helpful. The author might say, "What I was trying to do here was. . . ." and the ensuing dialogue can result in a solution. Pedagogical concerns might suggest the type of feedback you give a student at a specific time.

Perhaps there should be a fifth category—no feedback. Sometimes a writer merely needs to hear how the work sounds when read aloud. John Steinbeck tried out material on his dogs. (He said Angel sat and listened, but he felt that Charley "was just waiting to get a word in edgewise," and a "red setter chewed up the manuscript of *Of Mice and Men*" [1977, 20]). You can designate a "reading day" in a workshop when students can try out new work without any responses, although some informal feedback may occur, perhaps after class.

Providing good feedback means knowing when to *discourage* revision. Writers sometimes delete a wonderful line or tinker until they tinker the life out of a piece. And sometimes the best feedback is just to convince a writer ⊙ keep going; Nabokov's wife talked him out of putting the first chapters of *Lolita* into the garden incinerator (1977, 105).

Feedback can also help a writer avoid logical or factual errors. Isak Dinesen received such assistance while dictating *The Angelic Avengers*: "I'd start one day by saying, 'Then Mr. So-and-so entered the room,' and the stenographer would cry out, 'Oh dear, but he can't! He died yesterday in Chapter Seventeen'" (1977, 7). Even Jack Keruoac, hardly one who delighted in being edited, appreciated the discovery of "logical errors, such as dates, names of places" (1977, 363–64).

The Roles of Editors in Publishing

Good editing requires an amalgam of acquired skills and cultivated talents. Most published works are scrutinized by line editors and copyeditors. The larger editorial questions are generally dealt with first, followed by the more specific ones.

The editing process can be examined in the same way we've learned to examine the writing process—by listening to what editors say about what they do. A line editor might begin, especially for a full-length work, with what Kathleen Anderson—of Poseiden Press, a division of Simon and Schuster—calls a "conceptual edit" (1986, 7) and make suggestions involving pacing, characterization, general use of language, or scenes to be written. Conceptual edits are followed by—or, for individual stories and poems, often combined with—line-by-line editing. The line edit may involve executing strategies determined in the conceptual edit.

Gerald Gross's valuable book *Editors on Editing* is subtitled "An Inside View of What Editors Really Do." In the chapter on line editing, written by Nancy Evans, several line editors discuss their jobs. Anne Freedgood says that she looks for soft places in a manuscript and makes such comments as, "I'm not convinced here." "I don't see how you got from here to there." "What are you trying to say in this paragraph?" "The order here is confusing." "Are you sure you shouldn't introduce this factor before that factor?" "This is where you lost me." "This is where I got bored." "This, I think, you've already covered" (Evans 1985, 103).

James D. Landis looks for loose ends, noting, "That's one thing writers like most, the editing of loose ends." Marian S. Wood thinks a good line editor answers the question "What's wrong?" with such specifics as, "This character is flat. . . . This one doesn't make sense." "You lose your tension here." "There are too many peripheral characters early on." "I don't understand the point of this part of the plot." "I think you may be repeating yourself here" (Evans 1985, 110).

Pat Strachan states that "the function of editing is to discover what the writer is trying to do" (Evans 1988, 112), a sentiment echoed by many other editors. Next, Strachan says, "you try to help him or her to do it a little bit better—in the book as a whole and sentence by sentence" (112). Strachan believes that "an inexperienced writer's main faults are overwriting and overexplaining" (113), an opinion shared by many creative writing teachers.

After line editing comes copyediting, where attention is focused
on the mechanics of grammar, usage, punctuation, and spelling. A
good copyeditor paves the way so that the reader will not be offended by misspelling and grammatical errors or stumble on clut-
tered syntax and poorly placed punctuation.

In *Editors on Editing,* William Bridgwater defines copyediting as
"basically the mechanical marking of a manuscript so that it is in literal and literary form ready to go to a printer" (Evans 1985, 69).
Bridgwater cautions that "if the task sounds easy, you do not understand it" (69). Copyeditors must know accepted usages, but weigh
them against the author's literary style. Bridgwater points out that
"unusual" employment of punctuation "has a long and honorable
tradition. Punctuation is part of the text . . ." (79).

Changes that the copyeditor feels must be made can go right on
the text; other suggestions can be put in the margins or on "Post-it"
notes. Sometimes a copyeditor will tighten or otherwise revise a
sentence and augment the proposed change with a comment such
as "au [Author]: Change OK?"

Line editing and copyediting can be seen in the context of the
writing process as described by Donald Murray, who denotes *internal revision* as "everything writers do to discover and develop
what they have to say, beginning with the reading of a completed
first draft" (Murray 1978, 91); and *external revision* as the stage where
writers "pay attention to the conventions of form and language, mechanics, and style" (91). The line editor participates in the internal
revision stage, and the copyeditor is involved with external revision.
The key ingredient to making the editing process work is for the author, who has often finished with external revision when the editor
steps in, to be willing and able to reopen the process.

The main distinction between feedback in the editing process and
in the writing process is that, in an editing session, the piece is of primary concern, and in the workshop, the growth of the student is
most important. Teacher/writer Richard Ploetz says, "With young
writers I'm not judging potential masterpieces, I'm midwifing the
craft."

The Dynamics of Feedback

It can be disconcerting to think of the thousands of comments I have
made to writers—as teacher, editor, or friend—without knowing
their long-term effects, both beneficial and detrimental. I can vividly

remember isolated remarks made to me that have helped and hindered my own growth as a writer; those who made the comments may barely remember *me*, much less what they said to me.

One of the editors of my college literary magazine doesn't know that, when he dismissed my e. e. cummings-influenced poem by saying "I don't like word games," I stopped writing poetry for two years. When I started again, in my senior year, I mustered the courage to show my spare, heartfelt poems to a young member of the English department. A dismissal by him might have broken me as a poet. But he told me how much he liked the poems, that they were "good."

I was halfway out the door when he added, "I don't want you to misunderstand. These poems are not *good*. Not by critical standards. But I sense in them that you can be a good poet. I can feel it." That was the most important comment someone ever made about my work. Without it, I might have continued to jot things down occasionally, believing I was writing good poetry. Or I might have disregarded his critique, thinking, "He was just being nice." Instead, I left feeling slightly discouraged that I hadn't emerged from my shell as a full-blown poet, but excited about my potential if I kept at it.

Similarly, a novelist told me that a pivotal comment for her was a teacher's praising the dark strain in her work, which was something she had felt unsure about. A remark like "How depressing" might have stifled her.

Some teachers and editors have a set style of feedback —be it combative and prescriptive or gentle and descriptive—varying slightly from student to student. Others are more like the therapist who told me that rather than being a Freudian or a Jungian, when he was with a patient named Smith he was a Smithian, and other times he was a Jonesian or Schwartzian.

Most students can best be helped when flaws are pointed out within a positive and self-deferential context. Note how poet Louis Zukofsky phrased his criticisms of poems by William Carlos Williams:

> Here y'are! Don't accept the detailed criticism in the manuscript unless it verifies your own misgivings, doubts, etc. I've written on the ms. lightly so it can be erased and you can still use the copy. The verse is excellent. But I think it would gain if the ideas it presents were not frequently repetitious. There is some of your finest writing here embedded in a discursive form which still doesn't form a setting. (Baldwin 1979, 135–39)

When criticizing a problem in a manuscript, if possible I point to a place where the author did the same thing well: "You're vague here, but in this paragraph you have a wonderful detail." This acts both as an illustration of the criticism and proof that the student is capable of responding to it.

Students have to determine the right step in the writing process at which to bring in a piece to workshop. Richard Ploetz says that, for him, exposing an early draft can "spoil it and I want to put it away for a long time." For another student, bringing in a mature draft might mean that the story has become frozen and the author resistant to change.

Waiting a week or so after last touching a story may enable the author to be more open to suggestions. After an exhausting bout with a story, authors may feel that this is the best they can do and become discouraged at even the slightest hint that it's not enough. A student told me she once showed a friend a story she'd just put everything into. Her friend said, "It's good but it needs tightening," a favorable evaluation that had the effect of a knockout punch. Writers learn that the most recent draft usually isn't the ultimate draft; stories can be improved upon.

Inexperienced writers can monitor and become familiar with their reactions. I used to find that my initial reaction to criticism was often to be closed and petulant; after cooling down, I'd implement some or all of the suggestions. Even now, as someone comments on my work, I sometimes feel myself regressing. But I am able to be civil and file away the suggestions for use when I grow up again.

Sometimes a student shows me a freshly-written piece and I can sense that the student won't tolerate feedback well at that moment, perhaps because he or she seems excited by how well the piece turned out or is emotionally caught up in the material. I might read through it quickly and say, "I like this; next week I'll have some specific thoughts about it."

Students should consider all manuscripts brought to class as "works in progress," and realize that valid criticisms provide opportunities to make the piece better, and this is what they're paying for. (If a piece feels particularly inchoate to the author, it may help to label the manuscript as a "working draft.") Reactions should be in the spirit of "This is what you can do next," not "This is what you did wrong."

Sometimes, no matter how much criticism a piece receives, and how many drafts it goes through, it remains less than a great success. New writers, particularly, should perceive these experiences as part of the growing process, rather than as final judgments ("This is how good I am and will ever be").

Pain is often a by-product of the feedback process. John Berryman didn't read reviews until he was thirty-five because ". . . I had no skin on. . . . I was afraid of being killed by some remark" (1977, 297). I've been surprised by students who, after what I'd thought was an invigorating, helpful, and encouraging session, told me they felt discouraged by the class.

Maybe the Army has the right idea: writing students can go through a workshop boot camp featuring literary skin-toughening exercises, where each writer looks his or her neighbor in the eye and chants, "This has potential but it needs work! Needs tightening! More details! Doesn't work for me!" For the ultimate survival exercise, the recruits could read what they think is the best piece they've ever written, and have it be met by silence, paper shuffling, furtive looks at watches, and finally the comment, "It's easy to read; what kind of printer do you have?"

We have to accept that there will always be injuries caused by critical shrapnel lodging in authors' egos. The least we can do is keep in touch with our students about how they are reacting, perhaps by having them keep journals and by occasionally devoting class and conference time to discussing reactions to feedback.

In addition to knowing how to respond to a writer's work, one must also know how *much* to say. Feedback can be compared to time-release pills: if all the medication goes into the bloodstream at once, the cure can be worse than the disease. A teacher/editor needs to consider how large and frequent the dosages of criticism should be.

It's the same in other art forms. George Balanchine, commenting on how he responds to dancers, said:

> If it's a young person I let her do it the first time. I don't tell her everything—it's impossible to do that. I'll say, 'If you do a little bit more turnout, then let's see what will happen.' So next time she'll turn out a little more, and I say, 'Now you're looking very good, but that's not everything. Why don't you look straight and go this way instead of that way?' That's what we do. We don't talk about beauty or 'Serenade,' you know. (1983, 71)

Not all feedback is appreciated. Hemingway, on a letter from Fitzgerald full of suggestions for *A Farewell to Arms*, wrote, "Kiss my Ass EH" (Bruccoli 1978, 83). And legend has it that on a Robert Benchley manuscript, *New Yorker* editor Harold Ross wrote, "Who he?", next to a mention of Andromache, below which Benchley wrote, "You keep out of this."

A writing teacher's schedule sounds pretty good—if you only count the time in class. But far more time is spent reading and commenting on student papers. Making notations on manuscripts is a form of writing that is rarely discussed. I find myself being influenced by my editors and teachers, and by such examples as the Zukofsky comments I quoted and the letters of Maxwell Perkins. Writers grow by reading, yet rarely do we read the comments written by other teachers on students' creative writing. I asked a few of my colleagues to share some of their emendated papers.

Playwright Robert Montgomery's comments, such as "This will be enjoyable to rehearse and to see," taught me to visualize the production process as I am reading scripts. Such comments have the effect of making the writer feel real. (I actually typed "feel read"—it's the same thing.)

Montgomery writes such reactive praises as "This is a real nice touch," "inspired idea," and "I laugh out loud"; and such descriptive praises as "I love how the friends diffuse this fight." Negative comments especially work well in the first person. Montgomery writes, "I'm missing what purpose these lines serve," and "This is a crucial moment and I'm wondering if you haven't rushed it a hair." Some of his comments are prescriptive, suggesting that a gesture should replace a character's words or that two characters continue with a conversation "if something comes to you."

Montgomery says he favors pointing out the good first, then, "when the relationship gets more history, specific negatives can be brought up more, although with some students negatives can be brought up sooner or immediately." By pointing out the positive in a piece, by implication you are isolating the less successful passages; as Montgomery says, "Knowing how well we can write is also a way of ex-ing the not-so good."

Poet Colette Inez's prescriptive comments include "pare down a bit?" and "another simile?" Notice the question marks. Some writers tend to accept uncritically all criticism—you say "I wonder about this image," and they're crossing it out—while others are chronically resistant. For both, it helps to put question marks with some comments, especially when not certain about a suggestion: "Would this character do this?" rather than "This character wouldn't do this."

Like Zukofsky, Inez couches negative comments with positive sentiments, such as: "You create a suspenseful opening. . . . Now strip away all the inessentials." Reactive comments often occur at the end of a piece, such as Inez's "Much to admire. . . . Revise, please."

Perhaps the most common form of written feedback is the bracketing of possible deletions. Nonfiction writer Nora Sayre says that she indicates "the repetitions . . . also the cliches. The students immediately start tightening their own work." Sayre learned this editing technique from her first editor and used it when she worked in publishing.

The basic workshop format is for a piece to be read, followed by comments by the students and teacher. Sometimes I will frame specific areas to be looked into ("I'd like some comments on the visual aspect of the poem"), or I'll ask students to point out specific lines or sections that work really well or don't work at all. I've said to classes, "There are moments in writing when you smile to yourself and say 'I've really nailed it'; pick out a place in this story where the author might have felt that way." The author generally remains quiet, except to ask questions, until the end of the discussion, when he or she can open up.

Although the instructor's role in a workshop can range from moderator to dominator, his or her opinions tend to be the most highly valued. Students shouldn't accept every one of the instructor's comments as literary shibboleth, any more than they should reject out of hand any comment made by fellow students because "What do they know?" The ultimate arbiters of any piece of writing are readers (who often disagree), and the workshop members are careful readers.

Teachers and students should make it known when a comment is colored by personal preference, whether it's an aversion to "minimalist" fiction or to fantasy. Thomas Wolfe would have had trouble in a workshop disinclined toward adjectives. If we just don't connect to a piece, we shouldn't strain for comments that the writer might take more seriously than he or she should. An editor once rejected a story of mine without his customary notes, saying, "It's just out of my line of vision."

I try to foster a workshop atmosphere where it's safe to take risks, by encouraging students to tread unfamiliar or foreboding territory in form and content, and not to be afraid of the simple (even though it might not engender effusive "analysis"). One of the most interesting and satisfying reactions I ever received to my own writing was when a poet I admired singled out one of my poems and said, "I really like that one. I got the feeling that you didn't know what the hell you were doing," the implication being that what I was doing was interesting.

One impediment to risk-taking is that the barometer for success in a workshop is often whether or not the other students can eruditely delineate what is going on in a piece and why it is or isn't working, whereas much wonderful literature is evocative yet baffling, or breaks rules but somehow packs a wallop. One way to encourage risk-taking is to be tolerant of reactive feedback in discussions. If everyone says basically "Wow, I'll remember this one," then the author might want to get an SASE ready.

Another way to encourage risk-taking is to give what I call "notebook assignments," which call for first or second drafts of exercises that may never be taken further. Examples include a monologue based on something overheard in the street, or a series of dream images. Or, students can be asked to write in class. In both cases, no one expects a polished, cohesive piece, and students often generate material they might not have otherwise approached.

Many students take a risk merely by exposing their writing, which often emanates from deeply felt experiences or embarrassing fantasies. I quote to classes a fifth-grade student of mine, who wrote: "To be a writer you have to write anything and everything. People like to read embarrassing moments. They'll give you credit. Later on, you'll be very famous."

Sometimes, the risk is in *giving* the criticism. The following comment by a student evinced an audible reaction from several others when I read it to the class: "I often feel guarded with my criticism of others' work, for fear that anything too harsh (honest?) might result in reciprocal attack on my work." There's no way to stop such retaliation, but it is extremely rare, and there are always other students to dilute the effect.

I told a workshop early in the semester that we should agree that we are going to wind up being a tight group and wishing we had come together sooner, so why don't we start now? I said it jokingly, but it helped some students who were holding back to open up more quickly than they might have.

Applying the Editing Process to
Creative Writing Classes

Student writers are often expected to plow through without the individual attention that their presumed superiors get from editors. I have incorporated peer editing into my workshops at Columbia University and at an elementary school, and I developed and taught a course in literary editing and publishing at Columbia.

In my college workshops, I team up students to edit each other on at least one story. I discuss with the class some of the basics of editing, including copywriting; I hand out a simplified sheet of editing marks. The students exchange manuscripts a week or two before the stories are due in class, and are on their own as to the nature and extent of their interactions. Each student keeps a journal of the editing experience.

Student editors can usually spend more time with each other than is possible in conference, and they can meet in informal settings on equal footing. A student editor, working intensively on one manuscript—unlike the teacher, who may have dozens at a time—is in a better position than the teacher to establish a true editorial partnership. The student editor might experience what editor Kathleen Anderson refers to as being "broken in" to a book, when she finds herself "transported" within it and anticipating "the characters' every move and reaction" (1986, 7). Knowing that an editor will see the piece before the class does can make it easier for the writer to get through the first draft.

Some student editors are timid about actually marking someone else's story, so I make it clear that they are not editing the story; they are editing a *copy* of the story. I also suggest using easy-stick/easy-remove "Post-it" notes, which provide more room for comments and make the edited manuscript look more professional. It is crucial that all editors and authors understand the fundamental law of literary property: authorship equals ownership unless a contract says otherwise.

Either the teacher can carefully pick out students who will best serve each other as editors, the students can select their own editors, or it can be done arbitrarily. I tend to abstain from being an editorial matchmaker; I simply pair students with the person they are sitting next to.

I've also used peer editing at the elementary school level. At P.S. 75, in Manhattan, where I direct a writers-in-residence program for Teachers & Writers Collaborative, I conducted a workshop in editing with experienced fifth- and sixth-grade writers.

The teachers maintained a folder of photocopies of student manuscripts that showed promise but weren't fully realized. Student writers could also contribute to the "editing folder." In the seminar we discussed editing strategies and critiqued edited manuscripts.

For example, an editor crossed out the word "child" in the sentence, "Child, this is the life." I pointed out that this deletion would tamper with the writer's voice. My favorite descriptive comment by a student editor was "sounds too goody-goody."

Sometimes we used role-playing, in which two editors selected a piece of writing from the editing folder. One played author, and the other played editor, and they explored the complexities and nuances of the editing process. By working with an actor rather than the actual author, the editor could experiment with approaches. This technique is also advantageous to the student playing the author, enabling him or her to examine the editing process from the other side.

Other times the editors would work directly with the author. First they'd mark up the manuscript, making comments, suggestions, and queries in the margins or on Post-it notes applied to the page. Providing the student editors with a Post-it supply was a breakthrough; the students felt "official" and perhaps safer about writing comments because they could be easily removed if the editor wanted to discard or revise the comment. The editor then showed the manuscript to the author, after which the two met to discuss the edit and evaluate what was and wasn't helpful.

Sometimes the edit was done with the author present. Nicole Santomasso said she might open a session by saying,

> Maybe we can do this together so if you don't like something you can tell me right away. And I'll explain to you everything I'm going to do, why I'm doing it. [She described the interaction:] You have to ask them what they think they could do to make the story better. And if they can't come up with anything, you tell them what you think they can do. And sometimes they might say, 'No, that'll ruin it.' You can take another copy and see how it would sound with the extra things in it, and if he doesn't like it, you say, 'I think you were right. This is good the way it is.'

At Columbia University's School of General Studies, the two-semester course in literary magazine editing and publishing touches on all the skills with which a literary magazine editor needs to be familiar. Discussion topics include: a survey of literary publishing; approaches to evaluating manuscripts and working with authors; line editing and copyediting; design (graphic arts, typography); proofreading; dealing with printers; and the business aspects of publication. I bring in editors to discuss their work, and students do papers on individual literary magazines and topics in editing, and hands-on design projects.

I assign students to write letters responding to manuscripts. The letters of Maxwell Perkins (recently reissued) are models of a thoughtful editor's mind at work, and are full of grace and wisdom. We critique the students' letters—"Are they clear and helpful?" I bring in manuscripts edited by professionals, and we discuss the editors' comments and how they are expressed.

One way for students to practice editing is by exchanging typed first drafts, written without using the backspace or delete keys. These stories are full of opportunities for intervention by an editor. Eventually, the students do the real thing. They act as editors for the creative theses written by graduating students in the program. This provides the students with an extended editing experience, often spanning several weeks, and is usually quite helpful to the authors, most of whom have never put together a large manuscript.

The students in the class also edit and produce *Quarto,* the literary magazine of the writing program, and often do other publishing projects, such as broadsides, postcards, chapbooks, and pamphlets.

The class bible is *The Chicago Manual of Style;* we also have *Words into Type* and several other style books available. At the end of the semester, students take a skills text in copyediting, proofreading, and typography.

Some students may find that their talent and disposition are more suited to editing than to writing; others may look to editing as an adjunct to their writing (most literary magazine editors are also writers). Plus, it is helpful in any writing program to have trained editors around.

Postscript

The final act of feedback, and for some students the most crucial, is grading. Pass/fail is the best method for graduate programs; the work itself will be judged as students apply for teaching jobs and submit their work to publications. Undergraduates, for the most part, receive letter grades.

At the end of each semester, I pore through my students' portfolios, which often include newly submitted revisions, and translate my response into a single letter (give or take a plus or minus). Generally, I first determine a "pure" grade on the writing, which may then be adjusted according to such factors as classroom participation, growth over the semester, the meeting of deadlines, and attendance.

At the end of a recent semester, dozens of portfolios decorated my desktop, as I struggled with the last few grades. Although office hours were over for the semester, a student dropped by on the chance I might be there. He was a "special student," enrolled only in my class. He was working in a bookstore and paying over $1,000 to take the course.

He said he'd been thinking about the comments I'd made on his short story, and wanted to make sure he had them clear in his mind as we wrote over intersession. He asked when grades would be out. When I told him I was giving him an A-, he smiled and I could sense the momentary feeling of weightlessness one has at the receipt of great news. "Is the grade that important to you?" I asked.

"It's my life," he replied.

And, I told myself, "Don't you forget that."

Works Cited

Anderson, Kathleen M. "Editing: The Teaching of Craft." In *Teachers & Writers*, March/April 1986: 7–9.

Baldwin, Neil. "Zukofsky, Williams, and *The Wedge*: Toward a Dynamic Convergence." In *Louis Zukofsky: Man and Poet*, 129–42. Orono, Me.: International Poetry Foundation, 1979.

Balanchine, George. Interview with W. McNeil Lowry. *The New Yorker*, September 12, 1986.

Berg, A. Scott. *Max Perkins: Editor of Genius*. New York: Pocket, 1979.

Berryman, John. Interview with Peter A. Stitt. *Writers at Work: The* Paris Review *Interviews*, Fourth Series, edited by George Plimpton, 293–322. New York: Penguin, 1977.

Bridgwater, William. "Copyediting." In *Editors on Editing*, edited by Gerald Gross, 69–88. New York: Harper and Row, 1985.

Bruccoli, Matthew J. *Scott and Ernest*. Carbondale: Southern Illinois University Press, 1978.

Cheever, John. Interview with Annette Grant. In *Writers at Work: The* Paris Review *Interviews*, Fifth Series, edited by George Plimpton, 113–35. New York: Penguin, 1981.

Dinesen, Isak. Interview with Eugene Walter. In *Writers at Work: The* Paris Review *Interviews*, Fourth Series, edited by George Plimpton, 1–19. New York: Penguin, 1977.

Evans, Nancy. "Line Editors: The Rigorous Pursuit of Perfection." In *Editors on Editing*, edited by Gerald Gross, 102–15. New York: Harper and Row, 1985.

Gefuert, Constance J. *The Confident Writer*. New York: Norton, 1988.

Kerouac, Jack. Interview with Ted Berrigan. In *Writers at Work: Fourth Series*, edited by George Plimpton, 359–95. New York: Penguin, 1977.

Maxwell, William. Interview with John Seabrook and George Plimpton. In *Writers at Work: The* Paris Review *Interviews,* Seventh Series, edited by George Plimpton, 39–70. New York: Penguin, 1988.

Murray, Donald M. "Internal Revision: A Process of Discovery." In *Research on Composing: Points of Departure,* edited by Charles R. Cooper and Lee Odell, 85–103. Urbana: NCTE, 1978.

Nabokov, Vladimir. Interview with Herbert Gold. In *Writers at Work: The* Paris Review *Interviews,* Fourth Series, edited by George Plimpton, 91–107. New York: Penguin, 1977.

Sacks, David. "An Interview with Jonathan Galassi." In *Poets & Writers,* November/December 1987: 21–24.

Steinbeck, John. Interview with George Plimpton and Frank Crowther. In *Writers at Work: The* Paris Review *Interviews,* edited by George Plimpton, 179–207. New York: Penguin, 1977.

Wheelock, John Hall, ed. *Editor to Author: The Letters of Maxwell E. Perkins.* New York: Scribner's, 1987.

20 The Book in the World

Valerie Miner
University of California, Berkeley

Ten years of my life have been consumed in correspondence
and litigation about my book, *Dubliners*: it was rejected by 40
publishers; three times set up, and once burnt. It cost me 3,000
francs in postage, with 110 newspapers, 7 solicitors, 3 societies,
40 publishers and seven men of letters about it. All refused to
aid me, except Mr. Ezra Pound. In the end it was published,
and in 1914, word for word as I wrote it in 1905. My novel (*Portrait of the Artist as a Young Man*) was refused by every publisher
in London to whom it was offered—refused (as Mr. Pound informed me) with offensive comments. When a review did decide to publish it, it was impossible to find in the United Kingdom a printer to print it

—James Joyce, in a letter

My life changed in the late 1960s when I was an undergraduate, majoring in English at the University of California, Berkeley. I had
come from a conservative, immigrant, working-class home, and was
the first one in my family to go through college. Berkeley was full of
surprises. I learned about Geoffrey Chaucer and John Milton. I
learned about Vietnam. I learned I was bright. I discovered I wanted
to be a writer. But I was confused. What did writing have to do with
the world that was exploding before my eyes? And how was writing
treated in the world? Did people *like me* ever become writers? No
one seemed to talk about these things. I hoped to be a novelist, but
this was something I didn't admit to myself, let alone to anyone
else. For there were many things I did not learn—subjects about
which I didn't know how to form questions—things about class,
race, sex, the relevance of art to society, the practical issues of being
an artist.

In the last two decades I have learned how to ask some of those
questions. I started by studying journalism, a form of writing in
which social relevance and practical issues were addressed together

in the classroom. I grew more politically active. I left the country in protest to the war in Southeast Asia. I lived abroad for seven years. My journalism took me to Canada, Europe, and Africa. Despite wide publication and much satisfaction, I still ached to write novels. So I began asking the questions about fiction on my own. Through writers' groups I gained the courage to finish and submit short stories. Eventually I began a novel. Today I have published five novels as well as a collection of short fiction and have coauthored four other books.

In the late 1980s, I find myself back at Berkeley as a teacher. Much has changed. Much hasn't. Fiction, for instance, is still usually confined to two contexts—the veneration of dead authors in survey courses and the ventilation of hopeful authors in creative writing seminars. So it is with some personal evangelism that I want my students to appreciate how fiction is published, to consider context influencing content, to acknowledge the social value of literary contribution, to understand how our individual writing ambitions are affected by the publishing profession and the book industry. For the last six years I have taught a course called "Social Issues in Publishing," in which we study the role of the writer in society as well as practical issues about the book as a cultural product.

"Social Issues in Publishing" is a field-based course where students integrate creative and academic work with internships in the publishing world. I teach a three-hour weekly seminar that knits together their literary concerns and their experience in the outside world. We consider aesthetic, social, political, ethical, and commercial issues from the perspectives of readers, writers, publishers, reviewers, booksellers, and librarians. We teach each other about the interplay of many factors in the development of a book.

Each week's seminar focuses on a tandem of "theoretical" and "practical" issues—revealing the artificiality of such distinctions. The theoretical issues include: literacy in the United States; regional identity in publishing; the economics of conglomerate houses and independent firms; the role of the critic in society; the treatment of under-represented cultures in publishing; First Amendment rights and responsibilities. On the more pragmatic side, we follow a book from author's conception to reader's bookshelf, dealing weekly with such topics as: creating and submitting a manuscript; editorial acquisition; literary agenting; editing, design, and production of books and journals; promotion and publicity for books; writing a critical review and responding to criticism; distribution channels.

The course involves a wide range of texts including fiction by Chinua Achebe, Alice Walker, I. B. Singer, Sandy Boucher, and Zhang KangKang; essays by George Orwell, Dorothy Bryant, and James Houston, as well as some of my own writing. We read three books that provide considerably different perspectives and approaches to American publishing: *Books* by Lewis Coser, Charles Kadushin, and Walter Powell; *The Media Monopoly* by Ben Bagdikian; and *The Passionate Perils of Publishing* by Celeste West and Valerie Wheat. Students select a biographical or autobiographical book about a writer (favorites are Sylvia Plath's *The Bell Jar* and Maya Angelou's *I Know Why the Caged Bird Sings*). They also bring in extensive materials from their placements—for example, books or journals on which they are working; a set of guidelines on manuscript preparation; a series of covers; a blueprint for sales promotion. Perhaps the most important test in the class is the field placement itself. Students are encouraged to approach the field as anthropologists—investigating various literary and social questions.

Internships

The internships are varied in size, environment, and function. This allows students to experience many angles of publishing in class discussions. Placements have included large publishers (Harper and Row and The University of California Press); independent publishers (Sierra Club Books); small independents (Heyday Books); journals (*Poetry Flash* and *The Feminist Bookstores News*); bookstores (Small Press Traffic, A Woman's Place, Bookworks) as well as literary agencies, a book distributor, and a writers' organization. I aim for a span of placements that illustrates different steps in the publishing process and represents different cultural and political communities.

Students work ten hours per week at placements that are chosen at the beginning of the term. They all do serious tasks under concerned supervision. At Harper and Row, for instance, we have had students reading manuscripts, writing jacket copy, and negotiating with potential reviewers for coverage of new books. At *Poetry Flash*, students have been involved in every stage of publication from editing to production and distribution. People at Small Press Traffic have had an opportunity to work in the literary reading series as well as on funding applications so vital to keeping arts centers alive.

Students accompany their supervisors to book parties, readings, and conferences. Thus, they are able to observe and ask questions about the role of the writer and the social treatment of books in many settings.

As a student wrote in the middle of the term:

> My placement . . . will be a valuable tool in my future develop-
> ment because of the exposure I have had to the intricacies of
> making a living while retaining the goals of the small, indepen-
> dent presses. Much of the material we have read in *Books* and
> *The Media Monopoly* emphasizes the publisher/editor's concern
> with mass appeal, advertising, and targeting the largest homo-
> geneous sector of society in order to maximize profits. Because
> small presses concentrate on content with creative and literary
> merit, the focus is much less on profit. . . . I have also come to
> understand the need for this avant-garde literary community to
> work together to promote alternative writing in general. There is
> a publication called *Small Press,* which unites the literary com-
> munity's concerns by advertising both small presses and alter-
> native bookstores which distribute their works. Another exam-
> ple is that Small Press Traffic advertises in *Poetry Flash* and this
> publication is available to the public at Small Press Traffic. The
> bookstore City Lights refers customers looking for small press
> books to Small Press Traffic.

Why do supervisors volunteer to work with students? One motivation is to provide a service, to expose students to experiences they
wish they had had when in school. Most supervisors find the students' help a valued contribution in a traditionally underfunded
field. And many of them simply enjoy the opportunity to think
about their work in different ways, to meet the challenges of students' endless curiosity. Several supervisors have found themselves
seriously rethinking ethical and aesthetic practices. One student
noted in the final study journal:

> I entered this [term] confident that my career as a writer was vir-
> tually assured. My books would be quickly snatched up and
> published, and soon I would be making the rounds of the talk
> shows. Then weeks later those illusions were shattered . . . re-
> placed by a real knowledge of the publishing business and its
> pitfalls. I have a much better idea of what needs to be done,
> both in my writing and after the writing is finished.

Weaving Together

My favorite part of the course is teaching students to integrate their
personal, philosophical, and aesthetic pursuits with their experience

in the publishing world. I try to facilitate this through writing assignments and a series of disruptions to "normal" course parameters. Early in the class, I hold a special evening session to which I invite supervisors and students so they can get to know each other informally. During the term, supervisors sometimes sit in on a class and talk about their work in greater depth. Students are required to visit and write about a specialty bookstore. They are asked to visit each other's placements. They also attend literary activities sponsored by each other's field supervisors.

Students write regular three-page study journals in which they address an assigned topic by discussing their field experience in conjunction with their responses to the week's required reading. For instance, the week we discuss regionalism in publishing, I ask them to consider their placements for any regional identity. Is there a special character to West Coast writing and publishing? If so, how is it different from books emanating from the "established" Manhattan presses? Why have New York publishers developed West Coast branches? How is West Coast writing received in different parts of the country? Will there be a civil war? (As someone who moved to England when I wanted to write fiction— because my Berkeley education had taught me that "serious" literature was British—I find some of these regional questions particularly pressing.) Writing the journal prepares the student to discuss the topic in the forthcoming seminar. Thus, when we talk about economics, students are prepared with an analytical framework from Bagdikian and West as well as their own firsthand information about who owns their placement and how this affects editorial decisions.

At first, the weekly discussions tend to be segmented, where we begin by talking about the texts and wind up checking in about the placements. However, as time goes by, students learn to bring their field experience into the discussion of the books and vice versa. Often they get into quite heated disagreements with the authors of class texts as well as with each other.

The field provides surprises about literary standards and economic constraints. One study journal revealed, "The level of creativity is limited. The final question is not how well a book is written or whether it will have a potentially good impact on its readers, but 'Will this book sell?'" After working for a bookstore and witnessing the sales process, another student observed, "There is such a small effort made in marketing literature. I realize art isn't like shoes or bread in the hierarchy of needs, but the literary reading section was so poorly organized—the classics all jumbled in with Berkeley small press volumes, simply because they happen to be alphabetically similar."

The Field-Based Term Project comes in three parts, all of which involve extensive sharing and interstudent learning. The paper allows students to investigate an issue from their placements, bringing in course texts, seminar discussions, and independent research. The first phase is a proposal (or query letter), which students photocopy and distribute to their seminar colleagues. Each student reads a proposal aloud and gets oral and written feedback from the others. This is an exciting session, where students give each other ideas for people to interview—books to read as well as comments about their writing. Several weeks later, after digesting criticism from other students and myself, the student brings in a prospectus—or a five-page project description—which is again shared with classmates. The final project is photocopied for each member of the seminar. We spend two weeks discussing the term papers, which are the *final texts* in the class. Thus, the student experiences publishing directly—as writer, editor, printer, binder, and distributor of the field-based project.

Work Load

By now you have discerned that this type of experimental education is a lot of work for the students as well as for the instructor. I estimate that the course takes students at least twenty hours a week, considering the ten-hour placement, the three-hour seminar, the time commuting to the field, the reading and writing assignments. I think students should receive substantial extra credit for the course work. However, at Berkeley, as well as at many elite institutions, we have had to fight an uphill battle even to maintain credit for experimental classes. Students earn four semester units for the course.

My own work is extensive. I have to create a balance of theoretical and practical inquiry. When I originally designed the course in 1980, I did so with the aid of an NEH Pilot Curriculum Development Grant, which was enormously helpful. I would encourage teachers to apply for whatever teaching improvement grants are offered by their institutions. But be forewarned—even after the course is set for one semester, it requires considerable ongoing work, partially because of the fluid nature of the publishing industry. In addition to teaching the three-hour seminar, I establish the internships with the supervisors. I stay in contact with them during the term. I visit placements. And there's a lot of individual work with students who have problems or questions about their placements. Of course, all of this means staying active in a literary community in order to be aware of current issues, practices, and people.

As I was writing this essay, the editor asked me to address the needs of teachers and students "in the heartlands, far removed from the publishing industry." My first response is to point out the many fine journals and publishing houses flourishing between the Hudson River and San Fernando Valley. But that's another article in itself. Suffice it to say, near most colleges are located at least one or two independent publishers. Even if teachers can't find these mad souls at first, they can set up internships at bookstores, radio stations, libraries, and college publications. You don't have to work at the Hogarth Press to acquire some of the very same lessons Leonard and Virginia Woolf learned about publishing.

The rewards are varied. Often I hear students say this has been their hardest and most enlightening course. Because of the intense interstudent learning, many people stay in touch with each other afterward. It's not unusual for students to start a postcourse writing workshop. Several students have created new journals and then asked me to solicit submissions from my current seminar. I am delighted to see a number of students getting published. And since I know that one doesn't make a living from serious writing in this country, I am also delighted to see them working as editors and booksellers, using some of the skills and perspectives gained in the course. Over the years I have developed great admiration for students' flexibility, common sense, creativity, and intelligence.

Context and Confidence

No doubt some creative writing professors will argue against literary fieldwork, saying we need to shelter the student from the marketplace. I'd recommend these people define their terms and examine their assumptions carefully. If they are saying we shouldn't teach formula courses about how to write genre novels, I would agree. I'm not teaching people to compromise their art to suit the bestseller list or the elite list of celebrated literary houses. Quite the opposite, I'm saying that writers need to know about the world around them to understand how to protect the integrity of their work.

As artists, it's crucial to understand how we function as social agents. As readers (presumably most serious writers are serious readers), it is essential to understand what does and doesn't get published and why. When teachers say students will be discouraged or misdirected by learning about the way a book is treated in our society and by considering the writer's cultural roles, I would suggest that these teachers are either naive or overprotective. By studying the *context* of the making of literature we can preserve good writers from early discouragement. We all know that it is not necessarily the most brilliant writer who succeeds; one needs a combination of talent and persistence. Perhaps more of us would persist if we knew more about the practical obstacles and challenges we were facing.

In the United States, writers get trapped in the schizophrenic conundrum whereby we think it is a privilege to publish and a personal failure not to publish. We celebrate the novel as solitary genesis, denying the society in which the work was provoked or inspired as well as the contributions of other writers and editors to the final product. By rarifying art and venerating the artist as supernatural being, we encourage the deadening solipsism plaguing contemporary writing. We cultivate an antagonism toward the artist and develop a sado-masochistic relationship with her or him. Often we demand that as proof or penance for the art, the writer be addicted, psychotic, desperately unhappy, or suicidal.

If this class isn't as dramatic as suicide prevention, it does defend against an attrition of the spirit. When we don't understand the social context in which our work is published, our art easily gets distorted by ignorance, cronyism, and fear. It takes nothing from the quality of our imaginations to admit that writing is work. In fact, the more we understand how our work is treated in the world, the more likely we are to survive and succeed as writers.

Another American legend worth examining is the notion that "any good book eventually gets published." If we live in a country where—as popular myth would have it—anyone can grow up to be president, certainly anyone can be a writer. The truth is that in either case you may succeed more readily on the basis of race, gender, social or geographic status. We have just begun to study the unrepresentative nature of the American literary canon. Literary fieldwork courses can encourage writers from marginalized groups by offering differing perspectives; they can direct students to some of the fine alternative publishers who are contributing to the development of a multicultural literature; they can offer writers without family financial cushions a sense of direction about making a living while they create great American novels. Field-based courses are not substitutes for, but supplements to, other courses in writing and reading. One of my students summed up the experience as follows:

> Then came Field Studies. And I had to ask and argue. Is this really what publishing is all about? It's ugly, rude. No better than business school. No more enlightened. No more genteel. I went out of my way to meet writers outside of the class, to think about young writers in the class, to talk to people in other fields. Feeling like I was becoming a minor authority on the publishing industry, I would tell everyone my new findings. Not that anyone cared. But I wanted to bounce it all around. For all the bad news, I still will write, with a little more commitment, being a little less naive.

Works Cited

Bagdikian, Ben. *The Media Monopoly.* 2nd ed. Boston: Beacon Press, 1987.

Coser, Lewis, Charles Kadushin, and Walker Powell. *Books.* New York: Basic Books, 1982.

Joyce, James. *The Letters of James Joyce,* edited by Stuart Gilbert. New York: Viking, 1956.

West, Celeste, and Valerie Wheat. *The Passionate Perils of Publishing.* San Francisco: Booklegger Press, 1978.

21 Literary Magazines and the Writing Workshop

DeWitt Henry
Emerson College

Any writing workshop or curriculum should include an analysis of some lively, living literary magazines for the practical reason, if none other, that these are nearly the only outlet for poets, the primary one for literary fiction, and the most likely place for discovery—publication for the previously unpublished. In addition to *Ploughshares*, which I have codirected and edited since 1971, and which grew out of my own workshop experiences as a student and later as a teacher with and without walls, there are about thirty literary journals of national significance. Beyond these thirty may be another three hundred of regional, factional, or personal significance, offering publication to almost any writer of talent and persistence.

Of course they can rarely pay more than a $50 honorarium and copies. They are sold more by subscription than by retail, and tops in circulation is ten thousand, with the average being fifteen hundred. They are not a guaranteed means to instant fortune and fame, but they are a means to it, and often to contact with influential readers, such as agents, "best of" anthologists, grants panelists, readings coordinators, writing chairpeople, trade editors, reviewers, other writers, teachers, students, and some percentage of "bookpeople"—independent-minded, reading adults, bless them each and all. Most of our better-known fiction writers with initial publications in the 1970s emerged from literary magazines, won some grants, some prizes, attracted the attention of trade editors like Ted Solotaroff, Seymour Lawrence, Gordon Lish or Carol Smith, published a first collection of stories or first novel, were well reviewed, won more prizes, and then were safe and proper fare for the larger magazines. Witness from the pages of *Ploughshares* alone the rise of Tim O'Brien, Jayne Anne Phillips, Carolyn Chute, Sue Miller, Pamela Painter, as well as the renaissance of Gina Berriault and other neglected writers. But this is both to and off the point. Yes, literary magazines are a viable "market"; yes, in some sense they serve as a farm team to be harvested at will by the major leagues; yes, for the talented, productive, and lucky, they advance careers; yes, they depend on unsolicited and unagented work for most of and for the best of what they publish.

Yet most important, the ideal issue of the ideal magazine embodies the value and possibility of writing well. The editors are writers, editing out of the same standards and passions with which they write. Literary magazines link writers of all ages, stages, styles, subject matters, backgrounds, and visions under the conviction that good writing matters more than anything else, except life itself. And there are other tenets: that at large, the circumstances of culture deny and compromise the development of talent; that something is rotten in the state of demand-oriented publishing; that poets are, indeed, the unacknowledged legislators of the world; that talent should and must be trusted and enabled; that richness is no proof of smartness, or vice versa; and that the judgment of quality itself is a matter of vision and opinion.

In surveying the field, students should be aware of the general categories of (1) academic reviews (*Hudson Review, Massachusetts Review, Kenyon Review, Poetry, Georgia Review, Virginia Quarterly, Sewanee Review, Partisan Review*); (2) eclectic creative writing magazines (*Ploughshares, Paris Review, Antaeus, Iowa Review, American Poetry Review, Pequod, Ontario Review, Grand Street, Missouri Review, Story Quarterly, Boulevard, North American Review*); (3) Black Mountain, surrealist, and experimental poetry magazines (*Field, Kayak, Chicago Review, Seneca Review, Ironwood*); (4) experimental fiction magazines (*Mississippi Review, Conjunctions, TriQuarterly, Fiction, Fiction International, Sun and Moon*); (5) feminist magazines (*Calyx, Woman Poet, Thirteenth Moon, The American Voice*); and (6) ethnic magazines (*Puerto del Sol, Quilt, Callaloo*), among others. In themselves, these categories offer a challenging range of possibilities, while within each category are equally important differences to explore. (Here I assume that the writing program can convince the campus library to subscribe to at least this many titles, not for "research value" in the conventional sense, but for "creative research" to support the writing of poetry and fiction.)

As instructor, I would single out magazines I follow myself, those which I look forward to and read as an extension of community and challenge. I would point to those, also, that I disagreed with or disliked as opposite in vision, weak in standard, or out of touch. I would point to special issues, where the focus seemed promising in generating stories (one of *Ploughshares'* most successful issues was on the problem of men imagining women and women imagining men). I would speak of writers I discovered in their pages, and whose books I later sought out and read; I would cite provocative ideas from interviews, craft articles, and book reviews outside the tradewinds of the media. I would also discuss trends I saw myself (as a writer) as they manifested themselves in the magazines—the waning of the metafiction debate; the complaints now about minimalism; the epidemic of the present tense; the growing interest in internationalism (and translation) in search of more urgent and deeply rooted subjects than those of our domestic culture watch.

In assigning magazines, I would have students ask whether any work in a given issue was as good as or better than their own; whether any stories or poems were as good as or better than work by their heroes; whether anything was bewilderingly good and different, a challenge to their assumptions in writing and reading; whether anything was offensive or plain awful; whether anything was marvelous to learn from, imitate, rise to, answer to; and overall whether there were clear editorial ideas or anything like an editorial vision. Among writers such questions should lead to disagreements that clarify and enliven motives, pose challenges, and increase the understanding of craft.

A *Ploughshares* subscriber sent a postcard recently responding to my latest fiction issue and praising all the stories as "page turners by masterful storytellers," except for Eve Shelnutt's story ("The Beguiling Idiot"), "which is so forced: it sounds like what someone learned to do in a workshop or the drivel in the O'Henry Best Story collections." Isn't this what we talk about when we talk about writing? What about the Stuart Dybek story in the same issue: how is that a "page turner?" What do you mean "forced"? Difficult to read? What about "poetic" as opposed to "dramatic" structure? I would argue that Shelnutt's intensity is authentic and the means to something deep and rare—something analogous, perhaps, to the means and aims of Eudora Welty's more metaphorically dense stories, such as "Death of a Traveling Salesman." The dramatic base is there.

A teacher's husband is away with his dying father; death is on the teacher's mind, as well as her life's meaning (she is childless) and a mounting sensuality, prompted by missing her husband, by the heat and beauty of the country summer day, and by the liberty of his absence. She wanders from her house into the countryside, encounters a retarded man in a field, feels both erotic and maternal attraction to him, and follows him into a deserted cottage, his home, where mutely he shows her the woman whose love and care are evident in the keeping of the cottage and in his embroidered socks—"his mother no doubt"—laid out on a table in death. But the power and richness of the story is in the accumulation of images, linking love, sex, death, and mothering, and dependence and responsibility. The narrator's husband's dying father is "envisioned, in a pink flash, the broken veins of his cheeks and nose . . . the wax-white of his forehead and ankles. . . . The skin had drawn tight and almost transluscent on his skull where like a baby's the pulse was visible. . . ." She recalls, "The old man wanted lilies when he died. . . . but inwardly she had protested, thinking it was a flower for a young boy, age seven, say, when the face first suggests the man who will carry it, a face which would be as white as the flower." When she first sees the retarded man, she takes him for a boy, but "he was a man with a boy's gestures, a boy of twelve. . . . Certainly they [she and her husband] should have had a child, who would surely have been male." The life stages of men are merged in her equally merged relations with them. Elsewhere, her love is frankly sensual, from feeling naked with students, to lying naked with her husband, to feeling young again in sexual sport, to imagining that workers can see through her dress, to feeling "errant sensuality," to wanting to touch the vulnerable palms of men's hands, to the erotic tension in her attachment to the retarded man. All this coheres as she recognizes the mother's devotion to her retarded son, not only in his clothes, home, and manners, but in his speechless grief; as she thinks of her own dying and feels her father-in-laws's "merciless" male imperative to voice her sense of self as a woman whose men will "have no idea of how much I loved you all"; and as, finally, she sees in the dead mother before her, "A face so like her own she bent to kiss the lips." This is not portentous, but rather mysterious, the expression of a passionate, lived, intuitive writer. The wonder is in the narrative compression and lyrical distortion, the dreamlike "errancy," the shifts of consciousness in time, and the layering of thought, all focussed by love and grief. Shelnutt knows what she means, but she also means more than she knows, and I can imagine no other writer telling this story, or this writer telling it another way. To the reader who disagrees, I would say turn pages *back*, to re-explore and respect the art, and as a writer to emulate its ambition and its standard, if not its manner.

As a source of models, literary magazines have an advantage in their very currency. This is what writers are doing now, in response to our shared times and circumstances (including a changing view of earlier writing)—not what Sherwood Anderson did in 1919, Hemingway in 1931, Eudora Welty in 1941, or Richard Yates in 1955. Here, in fact, are positive (and negative) examples of how writers themselves are now making use of classical models. One thinks of André Dubus, Tim O'Brien, Thomas McGuane, and Raymond Carver, all talking back to aspects of Hemingway, while also talking, through their different visions, to each other. Here, also, are examples of strongly felt themes, questions of courage in a nuclear age, of intimacy in a technological one, of conscience in a materialistic one, of class, race, gender, of historical identity, of "anything being possible" and nothing being meaningful—a contemporary awareness, at best, speaking to what we didn't know, or want to know, what we knew, and speaking from the front lines of the individual imagination. As examples they are mediated by the judgment of only a single editor, rather than by a legion of editors, commentators, and anthologists, and they openly invite the reader to like, dislike, and to argue back—in fact, to develop the courage of opinion, regardless of "authority." I like to think of the process of letters, generally, as one of discourse: writer talking back to writer, editor to editor, magazine to magazine. And part of writing well lies in learning the level, the stakes, and the idiom of this discussion and wanting to join in.

For her workshop at Western Connecticut State University, Barbara Winder assigns a story each week from *Ploughshares'* 10th Anniversary Issue (edited by Dan Wakefield). She reports that she has used Janet Burroway's *Writing Fiction* some semesters, but prefers the magazine, especially when she can invite a given editor to class; also she "can't see the value of students purchasing this text, when, for the same investment, they could buy several copies of literary magazines." She finds that analyzing stories from *Ploughshares* helps to "demystify the writing process." One week, analysis of a certain story allows her to ask students for a piece where one character wants something that the other character doesn't want to give; another week, one prompts the assignment for a story in which setting poses an insurmountable problem, or for a retelling of the model story from a different point of view. My favorite selection in this issue for a point-of-view exercise is "Coggios," a short-short story by Sharyn Layfield (reprinted in *The Ploughshares Reader: New Fiction for the 80's*), where an educated, sophisticated, independent and lonely female narrator idealizes the family-centered lives of working-class immigrant neighbors as a dream of what she has lost or never had: "I know the girls will never marry. Why should they?" But what would *her* story be from the point of view of one of the Coggio girls? What would their own stories be?

Where a danger of workshops can be indoctrination and mimicry, resulting in the MacPoem or MacStory, literary magazines at once help to expose those vices and to offer a breadth of models to combat them. How many of the stories are too much alike here? What is original and how? They also take the focus off the praised and famous (hence off "praise" and "fame" themselves)—the Barthelme, Carver, or Beattie story, the Merwin or Hugo poem—and put it back on craft and the responsibilities of craft.

Internships are welcome and needed support for literary magazines, once those journals have formal offices, where tasks are organized and students may report for work. (No joke—the *Ploughshares* office "floated" from private apartment to apartment for the first ten years.) And I agree with Valerie Miner, in the previous chapter, when she suggests that there is no better way to involve students in "the context of making literature." There are myths operative here, which I remain susceptible to—of noble mendicancy, of revolutions in a garret, of improbable effects from limited means. Yes, you can, with some talent and determination, produce that beautiful and professional-looking paperback magazine with type from a composition house (inputed perhaps on your own PC or on a borrowed one) and a lightbox on which to paste up single pages. You send the camera-ready pages to one of the Ann Arbor printers, and six weeks later an interstate trailer arrives with boxes of books. You label padded envelopes to your subscribers, drag presorted full bags in for mailing, and settle down to marketing the remainder and to editing manuscripts, selling ads, and applying for grants to pay the bills for the next issue. There's more, a lot more, which, lacking money, is fueled by a sense of mission, yet has increasingly less to do with writing and more with small business. If nothing else, the experience should temper the students' impulse to start their own magazine at the first sign of injustice (unless they are rich, of course, and can hire help).

More enlightening is the sheer volume of stories, poems, and essays submitted, most of which are inappropriate in quality or kind, suggest little acquaintance with the magazine beyond its address, and outnumber subscribers by twenty to one. In terms of quality, that so many people—intelligent, estimable people, such as doctors, lawyers, assistant professors, board members, *Playboy* bunnies, the previously published, let alone your former teacher, your friends—should lack or deny any sense of how poorly they write, must initially dismay and exasperate the intern and to some extent reassure him or her. No, he is not this bad; she is clearer about her talent and prospects than *this*. Where personal standards are offended, interns often turn to their own writing to prove and reassert real art; they turn to their masters, and yet the humanity of all those dreamers weighs heavily. A suggestion or note of encouragement can result in more submissions and neurotic mail; likewise, disparaging comments invite invective, litigation, and assault. The intern learns the purpose of the plain rejection slip. Yet, is the intern so different? Is he or she ready to be judged? At the same time, perhaps ten percent of the submissions will seem better in various ways than the screener's own work, and, though publishable, still fall short of *this* magazine's standard. When one story in two hundred does impress the intern as a sure thing, and then the intern passes it on, a higher reader or the issue editor may still turn it down. If this rejection is based wholly on a question of merit, and if a number of stories are competing for space in a single issue, the screener may learn a more exacting awareness of better and best from a more experienced editor/writer—and not in the classroom sense of whether Hemingway is "better" than Anderson or Lardner, but in the applied sense of whether a story is entered on the record or not, is nominated to be "literature," and is the subject for further discussion. In turn, the sharper standard may challenge and inform the screener's own writing. On this level, however, stories aren't only chosen for merit, but also for considerations of theme, style, how they ramify with other work in an issue, and personal taste. (This last mystery is rooted, like personality, in the events and issues of the editor's life.)

Sometimes, too, there is the need to feature recognizable "names," or a concern for balance in aesthetic or social terms; given quality, in other words, the variable of "needs" is a factor too, sometimes stated, sometimes guessable, often not. In addition, the intern may have the satisfaction of championing some work that prevails, or of seeing it prevail elsewhere. He or she may overhear or join in deliberations over work that has bypassed initial screening, whether the work is by a well-known writer, or more often by writers that the editor has been following, or perhaps even discovered. The intern watches these editor-and-writer transactions lead to revisions that strengthen a given story, and to copyediting and galley changes. And as an issue takes shape, the intern may discover in its contents some stories that have risen through and depended on this whole intricate process, whether or not they have passed through the intern's hands, and which ultimately make it all worthwhile.

What is the value, then, to the student's writing and career? The reassuring community of writers in the world, sharing his or her values in art and for the place of art in the lives of everyone. There is also the sharpening of the student's critical sense—a story of negative examples in flawed art to equal the store of positive examples supplied in the classroom. The student also gains a more detached perspective on publishing, so that rejection seems neither absolute, nor an assault on one's identity—nor, conversely, does acceptance seem a confirmation of ability either. Patience, let us hope, will be the value of all this, as well as confidence in his or her own talents, seasoned by acquaintance with others' talents at different stages and in different degrees—and the informed bet that if the student does good work, though the odds of publication seem steep at first, in the long run they are in his or her favor. The student will gain the ability, in brief, to look on publishing like a professional.

Finally, I have some suggestions on submitting work. (1) Know that what you send is good, not begging generosity, not hoping to be mended by another imagination. (2) Pick up to five magazines, ranging from most to least desirable, whose contents you follow and feel affinity with. Be especially alert for magazines just starting up, since they will be shortest in supply and seeking to develop contributors. (3) Submit your work simultaneously, along with a cover letter saying so; query by mail after ninety days, and if you get no response, send it elsewhere. Should your work be accepted, notify the other magazines immediately and withdraw it from their consideration. (4) Persist with any work you know is valid. (5) Subscribe to magazines you honor, whether they publish you or not.

And one parting suggestion on texts. Most magazines have large inventories of back issues, and those such as *Ploughshares*, *Pequod*, *TriQuarterly*, *Missouri Review*, *Antaeus*, especially, have a variety of special issues (Southern Writing, International Writing, the Essay, Realist Fiction) that amount to inexpensive mini-anthologies. Write, call, and ask—editorial phones and addresses are listed in *Literary Marketplace*, *The Coordinating Council of Literary Magazines Directory*, *The International Directory of Literary Magazines and Small Presses*, and elsewhere. Watch also for retrospective anthologies, like *The Ploughshares Reader: New Fiction for the 80's* or *The Ploughshares Poetry Reader*, which offer the "best" for classroom use along with the vitality, variety, and currency of the living magazine.

IV Maxims, Methods, and Goals

Writing ability is mainly a product of good teaching supported by a deep-down love of writing.

—John Gardner, *The Art of Fiction*

IV. Maxims, Methods
and Goals

22 Creative Writers' Report: Mastering the Craft

Ib J. Melchior
Paul Cook, Arizona State University
Richard F. Radford, Jr., Curry College
C. S. Adler
Stanley Cohen
Wallace E. Knight, Marshall University
Robert H. Abel, Mount Holyoke College

Finding Source Material

Fiction writing is a fraud. Only a small portion of what is written by those of us who are fiction writers is actually fiction. Primarily, a fiction writer is a sponge, soaking up surroundings and experiences and wringing them out over a typewriter. We are bombarded daily by events and concepts reported and discussed in our reading material that provide us with a wealth of story ideas. We are observers. At every gathering we attend there will be at least one person whose behavior, whose personality or whose actions, are remarkable in some way. Later, we conjure up those traits and those mannerisms and we endow our "fictitious" characters with them. The closer those characters are to reality, the truer and more convincing they will be. The more interesting. —IB J. Melchior

Getting Down to Editing

A good writing teacher has the opportunity to transfer his or her copyediting skills to the student, and usually this is best done in one-on-one sessions where the teacher takes a blue pencil and escorts the student through his or her story in an attempt to cultivate, in that student, the value of good editing. There is no substitute for this. "Touchy-feely" workshops are of no use whatever in this regard.

Writers and poets have an enormous opportunity to share their enthusiasm for the writers they've enjoyed, and in doing so, they are able to give the student a sense of the "thrill" of reading a good story or poem. Listening to Charles Wright discuss the *Purgatorio* allows one to approach Dante purely from the standpoint of one poet appreciating the work of another poet. —*Paul Cook*

Learning to be Objective

The title of the creative writing course I teach tells it all: "99% Perspiration; 1% Inspiration." In the first few class meetings I play a harsh devil's advocate, trying to scrub the stardust out of the eyes of the class participants and screen out the dilettantes. I emphasize that the primary requisite for writing is having spent their prior and present lives reading everything from Shakespeare to toothpaste tubes and being convinced (whether or not they have yet written a word themselves) that they could have done most of it better.

Writers who never expose their work to anyone tend to form an unnaturally high opinion of that work and therefore tend not to change, grow, and improve. The cafeteria roundtables and raps with classmates and teachers provide the group support needed to keep the writer writing and, *most importantly,* provide an audience. The "beauty part" of this audience is that the writer gets their criticism face to face. Constant criticism and comparison are heavy components of my classes as well as my own writing. If a person leaves me having obtained a degree of objectivity about his or her own work, I feel I've succeeded. —*Richard F. Radford, Jr.*

Steps in Maturing as a Writer

Life is chaotic, irrational, and not always under control, but when I capture a piece of it in words, *then* it's shaped and controlled. Besides, it's on paper where anyone can find it again. Moments pass, but words remain.

I don't know if I knew all that when I was seven years old and decided to become a writer. Then my decision arose from my love for reading. Stories were wonderful and I wanted not only to read them but to make up my own. Since the creatures of my imagination seemed more interesting than the real people I knew, my first efforts were about worlds and people I didn't know. The "write about what you know" dictum only took hold gradually in my stories when I became a teenager. That may be why nobody wanted to publish what I wrote until I was in my thirties. Or it may be that it took me that many years to experience enough so that my writing was interesting to others.

What I did best as a young person was description. Depicting a character, bringing a character to life on the page, was much harder and took me a few decades of writing to learn. I think that progression stands for most writers, although some go through it faster than others. Possibly that's something you need a fair amount of experience and observation of other human beings to do. Maybe that's why more artists and musicians produce exceptional work at an early age than writers of fiction. The writers are still busy learning to creep inside other people's skin and feel how they feel and think how they think and figure out how they'll act in given situations. That kind of learning only comes from living, vicarious experience perhaps, maybe more mental than physical, but experience nonetheless.

Professional writers learn to look at their own work in a critical way. For most writers, time brings objectivity. After a week or a year, the weaknesses stand out and they know what to rewrite even if they aren't yet skilled enough to know how. What I discovered in my early twenties was that rewriting never ruined anything. I'd save the first version in case I wanted to return to it, but I never did. Furthermore, most criticisms had a grain or more of truth in them and needed to be considered. A writer is a professional when he or she can take an editor's pages of criticisms, nod, and get right to work on the revision. —C. S. *Adler*

Analyzing Readers' Comments

A beginning writer's imagination is a lively bit of business, jam-packed with a profusion of vivid scenes, intriguing story lines, and unique, captivating characters; the beginner sees those scenes, images, and characters, and the pervading moods and other background elements with absolute clarity in his or her mind's eye. But just having a head full of ideas doesn't make our beginner a writer.

I believe a beginner cannot learn to write without interacting with readers. The beginning writer has got to expose his or her work to readers for feedback, analyze this feedback carefully *and realistically*, and by doing so, gauge the degree of success, accepting what's good, what's bad, what needs fixing, and what's beyond fixing.

It's possible for a dozen people to read something and come back to the writer with a dozen different reactions. This fact must be considered when looking for commentary. Inexperienced writers need to learn to never throw up their hands over a single negative response. They must learn to analyze the audiences' responses, and to see what they can learn from it. —*Stanley Cohen*

Read to Write

Robert Southey's brother Henry, a physician, once decided he'd like to write a book, so he asked the poet laureate how he should get started on the project. Southey gave him lengthy instruction in research, note taking, and organization, then added this advice: "Say what you have to say as perspicuously as possible, as briefly as possible, and as rememberably as possible, and take no other thought about it. Omit none of those little circumstances which give life to narration. . . ." People who write for a living are often asked similar "how to" questions. Their answers vary widely, of course, and Southey's strikes me as better than most.

No one ever became a writer of consequence without also being a reader. I'm not advocating a constant diet of Milton, Mill, and Montaigne when I say that—read trash if that's what you initially prefer. Read critically, though—keep asking yourself questions about the material and its construction and purpose. Think about ways to make it better. Soon enough you'll become more selective, more appreciative, and more attuned to the merits of good writing style and technique. —*Wallace E. Knight*

Learning to Revise

How does a person learn to live, to change, to grow? Revision happens when you finally see what it is you were writing about in the first place, or when you perceive that an attitude toward the subject can in fact be loaded, become denser with possible meanings and relationships to other parts of the work. It seems to me that revision for a novelist is always undertaken against the background of what it all adds up to, so that ideally every word really counts, and shimmers, and that it is not simply a matter of getting the color of a character's eyes or the grammar or a point of view adjusted, but of seeing where each piece fits (or doesn't) in the whole mosaic.

Developing three-dimensional characters involves a similar process—learning, knowing what actions and speech are consistent within a character's world view. Sometimes it is a matter of knowing if, and how, a person can change. This sounds awfully mechanical, and any character who does not have the potential to surprise the reader, and the writer, will sustain no one's interest for long. Characters in novels had better rattle the cages of the ideas that sustain them, or they will be cartoons. What makes for complexity in characters is what makes for complexity in humans, I suppose—their histories, their circumstances, their relations with others. In fact, a good answer to what makes characters "three-dimensional" has traditionally been "another character who says something about him or her," or who does something with, or to, the character being developed—or who *fails* to do something necessary or important when it might have counted. What would Quixote be without Sancho Panza? Their counterpart enlarges both of them by more than the sum of their parts. And what would Sophie be without her schizophrenic lover? A character is not an isolated element in a fiction—a character is always a character in relation to. In revising for more depth, and more reality, we should not narrow our focus too much. Perhaps it is not the killer we must change, but her mother; perhaps it is not the lover we must change, but his bank account. And if the writer does not also change in this process—does not enlarge his or her vision in consequence—then we have become the kinds of robot-characters we see in the movies, churning out over and over again what we already knew. That's when writing becomes a job. —*Robert H. Abel*

23 A Writing Program Certain to Succeed

Joseph M. Moxley
University of South Florida

In my introduction, I reviewed some of the criticisms of the workshop method and of creative writing programs in general. When I first wrote that introduction, now over four years ago, I believed we needed to evaluate whether our programs and courses lacked rigor, whether we were promoting a "culture of narcissism" or providing a haven "from academic requirements and from intellectual challenge" (see the remarks by Solotaroff and Gass quoted in the introduction). As a graduate of two creative writing programs, I shared the concerns of Solotaroff, Gass, Stern, and others who have criticized the workshop method. For me, it wasn't until I became familiar with the research and theories of rhetoricians and composition scholars that I learned about the creative process or about the composing process, and I wondered why there wasn't a stronger dialogue about the creative process or pedagogy among teachers and creative writing, composition, and literature students.

Rather than growing soft, fat, and sassy with our success and growth, I believed that we needed to examine how well our theories and practices accounted for the demands of composing or for the needs of students who want careers as professional writers. I wondered what alternatives exist within the traditional workshop format and how we can help our students transform their raw experiences into material suitable for fiction; how we can promote creativity and risk-taking; how we can teach critical reading; how we can select and introduce models of contemporary literature into the classroom. In large part, then, I conceptualized and developed this book to answer these and other related questions, questions which define the parameters of our discipline.

Based on the recommendations of the writers in this book and on all that I know about teaching writing, I would now like to highlight some of the most important principles, assumptions, and practices

253

that should form the foundation of a student writer's training. In my opinion, certain ineluctable conclusions have emerged from this book and from composition theory. As a result, I can make some concrete recommendations for the future about the teaching of writing and the development of writing programs.

Naturally, however, I do not wish to suggest that *all* of the following techniques should be used in *every* writing course or program. I recognize that what works well for one writer or teacher will not necessarily work well for every writer or teacher. We obviously cannot codify writing instruction. In fact, the recommendations of the authors in this book are at times contradictory. Witness, for example, the fascinating differences in Donald Murray's and Marion Zimmer Bradley's assessments of the value of planning and outlining. While Bradley considers planning to be essential, Murray prefers to discover his story while writing. Surely other equally distinguished and productive authors could present even more diverse modes of composing (and thinking). It is, therefore, not surprising that the pedagogical approaches of M.F.A. programs similarly indicate a lack of consensus about how to teach writing, as shown by Marion Perry's summary of the requirements of M.F.A. programs (see the appendix to this book). Perry's tables demonstrate the surprising degree to which we are unsure about the number of hours that should be required in writing courses that aren't workshops, in tutorials, in literature, thesis, and interdisciplinary courses.

With the preceding reservations in mind, then, I suggest that the following assumptions, theories of the writing process, pedagogical techniques, and discussions of our roles as teachers should form the foundation of our creative writing classes and programs. Moreover, given that most of the distinctions between "creative" and "noncreative/nonfiction" writing are arbitrary, I recognize that most of the following suggestions could also be useful to nonfiction writers and professional writing programs.

Assumptions

- The primary focus of all *writing* courses should be on the students' writing.
- In addition to writing courses, though, our students need an equally strong background in literature. In fact, their writing development won't reach its potential unless they have a solid background in literature.

- Writing can be learned, if not entirely taught. Our courses should teach students about the successful practices of professionals. Then, students can internalize the suggestions that work well for them.

- Writing is valuable in and of itself and does not need publication to validate it. Writing promotes thought, empathy, learning.

- To foster language development and literacy, all students in American high schools and colleges should enroll in at least one course in creative writing.

- We need to talk about writing holistically. Our discussions of discrete elements of craft—from diction, syntax, point of view, dialogue, plotting, and so on—must be placed in the context of the creative process. Writing is not learned atomistically from the parts to the whole, but holistically, from the whole to the parts.

- Writing and teaching are lifelong apprenticeships. Writers and teachers are perpetual learners; we read, reread, and continually question our techniques and beliefs.

- Writing teachers must be writers.

- We don't know enough about the *developmental stages* writers go through. Yet, from the research of Piaget and Vygotsky, among others, we understand that learning to consider the needs of external readers, to empathize, "to creep inside other people's skin," is both emotionally *and* intellectually demanding. And, sadly, we also know that some people never learn to escape the fog of egocentrism.

  C. S. Adler mentions that publishers did not want to publish her writing until her thirties because ". . . it took me that many years to experience enough so that my writing was interesting to others." Adler's comments are probably true to the experience of most writers. As teachers of young students, we need to be particularly sensitive to this developmental phenomenon; by asking questions about students' manuscripts, we can help them conceptualize the needs and opinions of others.

- Successful writers take risks, and we should be careful to give student writers room to do the same. In other words, we must be open to their goals and be sensitive to the kinds of *evaluative* and *substantive* responses that they need.

- Writers have to learn to draw on their felt sense, on that intu-

itive, prelinguistic, bodily feeling (see the remarks by Sondra
Perl quoted in chapter 2).

- One of the best "secrets of the craft" is perseverance. Successful writers must be disciplined and driven by a need to
create. And although we obviously cannot imbue students
with the creative spirit, we can certainly teach students how to
generate, incubate, and revise material according to a realistic
schedule by studying and learning from the working schedules
of successful writers.

  Ultimately, we should hope that all students leave our programs as Elizabeth Winthrop left hers, "carrying a suit case
bursting with short stories and the conviction that I was a writer."

- Writing is not solely a cognitive process, but a deeply affective
one. We don't know enough about how personality affects
composing strategies, but we do know that we intellectualize
beyond value when we ignore personality in our theories and
practices.

On the Writing Process

- *Writing is a generative, recursive process of forming meaning.* Many
creative writers do not think and then write; instead, they understand that new words and concepts will emerge as words
and images rub against each other in the web of meaning.

  Naturally, to help students understand the generative and
recursive nature of language, our classroom exercises and goals
must be grounded in an awareness of what *process* goals students are considering as well as their *content* goals.

- Although we may be uncomfortable doing so, we need to familiarize students with the mysterious nature of composing.
Students must learn that successful writers understand that
doubt and uncertainty are inevitable and fundamental features
of composing. Writers (and readers) seek the mysterious, the
surprise in life and fiction.

- There is no all-purpose writing process. Writers testify to an infinite number of strategies. William Holinger, for example, explains, "My own writing process varies considerably from one
project to another. I never write the same way twice; each new
story and novel grows differently."

On Teaching the Craft

- We should require productivity. John D. MacDonald, Ron Carlson, Marion Zimmer Bradley, and Elizabeth Winthrop consider regular writing to be essential: "The important thing in all writing," says Bradley, "is to get into the habit of doing it." Robert Boice has experimentally verified the innumerable anecdotal accounts of novelists: regular writing promotes creativity (see chapter 2).

- We should teach a variety of prewriting techniques, such as drawing, meditating, transcribing, maintaining a journal. Many of the writers in this book find it useful to keep journals to develop characters and stories. Stephen Minot recommends that we use journals to keep notes on the lines, images, and techniques that we enjoy in our reading.

- We can help students understand their writing process by sharing our own methods of composing. For example, Alan Ziegler and Sheila Schwartz suggest that we should show students our professionally edited texts in order to help them understand the role of criticism and the recursive nature of generating and editing material. Eve Shelnutt's discussions with her students about the sources of her fiction give voice to the unknown—how writers find source material.

- Student writers can share responses to each other's manuscripts in group work. Peer reviews promote critical reading and the development of essential editorial skills, and they help students to better understand the needs, interests, and expectations of audiences. Shy students can have the opportunity to ask questions that they might be afraid to ask in large groups.

- Naturally our primary goal should be to help students write the kind of material they wish to compose. Yet, we should also attempt to stretch our students' writing muscles. The works and productive strategies of the writers in this book forcefully illustrate the importance of writing in different genres. Much as we encourage students of expository writing to address different audiences and purposes, we should also challenge students of creative writing to write in different genres, such as children's literature, screenwriting, mystery and suspense fiction.

- In order to teach students a variety of writing strategies and prepare them for careers as writers, we need to encourage experimentation. As John Gardner has pointed out, we should be just as concerned with teaching students about the questions writers ask of their drafts as we are with the quality of their completed work (see chapter 2).

- To teach students to transform their experiences into material for fiction, we can use Wayne Ude's idea of having students write about one particular event from multiple points of view. Eve Shelnutt's memory exercises and her assignments that require students to write about the sources of fiction should also help us to bridge the gaps between personal experience, language, and fiction.

- While some, as Sheila Schwartz mentions, write to exorcise old wounds, many writers prefer to avoid autobiographical material and choose to do extensive research. To help these writers, we need to offer more information in our courses about the ways authors research their subjects.

- Much fiction is about people, about how we age, overcome obstacles, and achieve our goals. As Murray and Jauss caution in their chapters, literature students who are trained to identify themes sometimes consider theme to be a writer's method, not the end result of a process. Thus, we need to inform students that many authors discover their themes when composing. Even writers who write to address an idea or theme that obsesses them know that their fiction—above all else—must be interesting, entertaining, reader-based.

- To help foster a stimulating intellectual community for writers, literature, composition, and creative writing faculty can team-teach courses and offer reading and discussion seminars like the one Eve Shelnutt describes in chapter 1. We need to work together to develop ways to balance a background in literary criticism with models of contemporary writing and discussions of the composing process.

- Practicing the craft involves publishing. Yet, to ensure students have that all-important opportunity to experiment, creative writing programs have traditionally sheltered students from the concerns of publishing.

  Many of the authors in this book have argued convincingly that we need to reevaluate the importance of publishing, particularly in light of the importance that publishing plays to those who wish to pursue positions as writers or as academics.

For example, Valerie Miner contends that creative writing courses at advanced undergraduate and graduate levels should not ignore the demands or dynamics of the marketplace: ". . . I want my students to appreciate *how* fiction is published, to consider context influencing content, to acknowledge the social value of literary contribution, to understand how our individual writing ambitions are affected by the publishing profession and the book industry. By placing students in co-op positions with professional publications, we can familiarize students with the effect of the marketplace on contemporary writing."

At the same time, our students and colleagues should learn to consider writing to be a noble activity, whether or not it leads to publication. We clearly don't want our students pandering to the whims of the marketplace.

On Reading

- As almost every writer in this book has mentioned (see, in particular, David Jauss, George Garrett, Marion Zimmer Bradley, Stephen Minot, and John D. MacDonald), we need to teach students to read like writers. Yet, this doesn't mean we should teach literature courses for writers in the same way that we teach literature courses for literature students. After all, the student writer's focus should not be on theme or principles of literary criticism, but on the choices authors considered when composing. Writing students need to become active readers—to study the point of view, the tone, the plotting and other techniques that the authors employ. Writers need to question what effect the writer's personal and social history has had on that writer's choice of subject matter and treatment.

- We should emphasize that personal experience can be richly informed through extensive reading.

- As Minot, St. John, Miner, and Henry persuasively argue, students should be exposed to contemporary authors and aesthetic goals and some of the best contemporary literary magazines, such as *Ploughshares, Partisan Review,* or the *Kenyon Review.*

Our Role as Teachers

- The creative writing teacher is *not* a counselor; his or her position is not to commiserate or psychoanalyze, but to help students shape the material of their lives into a literary form. At the same time, much of student material is deeply personal, and as David Kranes warns, we must be sensitive when responding to student work. One-shot, reckless evaluations that disregard the personal risk involved must be avoided. As Donald Murray has pointed out, our responses should heal, not punish or maim.

- Our goal should not be to defend the tower—a particular code of aesthetics—but to help students write the kind of story that they want to write and to expose students to a variety of literary forms.

To foster a continuing dialogue about the creative process and pedagogy, we need a professional forum. Perhaps the National Council of Teachers of English or the Associated Writing Programs or the Teachers & Writers Collaborative or the Modern Language Association will be willing to help establish and fund a professional journal that publishes pedagogical and theoretical articles, literary criticism, and literature.

Appendix A
America's Master of Fine Arts Programs: Course Requirements

Marion Perry
Erie Community College, New York

Analysis of Tables

Table 1 lists the twenty-eight M.F.A. programs identified by the *Associated Writing Programs Catalogue,* and the number of hours required for each, as well as the type of degree offered as determined from the listings and from the publications of the programs. The first item of interest is the number of hours required by the programs for completion of the degree. Table 1 demonstrates that the hours vary from a requirement of 36 semester hours at four programs to 60 semester hours at five programs. The program at Sarah Lawrence requires an additional thesis for which no credit is allotted. The thesis would be worth at least 6 credits at other programs, meaning that the Sarah Lawrence degree requirement is equivalent to from 42 to 48 hours rather than the listed 36 hours. The four programs of the quarter system all require 72 quarter hours, which is equivalent to 48 semester hours. This means that of the twenty-eight programs, fourteen require 48 semester hours and two additional programs require 45 and 40 hours. The remaining twelve programs are nearly evenly split, with half requiring 12 more credit hours for completion of the degree and half requiring 12 less credits for degree completion.

Tables 2 and 3 describe the more specific requirements of the programs. It will be noticed that nearly all programs require some workshop hours overall. Since the thesis must be completed regardless of the credit granted, the actual difference in requirements among the programs is, in a number of cases, less than it may appear initially.

The other requirements are less specific. Most programs require some literature course work, some much more than others. The starting date of the programs is listed when it was available in the literature. In many cases, the dates are listed differently in the programs' various publications. Iowa, for example, indisputably the first program, has varying dates due to the nature of its establishment in a number of official steps, which occurred between about 1932 and 1939. However, Iowa celebrated their fiftieth anniversary in 1986.

Similarly, not all programs provide all information charted in the tables in the fourth edition of the *AWP Catalogue,* nor in their literature. Furthermore, M.F.A. programs are changing almost as rapidly as computer software: some universities that offered such programs five to ten years ago, no longer do so, while many others are adding programs. Emerson College, for example, did not have an M.F.A. program listed in the catalogue, but now has one.

Works Cited

Hammer-Sarosdy, Kathy, comp. *AWP Catalogue of Writing Programs.* Norfolk: Associated Writing Programs, 1984.

Perry, Marion. *Master of Fine Arts Programs: The Training of Professional Writers as Artists.* Ann Arbor: University Microfilms International, 1986.

Table I: Program Requirements

Program	Degree Description Studio/Academic	Hours*	Years in Residence
1 University of Alabama	Studio/Academic	48	3
2 University of Alaska	S/A	45	2
3 American University	S/A	48	2
4 University of Arizona	S/A	48	2–3
5 University of Arkansas	S/A	60	
6 Bowling Green State University	S	40	2
7 University of British Columbia	S	18–21 units	2
8 Brooklyn College, City Univ. of NY	S	36	
9 University of California, Irvine	S/A	72 quarter/hrs	2
10 Cornell University	S/A	40	2
11 Eastern Washington University	S/A	72 q/h	2
12 George Mason University	S/A	48	48 hrs
13 Indiana University	S/A	60	2
14 University of Iowa	S	48	
15 University of Massachusetts	S/A	60	
16 McNeese State University	S/A	60	2
17 University of Michigan	S/A	48	2
18 University of Montana	S/A	72 q/h	
19 University of NC, Greensboro	S/A	36	2
20 University of Oregon	S or S/A	72 q/h	2
21 University of Pittsburgh	S/A	36	2
22 Sarah Lawrence College	S	36+	2
23 Vermont College of Norwich Univ.	S/A	48	
24 Virginia Commonwealth University		48	
25 University of Virginia	S/A	36	2
26 Warren Wilson College	S/A	60	
27 Western Michigan University	S/A	48	
28 Wichita State University	S/A	48	

*Semester hours unless otherwise noted

Table II: Program Requirements*

Program	Workshops	Thesis	Lit Courses	Interdiscipline	Language
1 Alabama	18–24	to 6	24 or more	6	reading prof.
2 Alaska	3–6	6	27		
3 American Univ.	12–24	required	12	12 specified option	
4 Arizona	18–21	12–18	12–18		
5 Arkansas	15–18	6	24		
6 Bowling Green	16+	to 6		encouraged	
7 British Columbia	9–18 units	3 units			
8 CUNY/Brooklyn	12	required	12		
9 California	48 q/h	required	24 q/h		proficiency
10 Cornell	16	required	16–24		
11 E. Washington	15–20 q/h	6–12 q/h	15–20 q/h	10 q/h	
12 George Mason	15–24	6	15–24	3–6 specified	
13 Indiana	16+	4–12	16 or more	4 specified	
14 Iowa	to 24	to 12			
15 Massachusetts	24	6	24	6 related fld.	proficiency
16 McNeese State	12–15	6	27–30		
17 Michigan	24	required	12–20	6	
18 Montana	18+ q/h	12–15 q/h	9–20 q/h	6 q/h	proficiency
19 NC, Greensboro	6–12	6	12–18		
20 Oregon	9–36 q/h	18 q/h	18–45 q/h		
21 Pittsburgh	9–21	to 6	12–21		
22 Sarah Lawrence	required	required	arranged	encouraged	encouraged
23 Vermont College	required	required	arranged	arranged	
24 Virginia Commonwealth	15		12	12 specified	
25 Virginia	12	6	12		
26 Warren Wilson	required	required	arranged	arranged	
27 Western Michigan	12–18	6	6+		proficiency
28 Wichita State	to 12	2–6	12–26	6	

*Semester hours unless otherwise noted

Table II: Program Requirements*

Program	Other Wrtg. Courses	Tutorials, Dir. Rdg.	Written Exam	Oral Exam	Date Beg.
1 Alabama	up to 6	to 6	required	required	
2 Alaska	6–12	to 12	required	required	1968
3 American U	12–24	required	option	option	
4 Arizona	6–18	6–9			
5 Arkansas	9–12	6–9			
6 Bowling Green	18	5		required	1964
7 British Columbia		to 9 units	required	required	1965
8 CUNY/Brooklyn		12	required		
9 California	up to 8 q/h			required	1965
10 Cornell					
11 E. Washington	10 q/h		required		
12 George Mason	3–12		required		
13 Indiana	4 or more				1980
14 Iowa			required		1936
15 Massachusetts				required	
16 McNeese State	12–15		required	required	
17 Michigan					
18 Montana	to 9 q/h	to 6 q/h	required	required	
19 NC, Greensboro		6–12	required		
20 Oregon	to 9 q/h	to 27 q/h	required		1960
21 Pittsburgh	3–6				
22 Sarah Lawrence					
23 Vermont College					
24 Virginia Commonwealth					
25 Virginia				required	
26 Warren Wilson	8 or more	to 8			1981
27 Western Michigan	6–18	to 9			
28 Wichita State			required	required	1974

*Semester hours unless otherwise noted

Editor

Joseph M. Moxley, an associate professor of English at the University of South Florida, has published articles in *College Composition and Communication, Journal of Teaching Writing, The Journal of Technical Writing and Communication, College Teaching, Freshman English News,* and fiction in *Sign of the Times, Perigraph,* and numerous other journals and magazines. Moxley has recently completed a novel, entitled *Jake Gunner on the Gold Coast.*

Contributors

Robert H. Abel's books include *The Progress of a Fire* (Simon and Schuster, 1985) and *Freedom Dues* (Dial Press, 1980).

C. S. Adler is the author of twenty-four novels, including *Down by the River* (Archway Pocket, 1983), *Footsteps on the Stairs* (Dell, 1984), and *Shell Lady's Daughter* (Fawcett, 1984). Adler is winner of the William Allen White Award and the Golden Kite Award for *Magic of the Glits*.

Marion Zimmer Bradley is the author of over fifty books, including the "Darkover" novels and other science fiction/fantasy novels, as well as the mainstream novels *The Catch Trap* (Ballantine, 1979, 1980, 1984), *The Mists of Avalon* (Knopf, 1983; Ballantine, 1984), and *The Firebrand* (Simon and Schuster, 1987). She also edits an annual anthology, *Sword & Sorceress,* for *DAW,* and she has been publishing a fantasy magazine since 1988. Bradley has given workshops in story plotting, most recently at Omega Institute in New York and Harrisburg Area Community College in Pennsylvania. She has also taught several semesters of a science fiction course at the Urban School in San Francisco.

Ron Carlson is the author of a collection of stories, *The News of the World* (W. W. Norton, 1987/Viking Penguin, 1988) and two novels, *Betrayed by F. Scott Fitzgerald* and *Truants.* His work has appeared in *Harper's, Mc-Call's, Sports Illustrated, The North American Review, TriQuarterly, The New York Times,* and other magazines and newspapers. His stories have been included in several anthologies, including *Editors' Choice 1986* and *Best American Stories 1987* edited by Ann Beattie. Most recently he completed a screen version of his story "Life Before Science" for Columbia Pictures. Mr. Carlson was awarded a National Endowment for the Arts Fellowship in fiction in 1985. He lives in Tempe, Arizona, where he is on the writing faculty of Arizona State University.

Stanley Cohen is the author of *Angel Face* (St. Martin's, 1982) and *330 Park* (G. P. Putnam's, 1977).

Paul Cook is the author of *On the Rim of the Mandala* (Bantam Spectra, 1987), *The Alejandra Variations* (Ace Science Fiction, 1984), and *Titagel* (Berkeley, San Francisco, 1981). Cook is writer-in-residence at Arizona State University.

George Garrett is a professor of English at the University of Virginia. Garrett's recent books include *Poison Pen* (Stuart Wright, 1987), *Understanding*

Mary Lee Settle (University of South Carolina, in-press), and *Entered from the Sun* (Doubleday, in-press).

DeWitt Henry is the cofounder and director of *Ploughshares*, editor of *The Ploughshares Reader: New Fiction For the 80's*, and coordinator of the M.F.A. in Creative Writing at Emerson College.

William Holinger's novel, *The Fence-Walker* (SUNY Press), won the Associated Writing Programs' Novel Award in 1984. He has published many short stories and is the coauthor of *Short Season* (Scholastic, a young-adult novel written under the pseudonym Scott Eller). His articles on teaching creative writing have appeared in the *AWP Newsletter* and *The Writer*. He lives in Ann Arbor and teaches at the University of Michigan.

David Jauss is the author of *Crimes of Passion*, a collection of stories published by Story Press, and editor, with Philip Dacey, of *Strong Measures*, an anthology of contemporary American poetry published by Harper and Row. His stories have appeared in *The Iowa Review, New England Review/ Bread Loaf Quarterly, Prairie Schooner, Prize Stories 1983: The O. Henry Awards*, and other journals and anthologies.

Wallace E. Knight has published *Lightstruck* (Little, Brown, 1979), *The Literature of the South* (Scribner, 1979) and fiction in such magazines as the *Atlantic*.

David Kranes—novelist, playwright—is artistic director of Sundance Institute's Playwrights' Laboratory. His play "Cantrell" will be included in the *Best Short Plays of 1988*. His fourth novel, *Keno Runner*, will be published early in 1989. He lives in Salt Lake City and is on the creative writing faculty of the University of Utah.

John D. MacDonald authored some seventy novels, including twenty-one about his fabled hero, Travis McGee, and over 500 short stories.

Ib J. Melchior is the author of nine books with Harper and Row, and Dodd, Mead and Co., including *The Haiglerlock Project, The Marcus Device, Eva, Code Name: Grand Guighol*. He is the recipient of the Hamlet Award for Excellence in Playwriting, "Hour of Vengeance," 1982, The Shakespeare Society of America; and the Golden Scroll for Best Writing, 1976, the Science Fiction Academy.

Valerie Miner's novels include *All Good Women, Winter's Edge, Movement, Blood Sisters* and *Murder in the English Department*. Her book of short stories is called *Trespassing*. She has won an Australia Council Grant, a *PEN* Syndicated Fiction Prize and other literary awards. For the past ten years Miner has taught at the University of California, Berkeley. Her work has appeared in *TLS, The New York Times, The New Statesman, The Los Angeles Times* and other journals.

Stephen Minot's novels are *Chill of Dusk* (Doubleday, 1964), *Ghost Images* (Harper and Row, 1979), and *Surviving the Flood* (Atheneum, 1982; Second Chance Press, 1986). He has also published a collection of short stories, *Crossing* (University of Illinois Press), two college textbooks, *Three Genres* (Prentice-Hall, 1965, 4th ed. 1987) and *Reading Fiction* (Prentice-Hall, 1984), and has edited an anthology of short stories, *Three Stances of Modern Fiction*, with Robley Wilson, Jr. (Winthrop, 1972). Minot's stories have appeared in such magazines as the *Atlantic, Harper's, Redbook,* and *Playboy* as well as quarterlies such as *The Kenyon Review, The Virginia Quarterly Review, The Sewanee Review,* and *Antaeus.* His stories have been selected for inclusion several times in both the *O. Henry Prize Stories* collection and *The Best American Short Stories.* Minot taught creative writing at Bowdoin College and for twenty years at Trinity College, Hartford, Connecticut. He is now writing full-time.

Donald M. Murray, who has published two novels and is working on two more, is best known as the author of texts on writing, including *A Writer Teaches Writing, Write to Learn, Read to Write,* and *Learning by Teaching.* Murray, who won the Pulitzer Prize for Editorial Writing, has retired as professor of English at the University of New Hampshire to become a columnist for the *Boston Globe,* writing coach for the *Boston Globe* and the *Providence Journal,* and to write fiction.

Marion Perry is a graduate of the Iowa Writer's Workshop and the author of three books of poetry—*Establishing Intimacy* (Textile Bridge Press, 1982), *The Mirror's Image* (Serendipity, 1981), and *Icarus* (Textile Bridge Press, 1980). She is the author of more than forty additional published poems.

Richard F. Radford, Jr., is a poet and author of ten books, including *Promise of Spring* (E. P. Dutton, 1982), *Having Been There* (Scribner, 1979), *Golfer's Book of Trivia* (Quinlan, 1986), *Trooper* (Quinlan, 1987), *Drug Agent, USA* (Quinlan, 1988).

David St. John is the author of three collections of poetry, *Hush* (1976), *The Shore* (1980), and *No Heaven* (1985). He has received many grants and awards, including the Prix de Rome Fellowship in Literature. He teaches at the University of Southern California, Los Angeles.

Mimi Schwartz's books include *In Our Own Words: An Anthology of Women's Writing* (Helikon) and *Writing for Many Roles* (Boynton/Cook). Her essays have appeared in the *New York Times, College English, College Composition and Communication,* and *Journal of Teaching Writing,* among others. Schwartz is an associate professor of writing at Stockton State College in New Jersey and is currently working on a semi-autobiographical novel called *First Yankee in the Family.*

Sheila Schwartz's books are *How People Lived in Ancient Greece and Rome* (with G. Reuben; nonfiction YA; 1967); *How People Live in Mexico* (with Nancy Schwartz; nonfiction YA; 1969); *Teaching the Humanities* (1971); *Earth in Transit* (YA anthology; 1973); *Like Mother, Like Me* (YA; 1978); *Growing Up Guilty* (YA; 1978); *Teaching Adolescent Literature* (1979); *The Solid Gold Circle* (1981); *The Hollywood Writers' Wars* (completed for Nancy Lynn Schwartz;

1982); *One Day You'll Go* (YA; 1982); *Jealousy* (YA; 1983); *Sorority* (1987); *Bigger is Better* (YA; 1987); *The Most Popular Girl* (YA; 1987).

Eve Shelnutt's books include three short story collections, *The Love Child*, *The Formal Voice*, and *The Musician* (all published by Black Sparrow Press); *Descant*, a chapbook of fiction (Palaemon Press); *Air and Salt* and *Recital in a Private Home*, collections of poetry (Carnegie-Mellon Press). Shelnutt is also the author of three writing textbooks: *The Magic Pencil* (Peachtree Publishers); *The Writing Experience* (Macmillan); *The Writing Room: Keys to the Craft of Fiction and Poetry*. Shelnutt teaches in the M.F.A. Program at Ohio University.

Wayne Ude is the author of a novel, *Becoming Coyote*, and a collection, *Buffalo and Other Stories*. He has taught creative writing at Colorado State University, Mankato State University in Minnesota, and Lewis and Clark College in Oregon (the latter two as writer-in-residence). He currently teaches fiction writing at Old Dominion University in Norfolk, Virginia.

Elizabeth Winthrop has published more than twenty books for children of all ages. These include *The Castle in the Attic*, winner of the 1987 Dorothy Canfield Fisher Award, *Shoes*, and *Knock, Knock, Who's There?*, a young adult novel about growing up with the problem of alcoholism. She is a 1985 winner of the *PEN* Syndicated Fiction Award for her short story, "Bad News." Her first novel for adults, *In My Mother's House*, was published by Doubleday in 1988.

Alan Ziegler is director of the Writing Program at Columbia University's School of General Studies, and conducts workshops for Teachers & Writers Collaborative. He is the author of *The Writing Workshop, Volumes I and II*, on teaching creative writing. Ziegler's fiction has won four *PEN* Syndicated Fiction Awards and the Word Beat Fiction Book Award, and his stories have appeared in such magazines as *The New Yorker* and *Paris Review*. His books include *The Green Grass of Flatbush* (stories) and *So Much To Do* (poems). He coedited *Some* literary magazine and Release Press.